GNOSTICISM AND THE NEW TESTAMENT

GNOSTICISM AND THE NEW TESTAMENT

PHEME PERKINS

FORTRESS PRESS

MINNEAPOLIS

GNOSTICISM AND THE NEW TESTAMENT

Scripture quotations, unless otherwise noted, are from the New Revised Standard Version of the Bible, copyright © 1989 by the Division of Christian Education of the National Council of the Churches of Christ in the United States of America.

Excerpts from *The Nag Hammadi Library in English,* ed. James Robinson, copyright © 1978 E. J. Brill, are used by permission of E. J. Brill and HarperCollins, Publishers, Inc.

Cover design: Baker Group Design
Interior design: Publishers' WorkGroup
Cover photo: Courtesy Religious News Service.
Cover text: From the *Apocryphon of John,* courtesy of the Institute for Antiquity and Christianity at the Claremont Graduate School, Claremont, California.

Library of Congress Cataloging-in-Publication Data

Perkins, Pheme.
    Gnosticism and the New Testament / Pheme Perkins.
      p. cm.
    Includes bibliographical references and index.
    ISBN 0-8006-2801-2 (alk. paper) :
      1. Gnosticism. 2. Gnostic literature—Relation to the New
Testament. 3. Bible. N.T.—Criticism, interpretation, etc.
I. Title.
BT1390.P42 1993
273'.1—dc20   93-21890
                                                 CIP

#2829489{4}

Manufactured in the U.S.A.   AF 1–2801

97   96   95   94   93   1   2   3   4   5   6   7   8   9   10

CONTENTS

PREFACE

This book began as a graduate seminar at the Boston University School of Theology. At the time, I did not expect to write a book on the topic, but Adela Yarbro Collins, now at the University of Chicago, suggested that I undertake it. When the original plans for a series were discarded, she recommended the project to Marshall Johnson of Fortress Press. Dr. Johnson's enthusiastic support has certainly been instrumental in the completion of the project. I had the opportunity to complete most of the first draft while I was Rachel Rebecca Kaneb Visiting Professor of Roman Catholic Studies at Cornell University. Al Kaneb and the Near Eastern Studies Department at Cornell should also be warmly thanked for their support.

Like most scholars working in the field of Nag Hammadi studies today, I remain deeply indebted to the late George W. MacRae, S.J. No one could summarize the importance of research into gnostic origins for our understanding of early Christianity better than Prof. MacRae.

Since the publication of the full corpus of gnostic writings from the discovery at Nag Hammadi, scholarly work on Gnosticism has been a growth industry. Yet it has been over two decades since any single scholar has attempted to survey the significance of such study for understanding the New Testament and early Christianity. This volume certainly lacks the elegance of Robert McL. Wilson's *Gnosis and the New Testament* (1968). The individual chapters are divided into specific topic areas so that those who wish to catch up on what scholars are saying today about a particular area can read the sections of interest to them. Although much work remains at a preliminary stage, we have gathered enough new information to begin to change the terms in which we debate questions of gnostic origins and the development of New Testament Christianity. Consequently, I have tried to report our achievements over the past quarter century in a way that frames new questions for future research.

Pheme Perkins

INTRODUCTION

The second-century Apologist, Irenaeus of Lyons, complained that adherents of the gnostic sect known as the Valentinians had created a "clever imitation in glass" of the precious jewel of Scripture (*Adv. Haer.* 1.pref.). The author of a gnostic treatise accused the orthodox Christian bishops of being "dry canals" and misleading others by claiming an authority from God that is not rightfully theirs (*Apoc. Pet.* VI 79,22-31; *NHLE*, 376).[1] The populist orthodox bishops would eventually undercut the groups of spiritually elite Christians gathered around individual teachers that had been the mainstay of gnostic Christianity in the second century. Just as certainly, the shrinking horizons of the Roman Empire in the fifth century would sap the power from the great third-century reformulation of gnostic theology, Manicheism.[2]

Even before the discovery of a collection of original gnostic writings near Nag Hammadi in Egypt (ca. 1945),[3] scholars had begun to wonder if gnostic mythology and metaphor reflected a religious tradition that had emerged alongside Christianity in New Testament times. Discovery of a complete collection of Jesus' sayings and parables, the *Gospel of Thomas,* which contained shorter and formally more primitive versions of some of Jesus' sayings, awakened new interest in the issue. The echoes of familiar New Testament language in the meditative treatise *Gospel of Truth* and the many variations on the theme of enlightenment coming through the descent of a heavenly revealer also suggested the possibility of a pre-second-century gnostic origin for themes and images in the New Testament.[4]

The history-of-religions approach to early Christianity originally pre-

1

sumed that a genetic or evolutionary model was the key to understanding religious traditions. Texts, rituals, or doctrines were to be explained by situating them in temporal sequences. An earlier form of a phenomenon is the presupposition for its later development. The influence of phenomenology and comparative religions led to a shift in method. Scholars like Rudolf Bultmann were willing to look for patterns analogous to those in the New Testament material in religious texts that were either not contiguous with the New Testament or were temporally later. Mandaean myths about the heavenly revealer were used to explain the unusual picture of Christ in the Fourth Gospel.[5] The Nag Hammadi texts provided the possibility of finding evidence for earlier forms of gnostic mythology.

The Christian elements in a number of the tractates are quite superficial. But the mythological accounts of Wisdom's fall, of the emergence of the lower world and its god, and of the life of Adam and Eve all depend on Jewish traditions.[6] This line of argument does not require that any of the extant gnostic writings were completed earlier than the second century—only that the traditions upon which the authors built were formulated prior to that time.

When scholars ask whether Gnosticism influenced the writers of the New Testament, they may be asking one of three things. First, they may ask if the New Testament writers were influenced by religious ideas and images that had already taken shape in gnostic interpretations of Genesis. Or second, they may ask whether the New Testament traditions represent conscious opposition to gnosticizing views being propagated by others, as Bultmann insisted was the case in John. Or third, they may ask whether both gnostic speculation and the New Testament come from the same larger world of heterodox Judaism. In that case, what they have in common is due to this shared origin, not direct influence of gnostic speculation on New Testament writings.

Each of these approaches looks to a somewhat different type of evidence to make its case. In the first instance, the question is whether specific gnostic mythemes have been adopted by New Testament writers. Possible candidates might have included the fall of Adam and Eve under the demonic power of death; the Law of the creator god as an instrument of slavery, not life; the true origin of humanity in a heavenly world, not this one; the coming of a revealer from heaven to enlighten the elect; the need for a Spirit-guided interpretation of Scripture so that the elect can discover the wisdom hidden in the text; the sayings of Jesus as the key to such hidden wisdom.

Since the New Testament does not directly mention gnostic sects, it might seem more difficult to argue that its authors were opposing an early form of Gnosticism. This type of argument presumes that the unusual shape taken by the New Testament writings can be best understood as the conscious desire to stem gnosticizing developments. The New Testament Gospels use historylike narratives, especially those about the suffering of Jesus, to limit speculation about Jesus as a heavenly being. Son of man sayings are referred to the passion, as is the transfiguration story. Visions of the risen Jesus do not convey new teaching, as gnostic writers would later claim, but merely affirm Jesus' status with God. The wisdom sayings with their emphasis on inner transformation are combined with apocalyptic traditions about the coming of the Son of man in judgment. Speculation about the powers in heaven is cut off by the insistence that Christ has dethroned any such powers. The Law is not a cosmic phenomenon, whether divine or demonic, but a source of general moral precepts and exemplary stories.

The third approach does not require that a sociologically distinct religious movement made up of one or more gnostic sects existed in the first century C.E. Where New Testament and gnostic traditions share a common ancestry, they draw on a rich tradition of exegetical and mythological speculation that had taken shape in Judaism during the Hellenistic period.[7] These early traditions include speculation about Adam and Eve; the role of heavenly Wisdom coming to enlighten humans lost in darkness; and the development of baptismal rituals as a way of incorporating human beings into a new, heavenly race free of the constraints of this world.

If the New Testament and gnostic traditions develop out of the larger matrix of religious speculation and symbolism in the first century C.E., then it is not possible to determine whether there is a direct, genetic link between the two movements. It is evident that a number of the Nag Hammadi writings are only superficially Christianized. However, it would be impossible to describe the basic elements of gnostic myths about the origins of the material universe and the bondage of human beings within this world without reference to Jewish traditions of exegesis. These traditions are not limited to the biblical texts.[8] In their second-century forms both Gnosticism and Christianity appear to be unlikely offshoots of Judaism.[9]

From the perspective of second-century gnostic writers, most Christians have betrayed their origins by remaining captive to the malicious creator god. Polemical traditions once used against the god of the

Jews have new life as evidence against orthodox church leaders.[10] The anti-Jewish polemic of the Fourth Gospel would serve second-century Valentinian exegetes as evidence against orthodox Christianity. But looked at from the outside, both gnostic mythologizing and early Christian traditions demonstrate a religious impulse to break with inherited religious traditions. Both claim that the authorities in charge of the inherited tradition have failed to accept the revelation of a heavenly figure that provides the key to salvation. Both insist that inwardly the enlightened possess a freedom that exalts them over the rulers of this world. This self-understanding makes both groups appear alienated from the world in which they live. Consequently, many interpreters see social dislocation, subjection to foreign rule, and religious and cultural fragmentation as the engines that drove people to create remarkable, new forms of religious belief and practice in the first century C.E.

Gnosticism appears more radically dissociated from the world, its scriptures, its centers of power, and its dominant religious categories. Nonetheless, analysis of the traditional material within the second- and third-century gnostic texts provides us with an opportunity to observe the larger framework that shaped the New Testament as well. Hans-Martin Schenke has proposed that the major religious impulse behind Gnosticism in this period is ecstatic identification with a heavenly source of redemption. He has argued that the originating mythological system of Sethian Gnosticism is so distinctive that even its Christianized forms found in the Nag Hammadi tractates have not been assimilated to Christianity.[11]

Even though the Nag Hammadi texts are not evidence for a pre-Christian Gnosticism in the same sense in which the Dead Sea Scrolls provide evidence for messianic expectations in a Jewish sect prior to the emergence of Christianity, it is no longer possible to account for everything in second-century gnostic writings as derived from Christianity.[12] They provide a different constellation of traditions from the remarkably varied religious landscape of the first and second centuries. New Testament writings are evidently neither advocating gnostic ideas nor combating the formal systems that would emerge in the second century. But the religious currents that appear in the gnostic writings are also part of the environment of the New Testament.

Although gnostic speculation may not have caused any particular writing in the New Testament, gnostic mythologizing does form part of the horizon within which the New Testament should be interpreted. Students of Christian origins have become accustomed to comparing the New Testament material with a wide variety of Jewish and Greco-Roman sources. The same efforts of analysis and comparison should be applied to the gnostic material.

I begin in Part One by investigating the arguments for a non-Christian Gnosticism that emerged prior to or concurrent with early Christianity. Part Two treats those sections of the New Testament where gnostic influence is generally detected: the tradition of Jesus' sayings; the opponents in the Pauline corpus; the images of Jesus as heavenly redeemer; and the revelation discourses of the Fourth Gospel. Part Three treats the emergence of a self-consciously Christian Gnosticism and its conflict with orthodox Christianity.

PART ONE ————————————————————————

GNOSTIC ORIGINS

1

The Search for Pre-Christian Gnosticism

The quest for the origins of Gnosticism is as old as the second century C.E. Gnostic Christians often claimed that their teaching was secretly revealed by the risen Lord.[1] Following a pattern common in Jewish pseudepigraphal literature, other gnostic writings allegedly contain revelations from primordial times that were hidden until the appearance of the elect in the last days.[2] On the other side, Christian heresiologists constructed a genealogy of gnostic sects originating with the arch-opponent of the apostles, Simon Magus.[3] These accounts all recognize that like Christianity itself, Gnosticism is a new phenomenon, not a variant of an existing religious group. Unlike Christianity—and later Manicheism—gnostic writers do not refer back to the life or revelations of a particular historical individual as the foundation for their faith. The schools attached to particular teachers like Valentinus, Basilides, or Ptolemy are associated with exegesis and interpretation of an inherited tradition, not its creation.

Simon Magus

The accounts of Simon Magus may constitute a departure from the usual pattern, because Simon is said to found a sect. His female companion, Helena, was alleged to have been a Tyrian prostitute redeemed by Simon. Her story enacted the mythic drama of the fall of wisdom or the soul, its wandering in the world, and its redemption.[4] The life of the founder was told to provide a cult legend for the sect of the Simonians.[5] Irenaeus or his sources added details that make the life of Simon parallel to that of Christ: descent of a divine being into the world in human form and suffering in Judaea (*Adv. Haer.* 1.23.3). Hippolytus mocks the claims of a parallel to Christ. He alleges that when he was faced with refutation by Peter, Simon had instructed his disciples to bury him alive under a mound of earth. His promise to be resurrected on the third day was not fulfilled.[6]

The process of assimilating the Simon legend to the dominant story of Christ may have been fostered by both sides. Devotees of the cult may have sought to undermine competition from Christians. Christian reports sought to show that Simon copied Christ without fulfilling any of his promises. The Simonians were said to have worshiped their founder as a manifestation of Zeus. Christians at Rome mistook a dedicatory inscription to the old Roman god of oaths as a dedication to Simon.[7] Patristic reports about Simon's successors Dositheus and Menander repeat elements of the Simon legend.[8]

Both too much and too little has been claimed for this evidence. Some scholars have viewed the Samaritan origin of Simon and those directly associated with him as sure evidence that he is a pre-Christian cult figure who should be identified with the Samaritan magician of Acts 8:9-25.[9] The obvious assimilation of the Simon legends to the life of Christ has been used by those opposed to the hypothesis of first-century gnostic origins as evidence that gnostic sects are secondary deformations of the Christian tradition.[10] Claims about the historical Simon and Samaritanism clearly cannot be made with any reasonable degree of probability.[11] On the one hand, second-century writers, both gnostic and Christian, were convinced that the fundamental structures of gnostic speculation and cult arose outside Christianity. On the other hand, identifiable gnostic sects do not appear prior to the emergence of Christianity. Simonianism as it was known in the second century reflects the efforts of such a group to copy a more successful Christian rival.

Jewish Syncretism

The quest for a pre-Christian Gnosticism played a major role in the history-of-religions school.[12] The history of Christianity was no longer understood within a dogmatic framework. That perspective focused attention on the doctrinal conflict between emerging orthodoxy and its opponents in the second century. Instead, the study of early Christianity was to account for the emergence of Christianity as a religious phenomenon within the syncretistic religious pluralism of the Greco-Roman world. That world was no longer conceived as the linear descendant of classical Greece and Rome but as the melting pot of religious impulses from the eastern provinces like Syria and even beyond the boundaries of the Roman Empire, such as Iran.

Admittedly, the surviving sources for the study of Gnosticism within the Roman Empire are all marked by the second- and third-century conflicts between gnostic groups and Christian orthodoxy. Even the Nag Hammadi codices may have been copied and later buried by Pachomian monks.[13] Publication of the biography of Mani shows that the founder of Manicheism had been brought up in a Jewish Christian baptismal sect said to have been founded by the prophet Elkesai in Syria around 100 C.E.[14] What little evidence exists for Mandaean origins also points back to the Judaizing baptismal sects of the late first and early second centuries C.E.[15] Rabbinic attacks on a heresy known as "two powers in heaven" seem to embrace both gnostic and Christian speculation.[16] Origen's reply to Celsus's attack on Christianity charges that Celsus has confused Christianity with gnostic sectarianism.[17]

The two-powers speculation, the baptismal sectarianism out of which Manicheism and Mandaeism emerge, and even much of the gnostic speculation presented in Celsus's refutation of Christianity, are not centered on peculiarly Christian practices, themes, or doctrines. They are concerned with cosmogony, creation, the soul's plight in a world of darkness, and return to the heavenly world. The dualistic picture of the world in the Qumran scrolls, where spirits of light and darkness contend for the allegiance of humanity, provides further evidence for a diversity of expression within first-century Jewish circles. Heterodox Judaism is frequently invoked as an explanatory category in reconstructions of both gnostic and Christian origins. That the Pseudepigrapha have been preserved and in some cases edited by Christians or that direct contact with either Philo or the sectarian writings found at Qumran is improbable has not dampened enthusiasm for using these works as the primary background for understanding the New Testament.

Some history-of-religions scholars insist that gnostic evidence must be considered as well. Four elements in the New Testament suggest some contact with an early form of gnostic speculation:

1. the presentation of Jesus as heavenly redeemer;
2. the anthropological terminology of the Pauline tradition that

speaks of humans as trapped by the flesh and the Law of the
creator god;

3. expressions of realized eschatology that speak of the believer
   possessing eternal life or ascending into heavenly realms;
4. and the dualism of light and dark, elect and unbelievers, those
   who belong to heaven and those who belong to "this world,"
   which permeates the Fourth Gospel.

All the alternate explanations for each of these phenomena that have
been given refer to sectarian forms of Jewish expression: Jewish wisdom speculation, apocalyptic speculation, Philo's amalgam of Judaism
and Greek philosophy, or a pre-rabbinic Jewish mysticism and angel-
ology. Each of these sources reappears when scholars attempt to
account for the mythological speculation in gnostic writings.[18] Even if
the New Testament writers were not dependent on gnostic mythologizing, gnostic sources may provide evidence of first-century use of Jewish traditions. Uncontrolled by a scribal tradition as in Essene or rabbinic writings or philosophical reflection as in Philo, gnostic
individualism and esotericism with its profound concern for saving
revelation may be closer to emerging Christianity than the Jewish
sources commonly invoked in explanatory models.[19]

Gnostic Mythemes and Alienation

The history-of-religions approach to gnostic origins has also been
strongly influenced by Hans Jonas. Jonas rightly insisted that the conventional divisions of religious movements into sects and schools did
not touch the most significant features of religious life in the Hellenistic world. What is required is a phenomenological approach to the
various expressions of gnosis. Scholars must investigate the core elements and diverse expressions of gnosis as a religious phenomenon.[20]

The second-century gnostic texts presume a communal process of
mythmaking in which an established set of stories about the origins of
the cosmos and the fate of humanity is available for reflective analysis.[21]
Gnostic mythology takes shape in a cognitive environment accustomed
to philosophical discourse about origins. Consequently, it has an abstract
character that differentiates it from more primitive mythologies. Those
who repeat the gnostic myths are aware of the mythic as well as the
theological character of the activity in which they are engaged.[22] The
interpreter faces a daunting task of charting a narrative that lacks

the fanciful realism of primitive mythology. The gnostic landscape is populated with figures that bear abstract nouns as names or formations apparently derived from popular magical or angelic names created around Semitic roots.[23] Concrete narrative details frequently depend on allusions to Genesis stories and to other mythic figures.

Once the hurdles of language and inadequate, preliminary translations that make little attempt to clarify the narrative sequence or literary structure of the text are overcome,[24] the structural features of a consistent mythology become evident. Based on a collection of texts in which Seth (or his sister Norea) is the eschatological Immortal Human, ancestor of the gnostic race, many scholars agree upon a sequence of mythemes characteristic of Sethian Gnosticism.[25] They include the transcendent divine world and its aeons; the emergence and functions of divine Wisdom; the creation of the material world, of its rulers, and of Adam; the salvation history of the descendants of Adam; and enlightenment through a baptismal ritual.

The mythemes that are concerned with the creation of Adam, the origins of evil in creation, and the salvation history of Adam's descendants are clearly related to traditions that appear in Jewish sources as early as the first century B.C.E. Contemporary students of mythology recognize that there is no single version of a myth. Myths exist as collections of variants. At the same time, a socially established mythic corpus does have established mythemes that constrain what may be said within a given mythic world:

> Within the system of myths, there may be a systematic definition of the contents of the given "words"—the figures like Apollo and Dionysus or the story "bits" that Levi-Strauss calls mythemes, the killing of the Python by Apollo or the sewing of Dionysus into the thigh of Zeus. Myth itself, once formulated within a society, is given a system, a sort of lexicon, where relations between words are more fixed than in a language: the words "Dionysus" and "Zeus" may be combined in a sentence much more freely than the mythemes about them can be.[26]

This feature of mythic expression makes it impossible to establish a chronological ordering of the variants of a mythic system. Since myth is predominantly a social language, however, the emergence of a new system with a relatively fixed grammar implies the existence of a community of users. Consequently, the question of whether there is a pre-Christian Gnosticism can be reformulated in terms more appropriate to this understanding of mythology. The issue is not so much one of detecting "influences" in particular examples of religious language. Rather, the question is whether there is a coherent set of mythemes and an established grammar for using them. The use of philosophical topoi and intrusive exegetical comments as well as recasting of material into other formal patterns such as a revelation dialogue suggest that the surviving gnostic texts do draw on such an established mythic language.

Gnostic mythologizing presents its own peculiar difficulties to the analyst. Material creation is not only rejected as the true dwelling place of humanity—it is rarely depicted. Concrete images or descriptive passages that might provide clues about the community or its place in the world are lacking. The gnostic uses abstract language to externalize consciousness.[27] Does this isolation from the commonsense world of creation imply a radical experience of individual and cultural disintegration?

Modern interpreters have often felt that Gnosticism presaged the alienation of twentieth-century nihilism.[28] At the same time that he suggested that the New Testament writers must be read within the context of the powerful new gnostic mythologizing, Rudolf Bultmann taught New Testament scholars to reject mythological language as a vehicle for expressing the kerygma. Theologians and exegetes alike quickly took the reorchestrating of ancient Near Eastern mythemes, like the divine warrior's battle with the chaos monster, as evidence that biblical writers practiced their own form of demythologizing, challenging the mythic foundations of imperial ideologies. Gnostic mythology is even more clearly aimed at deconstructing a tradition than any canonical example. The mythic legitimacy of the creator god and his servants will imprison those who do not know how to detect the true account of fall and salvation hidden in the narrative.

The reduction of images that takes such an extreme form in gnostic writings has analogies in the New Testament. Use of mythic-sounding terms without the vehicle of a mythic narrative is sometimes taken to be evidence for the dynamic of demythologizing within the New Testament:

> The New Testament, despite a new recourse to mythological representations, principally to those of Jewish eschatology and the mystery cults, begins the reduction of images which serve it as a vehicle. The description of man outside faith puts into play what can already be called an anthropological interpretation of concepts like "world," "flesh," and "sin" which are borrowed from cosmic mythology. Here it is St. Paul who begins the movement of demythologization.[29]

But is this observation correct? The much more explicit deconstruction of traditional myths in gnostic discourse belongs to a movement of remythologizing the world. If one reads terms like "world," "flesh," and "sin" as "world," "body or desire," and "error," the words taken from Paul become commonplaces of the gnostic myth of origins. Breaking religious terminology away from its established mythemes makes it available for new patterns of mythological speculation.

A Demonized World

The basic mythic pattern that brings these terms into relationship with each other in gnostic myths involves the error or fall of Wisdom. The material world and its rulers emerge from the displaced power of Wisdom. The demonic powers create the psychic and material Adam. The archons have a glimpse of the Immortal Human that leads them to give Adam a form superior to their own. After Wisdom secretly provides Adam with the spirit, the powers recognize that their creation has a power superior to their own. They seek further means to imprison humans in ignorance. The brief tale of the fallen angels of Gen 6:1-4 becomes the attempt of the lustful archons to pollute Eve by raping her.

Elaboration of the story of the fallen angels is already evident in Jewish apocryphal traditions from the early second century B.C.E. (cf. *1 Enoch* 6–10; *Jub.* 4–7). Angelic beings defile themselves by sexual union with human women. They also reveal secrets to the women that will be the source of evil in human history: jewelry, cosmetics, and other arts that further seduction; gemstones and metallurgy that favor the accumulation of wealth and the production of arms; the arts of magic, astrology, and medicinal herbs. The offspring of these unions, the "giants," spread bloodshed, oppression, and even cannibalism on earth until its inhabitants cry out to heaven for relief. *Jubilees* considers writing to be one of the ambiguous arts. Cainan's father had taught him to read. When he discovered engraved stones, he read and transcribed the astrological lore left by the fallen angels (*Jub.* 8). Some variants of the tale blame human women for the angels' fall.[30] Reflective analysis led to the conviction that since sexual intercourse between human and spiritual beings is impossible, the crime must have occurred because the women lusted after the angels they had seen while they were having intercourse with their husbands (*T. Reuben* 5:7).

In gnostic mythology the angels are demonic powers who seek to introduce passions into humankind and thus enslave the gnostic race, which the Demiurge was unable to eradicate. The creator god devises the scheme with his powers, but the rest of the episode is clearly a variant of the pre-Christian Jewish tale:

> And the angels changed their likeness into the likeness of their [the women's] husbands, filling them with the spirit of darkness, which they mixed for them, and with evil. They brought gold and silver, and a gift, and copper and iron and metal with all kinds of things. And they steered the people who followed them into great troubles by leading them astray with many deceptions. They [the people] became old without having enjoyment. They died, not having found the truth and without knowing the God of truth. (*Ap. John* II 29,26—30,4; *NHLE*, 121–22, my trans.)

Another gnostic variant of the story identifies the demons as the seven planetary rulers. Their hostility to Adam causes Wisdom to throw them out of the heavens to earth. There they begin to operate as sinful demons (*Orig. World* II 121,28-35; *NHLE*, 186; cf. Rev 12:9-17). This activity keeps the world in bondage until the coming of the revealer:

> Now when the seven rulers were cast down from their heavens to the earth, they made themselves numerous, demonic angels to serve them. And these instructed humanity in many kinds of error, magic, and potions; and the worship of idols and bloodshed and altars, temples, sacrifices, and libations to all the spirits of the earth. They had as their coworker fate, who came into existence through the harmony of the gods of injustice and justice. Thus when the world had come into being, it distractedly erred at all times. For all people on the earth worshiped the spirits from the creation to the consummation—both the angels of righteousness and the men of unrighteousness. Thus the world came to exist in distraction, ignorance, and stupor. They all erred until the appearance of the True Man. (*Orig. World* II 123,3-24; *NHLE*, 186–87, my trans.)

In order to counter the influence of the demonic powers, the Immortal Father sends gnostic spirits into the world to reveal knowledge. The powers try to pollute these beings by mingling their seed with them, but this plan fails.

The mythological development of the tale of the fallen angels and human women in its gnostic variants is preoccupied with defilement. The archons use lust to attack the purity of the Sethian race. The body is the entry point for the counterfeit spirit created by the chief archon and the other passions that trap humanity in ignorance.

Another mytheme in the gnostic account associates the tree of knowledge with the seduction (or attempted rape) of Eve by the powers.[31] The rape of Eve appears in Jewish legends that attribute the birth of Cain to intercourse between Eve and the serpent (Satan).[32] This tradition may also have been known to the author of the Fourth Gospel.[33] What appears as a free-floating motif in diverse Jewish contexts becomes a fixed mytheme in the gnostic myth of origins.

This mytheme carries with it a strong element of Docetism, which is quite independent of the later Docetism by which gnostic writers separated the immortal spiritual Christ from the crucified. When the powers see the spiritual Eve, Adam's true helper, talking with him, they decide to defile her. She escapes into the tree, leaving behind a material shadow that they defile with their sperm (*Hyp. Arch.* 89,17-28; *NHLE,* 164). The author of *On the Origin of the World*, a reflective exposition of gnostic *mythologoumena*, explains how the archons thought they would entrap Eve and force her to serve them. If her light-being were defiled with their seed, she would be unable to ascend to her light. They put Adam to sleep and invent the rib story, which comes to him in a dream, so that he will dominate Eve (*Orig. World* 116,13-25; *NHLE,* 182).

In one version of the myth, the rape of Eve is repeated when the chief archon attacks Eve's daughter, Norea. Norea is a well-attested figure in Jewish legends (under the name Naamah). She is variously the sister of Seth and wife of Noah, a dual identification evident in her gnostic appearance in *Hypostasis of the Archons* as well.[34] Norea repels the attack by cursing the rulers of darkness. She reminds them that they did not violate her mother, only a false image. She calls out to the true God for help and is rescued by one of the heavenly angels (*Hyp. Arch.* 92,18—93,1; *NHLE,* 166–67). The conflict between Eve (or her daughter) and the archons displays a profound anxiety over the extent to which the human body is threatened or invaded by powers that are not under human control.

Although some scholars correlate concern for the integrity of bodily boundaries with rigid social boundaries,[35] these stories depict a human community with little ability to protect those boundaries. The myth of the fallen angels would enjoy widespread popularity among second- and third-century C.E. Christians because it provided a fit with their experience. Individuals required protection of a powerful guardian angel in order to negotiate life in this world successfully:

This story of the mating of the angels with the daughters of men and of its dire consequences for the peace of society was not a distant myth: it was a map on which they plotted the disruptions and tensions around them. When Tertullian reported the exile of astrologers from Roman cities, he treated the measure as an attempt to "mop up" anomalous and disruptive elements which directly continued on earth and in his own age, the exile of the fallen angels from heaven. The Christian therefore stepped from a world shot through with "loose powers" made dangerous by incomplete and destructive skill learned from anomalous sources, into the firm protection of a guardian angel.[36]

The map of the dangerous powers let loose in the world requires a ritual community to provide access to divine protection. The angel who comes from the world of light to rescue Norea and to reassure her that she and her descendants do not belong to the matter of the archons must represent a power that can also be tapped by believers. Baptismal rituals are among the most pervasive elements of the early Sethian tradition. Disputes over the effectiveness of water baptism as well as claims to possess the "true waters of baptism" in contrast to other sects continue throughout the second and third centuries. Mani condemns the baptismal waters of heretical sects, including the Elkesaites, as ruled by the king of the archons of the water.[37] But for the sects that practiced baptismal purification, the ritual provided protection from the influence of the demonic powers. *Apocalypse of Adam* refers to the seed of Seth, those who have never been enslaved to the creator, as "those who will receive his [Seth's] name upon the water" (V 83,5-6; *NHLE,* 285).[38] The ritual that accompanied baptism is reflected in the prayer formula from *Gospel of the Egyptians:*

> This great name of yours is upon me, O Self-Begotten one, without deficiency, you who are not outside me. . . . I have mixed myself with the Immutable. I have armed myself with the armor of light. I have become light. For the Mother was in that place because of the beauty of grace. Because of this I was formed in the circle of the riches of light that is in my bosom, that forms the numerous begotten ones in the light into which no accusation reaches. I will truly glorify you. (CG III 66,8—68,1; *NHLE,* 218, my trans.)

Summary

The formation of gnostic mythology and its initial ritual expression in rites of baptismal purification are not dependent upon emerging Christianity. History-of-religions studies of mythology make methods of analysis based on the source and redaction criticism of traditional Gospel studies questionable. Variants of a mytheme cannot be ordered in a chronological sequence. But the structural elements in gnostic mythologizing are distinctive versions of first-century Jewish material concerning the origins of the world.

The plight of divine Wisdom and her offspring provides a narrative line that enabled gnostic storytellers to see their own experience in the trials of Adam, Eve, and the demons. Although the abstract character of gnostic mythologizing makes it difficult to apply anthropological methods for analysis of myth, the strongly docetic cast of gnostic myth suggests a communal sense of separation from the larger social world. Demonic powers threaten those who lack the protection of ritual identification with a powerful heavenly protector.

2

Gnosticism and
the Jewish Connection

The search for the origins of gnostic mythology leads to Jewish sources that were taking shape in Palestine as well as Alexandria at the turn of the millennium. Scattered legends and exegetical traditions from Judaism have been reshaped into a coherent set of mythemes whose primary intent is to undermine the authority of the very tradition upon which the gnostics are so dependent. The revolt against the creator is clearly an essential element in gnostic mythology. At the same time, the very revelation said to support the creator's rule can be rightly understood to point to a different divine world and to the superiority of gnostic humanity. Such hostility suggests an audience that is still sensitive to the authority of Jewish Scripture but does not consider itself part of the Jewish community.[1]

A Samaritan Origin?

The sociocultural proximity of Samaria provides a context for conflicts over a shared religious tradition. The Fourth Gospel uses this hostility in its account of the conversion of a Samaritan woman and her village (John 4:9, 12, 20, 25). Some scholars have taken the Simon Magus/Dositheus legend as evidence for a historical link between gnostic origins and Judaism that runs through Samaritanism.[2] Gnostic tradition is not a complete denial of Jewish tradition. If the creator is identified with an angelic mediator who bears the divine name, then his arrogance and ignorance typify a fallen angel. Wisdom is still able to trick the lower powers and use both creation and revelation to bring about salvation. Some gnostic myths contain a mytheme in which the creator (or his offspring) repents when shown the heavenly world.[3] The name Sabaoth designates the repentant archon, who is enthroned in his own heaven, as god of the Jews. His imperfect revelation is nevertheless based on some knowledge of the heavenly world.[4] Similarly, the enthronement of Sabaoth in the seventh heaven draws on Jewish traditions about the divine throne chariot (*Hyp. Arch.* 95, 26-28).[5] The more extensive description of the throne chariot found in *On the Origin of the World* depends on speculation about the angelic hierarchies around the throne of God that can be found only in first-century Jewish sources. The seventy angelic guardians of the nations play a major role in this configuration (*Orig. World* 104,31—105,16; cf. *T. Naph.* 8:4-5).[6]

Those scholars who seek to trace the Jewish-Gnostic connection through Samaritanism suggest that like the later Cabalists, the essence of God was thought to dwell in his name/glory. The angel of the Lord in Exodus 23:20-21 possesses the divine name, which Simon Magus claimed was his own. But what can actually be known of Samaritanism in the first century C.E. does not support the conclusion that Sethian gnostic mythology arose within their circles. For example, a central element in the earliest gnostic mythologizing is descent of the gnostic race from the pure seed of Seth; early Samaritan sources have no evidence for such a use of the Seth figure.[7]

Simon was also alleged to have claimed the divine epithet "the standing one," a term Philo used to designate divine immutability. The theme of stability as characteristic of the soul that draws close to or enjoys the vision of God is evident in ascetic writings and philosophical mysticism throughout antiquity.[8] Clement of Alexandria, who is familiar with this common tradition, says that Simon Magus and his followers sought to copy the divine "standing one" (*Strom.* 2.52.2). Fossum uses the association between a praxis of "standing" in Simonianism and its appearance in the Platonizing Nag Hammadi text, *Three Steles of Seth*, to bolster the case for a Samaritan connection.[9] But the divine title does not appear in earlier references to Simonianism. Further, divine entities are commonly described as "standing." Its appearance in several different gnostic contexts suggests that it represents assimilation of the tradition to a somewhat later Platonizing mysticism.[10]

Linguistic Evidence
for Palestinian Traditions

The strongest arguments for a connection between gnostic mythologies and a Palestinian environment are linguistic. Names and wordplays that depend on Semitic languages cannot have been taken from early Christianity or from Alexandrian Judaism, which used Greek. The puns on the name Eve (*ḥwh*) allude to the cognate terms "snake" (*ḥwy'*) and "instructor" (*ḥwḥ* or *mḥwḥ*).[11] Another wordplay designates the son of Eve "lord" (*yhwh*) whom another calls "beast" (Aram. *ḥywḥ*).[12] Other Semitic names are associated with angelic and female figures in Sethian mythology. The angel who rescues Norea, Eleleth, one of four light-angels, has the Aramaic name *'illith*, "the tall one."[13] Norea's name appears in several forms. The Semitic name for Noah's wife is Naamah. A Naamah also occurs in Gen 4:22 as the daughter of the Cainite Lamech. This Naamah was reported to have produced a demon son from a liaison with a demon. Noah's wife was said to be in league with the devil in order to prevent the building of the ark. According to Pseudo-Philo, Adam and Eve had a daughter "Noaba," probably a Latin corruption of the Greek "Noema," which is the Septuagint form of Naamah in Gen 4:22.[14] The original Greek form of the name appears to have been *Hōraia* ("pleasing"), a direct equivalent of the Hebrew Naamah, to which the initial *nun* was added.[15]

Medieval midrash provides further evidence of the persistence of the story of Seth's sister and the fallen angels. One of the leaders of the fallen angels, Shemhazai, attempts to seduce a young maiden. She escapes by pronouncing the tetragrammaton. She is then taken up to heaven, as Norea is in one variant.[16] Her name is given as Esterah, Istahar, or Naamah.[17] In the Armenian Adam book, *Death of Adam*, after the loss of Abel Eve bore Seth ("comforter") and a daughter, "Estera."[18] Although Naamah is usually a negative figure in Jewish tales, she becomes the "helper" of humanity in gnostic mythology.

Hebrew and Greek etymologies are mixed in *On the Origin of the World* (108, 22-25; *NHLE*, 178). The Light-Adam appears in the lower world causing the lower providence (Pronoia) to pour out her light/blood upon the earth. His name becomes "luminous man of blood," playing on the Hebrew words *Adam*, *dām* ("blood"), and *'adāmā* ("earth"). The earth itself is called by the Greek term *adamas* ("strong," "iron").[19] This etymological tradition is embedded in other gnostic writings. "Adamas" the perfect transcendent human is the first aeon praised in *Three Steles of Seth*. The name of this aeon is also formed by prefixing the Hebrew word *gēr* ("stranger"). The Sethian race derive their stability in the divine realm from Adamas. In the Naasene teaching, etymologies based on the term *adamas* are attached to the allegorical interpretation of *Odyssey* 24.5-8. Speculation about the creation of the human in the image of the heavenly Adamas is combined with allegories that mix passages from Homer and from the Old Testament:

> The "rock," he says, is Adamas. This adamant (*adamas*) is the "cornerstone which has become the head of the corner" (Isa 28:16; Ps 118:22; Matt 21:42)—for in the head (*kephalē*) is the brain (*enkephalon*) which gives the characteristic form, the essence from which every fatherhood is given form [Eph 3:15]—whom, he says, "I lay down as adamant (*adamas*) at the foundations of Zion" (cf. Isa 28:16), which is an allegory, he says, for the creation of the human. Now the adamant (*adamas*) laid down is the "inner human," and the foundations of Zion are the teeth, as Homer mentions the "fence of the teeth" (*Iliad* 4.350), that is, a wall or palisade, within which is the inner human (*ho esō anthrōpos*) who has fallen down from the primal Human (*apo ton archanthropon*) above, Adamas.[20]

Adamantine came to designate the immovable, divine realm or even the divine Father himself. The Light-Adam or primal human belongs to that realm.

Further evidence for the close connection between gnostic mythology and Jewish tradition has been compiled in Birger Pearson's study of Jewish sources in gnostic literature.[21] Literary features of Jewish pseudepigrapha such as the testament form, the heavenly journey, and the dialogue with an interpreting angel are carried over into gnostic writings. Both gnostic writers and their patristic opponents refer to writings that may have been Jewish. Hippolytus reports that Gnostics used revelations attributed to Adam (*Ref.* 26.8.1) and others used a "Gospel of Eve" and books in the names of Seth and Norea (*Ref.* 26.1.4-9). The books in the name of Moses used by gnostic groups may have included writings like *Testament of Moses, Assumption of Moses,* and the Adam book also called the *Apocalypse of Moses* (*Ref.* 39.5.1). Another sect is said to have used the *Ascension of Isaiah* (*Ref.* 40.2.2).

Gnostic writings themselves give fewer direct references to other writings. But *Origin of the World* claims to have drawn material from several earlier works, including an *Archangelic Hymn of Moses* (102, 8-9), a *Book of Solomon*, probably one of those linked to magic (107,3), along with other books that dealt with the powers in the heavens and fate. The *Pistis Sophia* refers to books of Jeu said to have been written by Enoch (3,134). These books may be further examples of apocryphal Adam literature. Writings by Enoch, Adam, Seth, and others are referred to in the Manichean texts of the following century.

Enoch Traditions in Gnostic Mythology

Enoch traditions were probably the source for the earliest core of gnostic mythical speculation. Nag Hammadi authors appear to know a *Book of Giants,* as do the Manicheans. Mani gained familiarity with Jewish pseudepigraphal traditions in the Elkesaite sect as he was growing up. *Apocryphon of John* appears to be directly dependent on the version of the fallen angels found in *1 Enoch* 6:2—8:4:

1. The chief archon decides to send angels to the daughters of men to produce offspring (*Ap. John* II 26,16-20; *NHLE,* 120). The angels desire the daughters of men and decide to produce offspring (*1 Enoch* 6:2).
2. When they do not succeed at first, they gather to make a plan (*Ap. John* II 29, 20-23). When one angel, Semihazah, hesitates, they all take an oath (*1 Enoch* 6:3-5).
3. Angels assume the likeness of the women's husbands and fill them with the counterfeit spirit (*Ap. John* II 29,30—30,2). Not present in *1 Enoch,* this mytheme appears in the *Testament of Reuben* (5:5-7), which makes it clear that the spirit that filled the women was the spirit of lust.
4. Angels teach humankind metallurgy and lead them astray (*Ap. John* II 29,30—30,2). They teach the women charms and magic. The chief angel teaches metallurgy and technological skills. The people go astray (*1 Enoch* 7:1-6).
5. Humankind is mired in mortality and ignorance. All creation is enslaved (*Ap. John* II 30,2-7). The people cry out to God in their misery (*1 Enoch* 8:4).[22]

Other echoes of Enoch material have been detected elsewhere in gnostic writings.[23] Mani's biography mentions apocalypses by Adam, Enoch, Shem, and Seth. The fragmentary citations have not been identified with any known Pseudepigrapha, although they may well have been Jewish apocalypses preserved among the Elkesaites.[24] The *Book of the Giants* reported to have been composed by the prophet Mani himself may have been derived from Enoch materials about the giants, such as those found among the fragments in Cave 4 at Qumran.[25]

The Manichean example suggests that Jewish material preserved in a sectarian context could continue to inspire new forms of gnostic mythology in the mid-third century C.E. Of itself, the presence of such Jewish tradition does not determine the relative date of any particular work. Nor does it require a pre-Christian origin for the emergence of Gnosticism. Mani has done what other gnostic writers also do: they incorporate earlier sources into their works. Consequently, any discussion of the Jewish contribution to the emergence of gnostic speculation must include those sources found in writings that are clearly the work of Christian Gnostics.

Anti-Jewish Midrash

Midrashic commentary normally fills the gaps in the text. 1QapGen recounts the unusual signs that accompany the birth of Noah, for example. It is related to similar traditions in *1 Enoch* 106 and *Jubilees*. Gnostic authors use the gaps and inconsistencies to undermine the text's authority. Birger Pearson has identified two midrashic sections in *Testimony of Truth*. The first treats the serpent in paradise (IX 45,30—49,7; *NHLE*, 454–55).[26] The second, which is extremely fragmentary, mentions David, Solomon, and the demons dwelling in the foundation of the Jerusalem temple (70,4-30; *NHLE*, 458). The demons are released when the Romans (= Ptolemy?) overrun the temple and empty the water pots in which Solomon had imprisoned them.[27] *Testimony of Truth* has taken over this material as part of an antiheresiological argument against orthodox Christians and non-Encratite gnostic sects. Damage to the concluding lines of the midrash on the serpent makes it difficult to tell how the author is applying this piece of tradition to his opponents. Since the source appears to have concluded with a comment on the serpent of Num 21:19, the transition to a comment about Christ was probably an allusion to John 3:14-16.[28] The opponents may have been orthodox Christians. The midrash is directed at the ignorant envy shown by the creator god. A similar argument appears in Julian the Apostate as evidence against Christianity.[29]

But the midrash itself depends only on Jewish sources. Its depiction of God in the paradise story may have been drawn up as evidence for the anthropomorphic and inferior nature of Jewish belief. Disputes about anthropomorphism in religious texts led to Platonizing allegories of ancient mythology. Philo preserves an antianthropomorphic interpretation of passages that fit the type encountered in the Genesis section of *Testimony of Truth*. Why does God get Adam to name the animals? Not because God is ignorant, but because God is like a teacher eliciting knowledge from a pupil (*Opif. Mund.* 149-50).[30] Although Philo insists that God has no resemblance to humans, the account of God breathing into Adam's face does refer to the spirit received by Adam's soul (*Leg. All.* 1.36-37). But the insistence upon antianthropomorphic readings of Genesis does not seem to have been the norm in the first centuries C.E. Jews were said to have thought of God in anthropomorphic terms. God's bodily form fills the entire cosmos.[31] Precisely the characteristics of the creator that *Testimony of Truth* mocks are the ones that might have been used within a Jewish context to argue for an antianthropomorphic reading such as that proposed by Philo.

Although the text is extremely fragmentary, *Melchizedek* (IX, *1*) may also draw directly on Jewish tradition. This text appears to depend upon the Jewish picture of Melchizedek as the eschatological, messianic figure.[32] Christ has been added as another figure among those in the heavenly realms.

Christianizing
Early Gnostic Traditions

Adding Christ to the heavenly aeons required little modification of the basic narrative in many gnostic texts. Had the original mythemes that shape gnostic speculation originated among Christians, one might have expected a more substantive appropriation of Christian themes. I have already mentioned that some of the strongest links to Judaism appear in the mythic accounts of the origins of the world in *Apocryphon of John* and *Hypostasis of the Archons*. Even the theology of divine transcendence with which *Apocryphon of John* begins might have its origins in Jewish Platonism. Philo of Alexandria provides for the Platonic interpretation of Jewish tradition about God in which divine transcendence is unknowable in principle.[33] Revelation is mediated through the Sophia figure, whose portrait is at least partly dependent on Jewish Wisdom speculation. Norea plays a similar role in *Hypostasis of the Archons*.

Because several versions of *Apocryphon of John* are extant, one can see even more clearly that the Christian elements in the framework of the text are secondary. When the framework story of Jesus' appearance to John and the dialogue on the different types of soul are removed, practically nothing Christian remains. The occasional glosses in the text differ between the long and the short version. The short version identifies Autogenes as the preexistent Christ (BG 30,14-17; Foerster, *Gnosis*, 1:109). This identification is lacking in the parallel passage in the long version (II 6,23-28; *NHLE*, 108). In the short version, the female heavenly wisdom figure, Epinoia, is the one who teaches Adam and Eve from the tree (BG 60,16-61,2; Foerster, *Gnosis*, 1:116). In the long version, Christ speaks to them from the tree (CG II 23,26-28; *NHLE*, 118).[34] The short version concludes with the Christ as the one responsible for the revelation that led to the formation of the gnostic race in the divine image. The long version ends with a poetic celebration of the three descents of the Mother, the perfect Pronoia, to awaken humanity.[35] Only the framework of the long version leads the reader to identify the "I" in this hymn with Christ.[36]

The fluidity of the Christianizing glosses in the two versions suggests that they are secondary to the account. They may even have been the work of individual scribes who were copying the text for a gnostic Christian audience. They felt it necessary to clarify the soteriological function of Christ by inserting glosses. But they had no established tradition of how to make the appropriate identifications.

The structure of some of the gnostic revelations also appears to derive from earlier Jewish models. *Apocalypse of Adam* is a testament of the dying Adam to his son Seth. This form is clearly a variant of testaments of Adam and other patriarchs that are common in Jewish apocrypha.[37] The basic structure of the *Poimandres* (C.H. I) follows the pattern of *2 Enoch*.[38] The prayers and formulae at the end of *Poimandres* also depend on the phrasing of Jewish liturgical models.[39]

In all these cases, the Jewish elements belong to the earliest traditions contained in the text. Not only has *Apocryphon of John* been Christianized, but it has also been molded by a Platonizing asceticism that sought to ward off the instability of the passions. *Poimandres* is now a Hermetic text. The Thrice-Great Hermes will mediate the saving self-knowledge. In its present form, *Apocalypse of Adam* may even be a restoration of the primary Sethian myth aimed to counteract the growing influence of Christianity.[40] In all three cases, it is possible to conceive of a saving revelation and cult without Christianity. It is not possible to say the same for the Jewish elements in these examples.

Summary

Gnostic sources show that the mythic structures of this emerging religious sect depend on Jewish traditions. The materials on which gnostic storytellers draw did not take the same shape among Jews as they did when incorporated into the gnostic myth. Linguistic clues such as names and puns as well as direct borrowing of literary models and exegetical methods show that a Semitic-speaking background must be presumed for the originating tradition. Gnosticism does not represent a second-century hellenizing of Christianity.

Some scholars continue to be attracted to the early Apologists' view of the origins of Gnosticism. Samaria seems to provide not only knowledge of Semitic languages, Mosaic traditions, and so on but also hostile distance to explain the ambivalence concerning the creator god that is central to gnostic speculation. But there is little evidence for Samaritanism itself as a revolt against either the creator or Moses. What little we know about Samaritan belief and practice in the first century C.E. does not support persistent attempts to undermine the presumed foundations of the tradition as gnostic writers do. Consequently, attempts to revive the Samaritan hypothesis simply lead to scholars attempting to explain one near unknown with a second unknown.

The overthrow of inherited meaning comes to form a central feature in gnostic speculation. Mani reorchestrates many of the earliest mythemes to provide crucial building blocks in his system. Mani has inherited this material from the Jewish Christian baptismal sect in which he grew up. The powerful hold of the gnostic mythemes becomes evident with the development of Manicheism. Finally, I have also shown that these stories can be Christianized very superficially. The Christ is inserted into the heavenly hierarchy but little else changes. Other elements in the growth of gnostic writings from the first century to the second- and third-century texts that make up the extant collection include assimilation of a philosophical understanding of the divine world and even a de-Christianizing return to the mythic structures of a non-Christian gnosis.

3

Gnostic Influence
and the New Testament

Although the written sources for gnostic speculation are later than
most of the New Testament, the formation of gnostic mythology takes
place in a Jewish context during the first century C.E. Because Gnosticism and Christianity emerged from the same environment, the question of influence is not whether New Testament writers were using or
refuting explicit examples of gnostic mythology. Both the New Testament understanding of Christ and the gnostic imagery of a heavenly
revealer were in the process of formation. In the second century some
gnostic writers sought to adapt their mythological tradition to the
more successful Christian figure of Christ as a savior. The religious
environment of first-century Christianity contained the formative traditions and mythemes of the later gnostic systems even though it might
not have identified them explicitly as elements of a threatening coun-
tersystem. It may even be the case that gnostic mythologizing could
not become a serious threat to Christianity until it had incorporated
some of the symbolic elements of Christianity with their ability to
reformulate a communal identity for the Gentiles that was opposed
to Judaism but retained the solidarity of the latter.[1]

Variations on the Redeemer Figure

Because one has to reconstruct the traditions behind second- and third-
century gnostic writings, the New Testament itself may even be the
best guide to answering the question of whether gnostic mythemes
influenced its writers.[2] In order to understand the significance of gnos-

tic speculation for believers, modern scholars have asked what religious or experiential criteria best describe the first-century beginnings of gnostic thought. Hans Jonas has reminded scholars that in the syncretism of the first century, gnostic *mythologoumena* can be combined in different ways. Each example serves to convey the special sense of redemption through enlightenment and of revolt against the God of the Old Testament that are so typical of Gnosticism.[3]

The New Testament and the Nag Hammadi writings preserve different, independent lines of development. For example, the Son of man tradition in the New Testament is developed along the lines suggested by Daniel 7. Gnostic use of the term owes more to the esoteric traditions found in *1 Enoch*. The New Testament preserves its Jesus sayings in the context of apocalyptic expectation. Gnostic sayings material develops the wisdom side of the tradition. Parallels between the New Testament and gnostic traditions often represent different developments of the common tradition.

Hans-Martin Schenke insists that a formative experience is required for the emergence of a new religious phenomenon.[4] In the case of Gnosticism, scholars used to emphasize the myth of a redeemed redeemer; most of the revealer figures in the new gnostic material are not trapped in the material world. Believers are saved by discovering that true humanity is achieved by identification with a heavenly figure. Consequently Schenke proposes the origin of gnosis as ecstatic identification with a heavenly source of redemption.[5] The encounter with emerging Christianity led to three developments. From the gnostic side, the redeemer figures were "historicized," identified with particular individuals. Jesus is the most prominent. The cult that grew up around Simon Magus represents another variant of this development. Although the earliest versions of the myth often have the heavenly revealer figures speak or appear from the heavens, assimilation to the Christian stories about Jesus required a more incarnational view of the activities of the redeemer. On the other side, Christians may have developed speculation about the preexistence of Christ in order to counter the proliferation of heavenly revealer figures.[6]

The second-century reaction against gnostic teachers and their disciples hardened the lines between gnostic and Christian speculation. The diversity among gnostic variants of what is essentially the same mythic pattern became evidence that Gnostics had fragmented into different heretical schools. This fragmentation was contrasted with an alleged unity of the orthodox Christian position.[7] By the end of the

second century C.E., the orthodox canon defined what was understood
to be an authentic presentation of Jesus and salvation. Other revelations could not claim authoritative status. In the first and early second
centuries C.E., however, pluralism of religious expression rather than
uniformity may have represented the common expectation. Second
temple Judaism generated its pluralism around the interpretation of
the Law as well as in the development of haggadah surrounding major
figures in the tradition like Adam, Enoch, Moses, the patriarchs, and
the prophets.[8] Helmut Koester's seminal essay advocated a similar
approach to the presentations of Jesus and the forms of religious orga-
nization in early Christianity.[9]

Gnostic Elements
in the New Testament

In Part Two, I examine the interdependence of gnostic and precanonical New Testament traditions. The fixed boundaries that would emerge
after the second-century struggles to institutionalize Christianity are
absent in the first century. Consequently, what appears deviant or
heretical in the later period may have been no more than one line of
development in the rich pluralism of the first century. Although the
Fourth Gospel came to be incorporated into the orthodox formulation
of Christian faith, its initial representation of Jesus was as daring a
departure from the Synoptic variants as gnostic mythologizing was
from its tradition. Frederick Wisse has observed that John can be
understood as participating in the same speculative freedom as the
gnostic writers:

> The author of the Fourth Gospel obviously did not feel bound by the
> early traditions about Jesus which were incorporated in the Synoptic
> Gospels, and his reinterpretation of Jesus is in many ways as daring
> as that found in Gnostic gospels. . . . As we see from their writings,
> Gnostics had little difficulty affirming the incarnation or the virgin
> birth, though as in the case of the author of the Gospel of John and
> many others in the early church, the real interest was in the divine
> presence.[10]

In attempting to understand how the New Testament authors reflect
the religious milieu that they share with emerging Gnosticism, one
must invoke the New Testament itself as evidence. This methodological necessity does not differ markedly from the use of the New Testament to understand other phenomena of first-century Judaism.

Although the discovery of the Dead Sea Scrolls has increased our knowledge of sectarian Judaism in this period, we are still dependent upon the New Testament for much of our information about the Pharisees and about Jewish life on the popular, village level.

Because the case for gnostic influence in the New Testament requires hypotheses that are formulated on the basis of the New Testament itself, one should not be surprised that scholars still disagree over the proper method of investigation to pursue. Walter Schmithals's analysis of the Pauline opponents has been a controversial reconstruction of the evidence. By insisting that the opposition to the Pauline mission was indebted to a single, gnosticizing understanding of Christianity, Schmithals has attempted to unify the various fronts on which Paul appears to argue, that is, against excesses of religious enthusiasm in the Corinthian community and against excesses in Judaizing practice in Galatians. The link between Judaizing and a false understanding of the preexistent, heavenly Christ appears to be presupposed in Philippians and Colossians. Because the Pauline letters attest to this conflict by the middle of the first century C.E., gnostic and Christian speculation are seen to be intertwined from the beginning.

Although other accounts of the controversy over Judaizing have seemed more persuasive,[11] Schmithals's treatment of the Pauline opponents can be seen to highlight significant developments in the religious environment of early Christianity. These developments are often overlooked when the New Testament is read against the Christian orthodoxy that emerged from the struggles of the second century. Paul's Corinthian opposition was clearly interested in spiritual identification with the source of heavenly revelation. The believer achieved perfection through that identification. These developments are sometimes traced to the influence of Philo's philosophical speculation about the role of wisdom in the soul of the wise or perfect. Yet the technical terminology of philosophical speculation is missing in the Corinthian correspondence.

Schmithals proposes to understand the "opponents" as examples of a gnosticizing Christianity rather than as heirs to the type of philosophical speculation found in Philo. He suggests six areas in which gnosticizing influence is evident: Christology, knowledge, pneumatic self-understanding, ethics, spiritualized eschatology, and ecclesiology.[12] Their ecstatic identification with a heavenly Christ led the Corinthian opponents to stress the freedom of the true believer from the restraints of the material world. Ethical conduct—whether the ascetic rejection of marriage or the liberated freedom of Christian women—demonstrates the superiority of the gnostic believer to the powers that claim to dominate this world. The individual attains immortality and freedom in knowing the Savior, not through the death of Christ on the cross or some future resurrection of the body. Schmithals holds that spiritual endowment was the basis for leadership in gnosticizing groups.[13] By this criterion, the Corinthian opponents rejected the authority of Paul, Peter, and other apostolic figures. Second Corinthians shows that Paul's status as a pneumatic was constantly challenged (2 Cor 11:5; 12:1-2). Although gnostic sectaries would certainly construe Christianity along the lines that Schmithals proposes, there is no evidence in Paul's text to suggest that these themes derived from early gnostic mythemes.

But Schmithals does not confine his proposals to the position of the opponents. Several features of Paul's theology depend on gnosticizing speculation. Paul does not entirely reject the charismatic legitimation of authority (1 Cor 2:10-16; Rom 12:5). Paul formulates his own variant of the identification of the individual with Christ. He frequently speaks of Christian life in terms suggesting that salvation is experienced as present through the Spirit. Baptismal formulae attest to the rejection of those divisions of gender, race (Jew or Gentile), and status that the demonic powers of the world used to keep humanity in bondage (Gal 3:28; 1 Cor 12:13; Col 3:10-11). Even more persistent and striking evidence of gnostic influence on Pauline theology can be found in the antithesis of the flesh and spirit. "Flesh" represents fallen humanity. In gnostic mythology its imprisoning power was due to the fact that it had been created by the demonic powers. But those who belong to the Spirit no longer belong to the realm of the flesh. Finally, Schmithals concludes that gnostic convictions about a heavenly redeemer lie behind the understanding of Christ as preexistent.[14]

These proposals bring us closer to the mythological perspective of gnostic texts, which I examine in more detail in chapter 7. Schmithals notes correctly that Paul's descriptions of spirit and flesh depart from the Essene examples to which they are frequently compared because the contrast is not between two spirits at war within the hearts of human beings. Nor can one derive this antithesis from the hellenized speculation of Philo, for whom the flesh is also of no consequence. The struggle occurs between God's Wisdom or Word and the contrary orientation of the soul toward the world of sense perception and pleasure.[15] Although Paul never invokes the mythological account of the origins of the flesh that are characteristic of gnostic speculation, his treatment and evaluation of the flesh is more congenial to the gnostic context than to the philosophical reflection of Philo.

The question of whether the Pauline picture of Christ requires the gnostic emphasis on heavenly revealers is more difficult to determine. Like the Fourth Gospel, Paul is not predominately concerned with the life of Jesus. His heavenly exaltation provides the final focus of Christian life. Paul's personal emphasis on the cross checks the tendency of some to turn the present life of the apostle and Christians into an immediate expression of heavenly glorification.

Cultic Innovation and Mythology

Because the evidence is predominantly documentary, comparisons are usually drawn at the level of ideas and images. Religious change becomes evident only when there is a change in the ideas and symbols being used by the members of a group. Yet I have already pointed out that elements of religious experience are fundamental to the emergence of Gnosticism. Helmut Koester shifts the terms of the debate by insisting that new mythic formulations emerge only as the rationalization of cultic practice.[16] Ethnic dislocation and the general religious syncretism of this period favored the emergence of new cultic forms that claimed to be rooted in antiquity. Koester provides a contemporary analogy in the cult of Palaimon/Melikertes. The cult is of Roman origin and developed in connection with the Isthmian games. Athletes and musicians would swear oaths in a mystery ceremony. A new cult myth was generated to explain the sect's activity. It held that the cult hero arrived from the sea on a dolphin. Named Melikertes, the god had been dead and now lives.[17]

According to this model of religious change, a community formed and changed its behavior. The changes then had to be incorporated within familiar myth structures. An example of this dynamic is evident in the Johannine Gospel and Epistles. Once expelled from the synagogue, the particular cultic practices of the Christian community took on central importance. At the same time, the community had to create a new mythic picture of Jesus as the redeemer figure from heaven. Once this transition had been accomplished, the field was open for the full-blown development of gnostic redeemer figures like those in the second century C.E. Analogous developments can be demonstrated for other groups. The speculative treatment of stock mythemes in

Gnosticism demonstrates that myths can be constructed out of the stock pieces that were part of their culture.

Koester's example of the Palaimon cult provides a glimpse of how myth and cult were interrelated in the Roman period. The games were said to honor the young boy Palaimon/Melikertes brought ashore by a dolphin. Ancient sources mention swearing an oath and entry into an underground shrine where the youth is alleged to be concealed, as well as ritual sacrifices to a black bull. Archaeologists have uncovered a circular temple, statues of a dolphin with a boy on its back, inscriptions referring to Sisyphus (the legendary sacrificer of the bull), and pits with ashes and bones of the bull. The number of lamps suggests that the sacrifices were nocturnal.[18] The myth itself and its associated rites might seem to be a piece of ancient etiology. But archaeologists have not discovered any remains of such a cult that date to the Greek period. It seems to have been introduced after the Romans refounded Corinth as a Roman colony. Koester has proposed that other details of the cult suggest even more precise information about its formation. The name Melicerta, derived from the Phoenician god Melqart, was probably associated with Palaimon through the association of the latter with Herakles. Tyrian Melqart was a dying/rising deity who had been called Herakles by Greek settlers since the time of Alexander.

Other Phoenician elements include the bull sacrifice in special pits. Such burnt offerings were not typical in Greek cults. The peculiar lamps are also not typical of Greek cults. But the cult would hardly be foreign to the Greek environment. Worship of the youth alleged to be dead yet alive in the sanctuary parallels veneration of a cult hero. Participants in the games swear sacred oaths in a secret ceremony that was said to involve initiation (Gk. *teletē*) and enthusiasm (*orgiasmos*). Consequently, Koester suggests that this cult was introduced by Phoenician settlers in the new colony. In this example it appears evident that the syncretistic myth is secondary to the cult. Created out of fragments of Greek mythology, it explains the rites associated with the games.[19]

Koester applies this example to the Fourth Gospel. Its myth of Jesus as heavenly redeemer emerged as a response to gnosticizing interpretations of the cult and of the sayings of Jesus.[20] Because the example derives from Roman Corinth, it should also illuminate the way in which Paul's Corinthian opponents understood Christianity. First Corinthians is unique among Paul's letters in its preoccupation with cultic behavior, claims to be "perfected" (*teleios*), and divisive manifestations of enthusiasm. We know that some Christians continued to attend ritual meals in pagan sanctuaries (1 Cor 8:10; 10:7, 14-22). Paul's athletic analogy (1 Cor 9:24-27) would also have reminded his readers of the Isthmian games. Although we do not have direct evidence for either the cultic practices or the mythic legitimations of Paul's Corinthian opponents, these may well have represented a mythic syncretism like that in Koester's example.

Corinthian preoccupation with freedom from sociocultural restraints could certainly have found powerful mythic expression in variants of the Genesis story such as occur in the earliest strata of the Nag Hammadi material. But Koester's example reminds one that cultic and mythological innovation was frequently local and particular. The grammar and symbols could be drawn from the broad range of Hellenistic religious syncretism while taking on a definitively regional accent. For a newly founded colony like Corinth, in which Roman colonists of diverse origins had to reinvent their own "ancestral religion," this impetus would have been even more pronounced.[21]

Recognizing the particularity and syncretistic creativity of local situations, one cannot presume that either Gnosticism or Christianity is a fixed entity that one may compare with the other. Koester observes that one must reject the older history-of-religions argument about whether a pre-Christian Gnosticism existed. Instead, one should focus on the gnosticizing process as it is evident in diverse contexts:

> Was there an original Gnostic religion with its original pre-Christian myth? The answer to this question must be negative. But there certainly were Gnostic religions and Gnosticizing interpretations of religious traditions and mythical materials, pre-Christian and Christian, Jewish and pagan. They may have been committed to different cults and they developed different myths, because in each instance, as also in the case of Melikertes in Isthmia, the formation of such myth is the result of interpretation of quite different materials, traditions, writings and rituals.[22]

This interpretation of Gnosticism as a family of cultic practices and their associated mythic legitimations remains difficult to document, although the persistent references to baptismal rites in early Sethian texts certainly indicates a cultic context. As a working hypothesis, it focuses attention on the fluidity of first-century Christianity. Wisse has attacked such interpretations of the gnostic phenomena by insisting that Gnosticism was not originally a form of religious practice. Instead, he argues that gnostic teachers came into conflict with second-century church leaders in Rome. Initially, gnosis was a school phenomenon. Teachers like Valentinus had been part of a diverse Christian community. When the church authorities sought to control teaching within the community, Valentinus and other heterodox Christians were forced out. Wisse insists that Gnosticism was not a religious phenomenon with its own cultic identity, though once forced out of the larger community Gnostics may have formed loose associations that fostered individual speculative thought and individual ascetic practice.[23] In Wisse's view the question is not whether particular New Testament writings reflect gnostic religious experience or the teachings of Gnosticism but whether their authors stand in the speculative tradition represented by gnostic authors.[24]

I have pointed out that gnostic mythology incorporates Jewish exegetical traditions that do suggest a speculative tradition. But Koester's example shows that new mythological formulations also employ fragments of earlier traditions, new identifications based on names and etymology, and the like. Further, new cultic forms emerge on the basis of established patterns. Jewish sectarian purification rituals as well as Christian cultic patterns might easily appear in gnostic sects. Without the archaeological evidence, we would not know that the cult of Palaimon/Melikertes was a new innovation in Roman Corinth. Variations on the basic structures in a mythic story are not necessarily signs of individual speculation. Within the collection of works characterized as Sethian, the speculative elaboration of inherited mythemes is readily identifiable in the redactional elements of works like *Origin of the World*. The inherited traditions of such writings presume a baptismal enlightenment that does not have typically Christian elements. Similarly, one should question the affirmation that the Fourth Gospel engages in individualist speculation rather than the symbolic explication of a community's faith.

Summary

The conflicts of the second century led to systematization on both sides. Conventional Christians as well as their gnostic opponents made conscious attempts to formalize the diverse traditions inherited from the first century. Gnostic teachers emerge within the sociologically more successful Christian communities. Their attempts to formulate a self-conscious Christian, gnostic identity are treated in more detail in Part Three.

Students of the first and early second centuries must remember that there was no fixed canon. Without an established sacred narrative, cultic practice, or creed, individual groups could develop the same heritage quite differently. Thus the question of gnosticizing influence in the New Testament cannot be asked as though there was an ideologically well-defined group of gnostic devotees against which first-century Christian authors wrote.

Finally, Koester has demonstrated that literary evidence for ideological or mythological change can postdate the more significant cultic innovations. Cultic change is both local and particular. When a sufficiently coherent group has developed ritual patterns of interaction, it may draw upon inherited mythemes to account for its own existence and practice. This phenomenon makes it highly likely that both gnostic and Christian practice in the first two centuries had regionally diverse embodiments.

4

Reconstructing
Gnostic History

The complex evidence provided by the tradition history of the new sources for the development of Gnosticism makes it difficult to formulate a comprehensive hypothesis about the development of the various forms of Gnosticism.[1] I have noted that the ubiquity of Jewish haggadic material at an early stage of gnostic mythologizing makes it impossible to maintain that if one can show that a motif in the New Testament, such as the dualism of the Fourth Gospel, has Jewish parallels then one need not consider parallels with Gnosticism. Many of the midrashic elements in early gnostic mythologizing are very close to their Jewish counterparts. Periodized salvation history, interest in cosmology, the origins of humanity, myths of the rebellious angels, and speculation about wisdom are all fundamental to the structure of gnostic mythologizing. They cannot be derived from the second-century interaction between gnostic teachers and orthodox Christianity.[2] Any hypothesis about the origins and development of Gnosticism must include its origins within a Jewish milieu.

The interactions between Christian and gnostic thinkers in the second century were probably facilitated by their common first-century heritage. It is not necessary to suppose that a specific event catalyzed the emergence of gnosticizing speculation. Social reality, cultic innovations, and shifting communal identities are reflected in and facilitated by the formulation of new mythic traditions. The bitterness directed at the Creator God of the Old Testament is no harsher than the polemic against "the Jews" in the Fourth Gospel. Hostility from outsiders intensifies the symbolic dualism used to account for the division between the group and its opponents. Anti-Jewish symbolism may have contributed to the convergence between Gnostics and Christians in the early second century. The gnostic mythology provided an explanation for the hostility of the Jewish community to the revelation of Jesus. Once "the Jews" came to symbolize a group hostile to the revelation possessed by a gnostic or Christian group, the symbolism might be reapplied to other opponents. Christian gnostic writers clearly understood their orthodox Christian opponents as slaves of the malicious creator.

On the Margins of Judaism

A history-of-religions approach to the origins of Gnosticism has to acknowledge the diverse manifestations of gnostic and Christian sectarians as phenomena within or on the margins of Judaism. Gnostic mythologizing appeals to the Old Testament as an authoritative text that is to be interpreted. Apocalyptic speculation within Gnosticism focuses on cosmological origins, the structure of the heavenly world, and the collapse of the world dominated by the evil angels. Unlike the New Testament, the Gnostics are not interested in the significance of events in world history as part of a divine plan. Heavenly Wisdom plays a central role in gnostic mythology. Her descent into the world below, lack of a suitable dwelling there, and return to the heavenly world echo the plight of Wisdom in *1 Enoch* 42. The combination of a tale of Wisdom's plight in the world with speculation on the cosmological origins of Wisdom and her place in the soul also has roots in Hellenistic Jewish speculation.[3] Unlike Philo's Platonic understanding of Wisdom and Word as the divine order in the world, the gnostic tradition is heir to a philosophical skepticism. The divine has no relationship to the material world, which itself is without any form or order discernible to human reason. This combination also differs from the underlying convictions of those New Testament passages that draw on speculation about cosmological wisdom. In the New Testament, the wisdom and order of God are evident in the created world (cf. 1 Cor 8:6; Rom 1:19-21).

Scholars have suggested other elements in gnostic mythologizing that were not mediated by Christianity. Those systems appealing to a dualism of two opposing principles at the origins of the cosmos may have been influenced by Iranian dualism.[4] The catalog of accounts of the birth of the redeemer in *Apocalypse of Adam* draws upon diverse mythologies, both Greco-Roman and Semitic.[5] Gnostic cult may also have been more open to elements from the lingua franca of Greco-Roman mystery initiations than early Christianity was.[6]

Scholars frequently ask whether the gnostic readings of Genesis could have arisen among Jews or only among non-Jews living on the margins of a Judaism to which they were hostile. It is difficult to imagine the details of the exegesis that gnostic mythemes share with Judaism being known among non-Jews. Certainly, no gentile Christian sources indicate an awareness of speculation about biblical passages and figures that goes beyond what might be reasonably available to readers of the Greek Old Testament and other commonplaces of Hellenistic Jewish propaganda. But Maurice Casey has recently argued that we need more differentiated categories to describe the options for self-identity available to those who might consider themselves Jews or be considered Jews by others. Some ethnic Jews may identify themselves as Gentiles; be considered apostates by those who insist on formal observance of Torah, Shabbat, and kosher as marks of Jewishness; and be considered as "Jews" by Gentiles who are aware of the familial origins of such persons or of their refusal to participate in some elements of pagan cult. Similar variations in perception are typical when one asks about how those persons who are ethnically Gentiles but embrace a Jewish life-style are considered.[7]

On a more differentiated scale, some early Christians were "Jews" both in their own self-identification and in the estimation of others. Those who married non-Jews had children like Timothy (Acts 16:1-3) whose identity was unclear. When Paul had Timothy circumcised, Timothy's identity was clearly shifted in the direction of Judaism:

> This must have increased the number of people who would perceive him as Jewish, a perception evidently held by Paul and by Timothy himself. Timothy could then engage in the Gentile mission, generally perceived by Christians as a Jew who, like Peter and Paul, was not observant when observance of the Law would have been dysfunctional in the Christian community.[8]

This example demonstrates that the question of whether gnostic mythologizing arose within or on the margins of Judaism is too global. The rebellion against the creator in gnostic mythologizing, which is frequently taken as evidence that the Gnostics would have identified themselves as non-Jews,[9] should be reevaluated. I have pointed out that gnostic mythology identifies Gnostics as the true descendants of the spiritual Eve, the seed of Seth. In one variant of the myth, the repentance of Ialdabaoth's son, Sabaoth, upon seeing the heavenly Wisdom provides an explanation for the true knowledge of the heavenly world that is mediated through the Torah.[10] Gnosticism may well have emerged among nonobservant, assimilating Jews.

This observation points attention to studies that attempt to discern the socioeconomic factors that contributed to the rise of gnostic sects. Historians of Greco-Roman paganism rightly resist the common Christian claims that paganism was so dysfunctional that people turned en masse to bizarre orientalizing cults. The alleged decline of paganism has been wildly overstated.[11] Conversions from Christianity to Judaism are also attested throughout this period.[12] I have already noted that a new cult might arise among the displaced populace of a new city in Corinth. Other scholars have noted the creation of classes of functionally literate persons who were displaced from their ancestral homes and traditions. The environment of the cities provided the context in which displaced persons who were noncitizens might turn the talent they were unable to exercise in the civic order to the formation of private associations.[13] The depoliticized intellectuals might also find gnostic mythology an expression of revolt against the exclusionary traditionalism of their social environment.[14]

Gnostic Teachers
of the Second Century

Reconstructing the history of Gnosticism remains difficult. Kurt Rudolph proposes a variant of the sequence of teachers that is typical of the church fathers. This approach considers the history of Gnosticism as a school phenomenon. Major founders or teachers are responsible for its emergence and development.[15] It is not possible, however, to construct a developmental sequence that explains the origins of Gnosticism. Individual teachers and groups may pick up elements from the stock of gnostic mythologizing independently of one another.

Rudolph suggests two lines of development in the first century C.E. The figure of Simon Magus in Samaria generated a gnosticizing cult, whose original myth appears to have described the activity of the divine Ennoia, who came into the world to rescue trapped souls.[16] The account of Simonian gnosis preserved in Hippolytus may have some relationship to the first-century figure, although scholars have not agreed on the possibility of actually isolating earlier elements of Simonian tradition.[17] Unlike second-century C.E. gnostic teachers,

Simon becomes the source of legends, especially in the anti-Paulinist tradition. Simon Magus appears as a surrogate for the apostle. He must be defeated by the superior power of the apostle Peter.[18]

The second line of development in the first century must be inferred from the New Testament itself. The gnosticizing tendencies that have been detected in writings of the Pauline tradition were probably mediated through Jewish baptismal sects. Gnosticizing elements referred to in the Corinthian correspondence as well as in the deutero-Pauline writings show that gnostic speculation had spread from Syro-Palestine to Asia Minor and Greece. Writings from the Johannine school also attest the existence of gnosticizing speculation in Asia Minor. The Fourth Gospel has contributed to Christianizing and historicizing the imagery of the heavenly revealer.[19] The Johannine epistles demonstrate an inner-Christian debate over the extent to which Christians are bound to the figure of the earthly Jesus.[20] By limiting Christian understanding of the Savior to the historical Jesus, the epistles set an important direction for the second-century conflict between the two movements. Some of the later writings in the New Testament, such as 2 Peter and Jude, as well as the epistles of Ignatius and Polycarp run into the second century. A gnosticizing Christianity is clearly evident in the churches of Asia Minor.[21]

The mid-second century C.E. brings a major shift in the development of Gnosticism. The mythologizing traditions that emerged during the first century in Jewish circles and became incorporated into the teachings of gnosticizing Christian sects by the end of the century and the early second century are taken up by several prominent teachers in Alexandria and Rome. Some, like Basilides, Heracleon, Valentinus, and Ptolemy, are known to have been Christians.[22] Just as the Simonian system had been elaborated in the second century, so the systems of these teachers were also developed by later followers. Rudolph holds that the account of Basilides given in Irenaeus is more likely to be original than the elaborate philosophical monism and emanations of Hippolytus's version.[23] Basilides and Heracleon fit the intellectual mold of Christian Alexandria. Both were concerned with biblical interpretation, although the commentaries attributed to Basilides have not survived. The eclectic philosophical mixture of Platonism and Stoicism that is evident in these thinkers also appears in the production of Sethian gnostic treatises like *Apocryphon of John* and *Origin of the World*. In both cases, the authors draw upon Platonic and Stoic philosophical topoi and refer the reader to earlier books.

Both Irenaeus and Hippolytus do quote or paraphrase their reports of gnostic systems from gnostic sources. Studies of Hippolytus's work on the pre-Socratics, where one has the possibility of controlling his way of working, indicate that when Hippolytus quotes directly his selections are so eclectic that they do not give an accurate picture of the systems from which he takes the quotes. But when he provides a summary of their system, his summaries generally cohere with what is known about the systems from other sources.[24] Hippolytus's original work against the heretics had followed the view of his predecessors that all the second-century schools descended from Simonianism. He appears to have acquired a collection of gnostic texts that included the Naasene sermon. Detecting links between this exaltation of the revelation humanity received through the serpent and the structures of mythology among the Sethians and the Ophites, Hippolytus attempted to create a new genealogy for the gnostic sects.[25] Although Hippolytus charges his opponents with introducing pagan philosophy and so corrupting the gospel, the reader can recognize that this philosophical defense of gnostic speculation in part only develops material that has been taken from the first generation. But the second-century gnostic teachers are no less eager than their Christian counterparts to exploit the differences between their faith and the reasoning of philosophers.[26] Hippolytus wishes to accuse his gnostic opponents of plagiarizing the speculative elements in their system.[27]

Valentinians

Within Christian circles those gnostics linked to the traditions established at Rome by Valentinus and Ptolemy and in Alexandria by Heracleon and Theodotos clearly appear to be the most dominant group. The diverse reports of the Valentinian system share some elements that scholars have suggested might derive from Valentinus himself:

1. The figure of Wisdom is divided into a higher and lower Wisdom. Events that can be said to occur within the higher world are duplicated in the lower world.
2. The mythic tale of the fall of Wisdom into the world of darkness is reformulated. Now her ignorance of the divine leads to a desire to grasp God that is inappropriate to her nature, though a suitable recognition of God's greatness.
3. Instead of the divisions of humanity into the immortal race of Seth and outsiders, the Valentinian school uses a division that

corresponds to the elements of the individual: spiritual (corresponding to reason or the mind), psychic, and material (fleshly).

Subsequent divisions within Valentinian circles reflect a concern for theological applications of this teaching to developing Christian beliefs. Eastern and Western schools took different positions on the nature of Jesus. For the Western school, Jesus was a psychic body into which the Spirit, the Logos of Wisdom, enters at baptism. For the Eastern school, Jesus was already endowed with a spiritual body at birth. The tripartite division of humanity and the involvement of Valentinian teachers with orthodox Christian circles led to elaboration of the category of psychic human beings. The spiritual humans were immediately drawn to gnosis. The material humans never could be enlightened. The psychic humans, apparently representative of the orthodox Christians among whom Valentinian Gnostics lived, were hesitant. They had to rely on faith and sacraments. They would be assigned a lesser place in the heavenly world than that of the Gnostics.[28]

Other moderating elements in the systematization of Valentinian thought have been attached to Ptolemy. He appears to have been concerned about the salvation of the psychics. The Savior did not come only to enlighten those who belong to the spiritual race. His activity will also bring about the redemption of those who are psychics.[29] This concern for the sympathetic outsider is also evident in the one exoteric writing that is extant: Ptolemy's *Letter to Flora,* in which he explains to a female inquirer (a wealthy patron?) the different sources of inspiration of passages from the Old Testament.[30]

Irenaeus also associates another figure, Marcus, with the Valentinians. But Marcus is the principal hierophant for a gnostic cult association. His only speculative additions to the gnostic system inherited from the early Sethian tradition may have been speculation on numbers and on astrological correlations or magic. Unlike the great second-century C.E. Valentinians, Marcus does not use the older mythologizing to exegete Christian Scriptures. Thus he appears to stand in closer continuity to the ritual/magic type of gnostic sect associated with Simonianism than to the move toward gnostic sects as schools gathered around a particular teacher.

Sethian Tradition History

Instead of laying out a possible schema for the development of Gnosticism following the lead provided by its ancient opponents, John Turner has proposed a model based on tradition history.[31] He analyzes the variations in the use of divine triads as well as the reuse of mythemes from Sethian texts in order to propose a schema for the development of Sethian Gnosticism into the fourth century. Each stage presupposes a somewhat different interaction between Gnosticism and Christianity. By the early first century C.E. Judaism in Syro-Palestine included baptizing sects: early Sethian Gnostics, Essenes, followers of John the Baptist, and Christians. The Samaritans also constituted a group on the margins of Judaism that was capable of negotiating over power with Roman authorities as well as having other contacts with persons in the Jewish community. At the early stage Sethian mythology includes the concept of a preexistent redeemer associated with Seth, identification with a heavenly Wisdom figure, the origins of evil as a result of the activity of the ignorant creator and his offspring, and cultic practices of baptismal ritual.

Late in the first century, Christianized versions of the Sethian myth emerge. The second century brings a shift in both Christianity and Gnosticism. The impact of individual teachers who would gather groups of interested members and would produce commentary on the traditional texts created the conditions for the conflict between Christianity and Gnosticism from the second century. It also was the period in which philosophical topoi were employed in developing accounts of the gnostic system. By the end of the second century, Christian church officials opposed the earlier independent teachers who sought to operate within the community. The antignostic polemics of the heresiologists seem to have succeeded in driving a wedge between Gnostics and the larger Christian community to which they had belonged. Several texts suggest anti-Christian developments.

During the third century, some Gnostics appropriated Neoplatonic categories. Ascent to a visionary experience at each of the levels of the divine triad becomes the mode of religious experience being sought by members of these groups. But orthodox Platonism also rejected the cosmological speculation of gnosticizing teachers. By the fourth century, Gnosticism can be said to consist in a collection of sects that had their origins at various points in this general pattern of development. Some had developed the early Sethian cultic stages or the Samaritan forms associated with the figure of Simon. Others reflect various stages in the Christianizing of gnostic mythology and cult, including the second-century syntheses by teachers like Valentinus, who clearly presented Gnosticism as a higher form of Christianity. Still others continued the philosophical mysticism of the emerging Neoplatonist groups. Epiphanius provides firsthand testimony to the existence of even more bizarre ritual groups that demonstrated their superiority to the rulers of this world in perverse sexual activity. On the other extreme, the ascetic character of gnostic treatises led to their preservation among ascetics in the Egyptian desert who may not have had any interest at all in cultic and ritual forms that are typical of other gnostic sects.

Turner's chronology follows a particular mythological and speculative tradition through the first four centuries C.E. The first two stages in its development overlap with the New Testament period. As already discussed, the exegesis of Genesis 2–6 as the originating history of humankind and the seed of Seth provided the foundational mythemes in the early mythology. Turner draws the basic outline of the Sethian mythic scheme from the report about the Sethian Ophites in *Adv. Haer.* 1.30 (Foerster, *Gnosis,* 1:87–93).[32] The ideal human being is represented by the heavenly triad of "Man," "Son of Man," and the "third Man." The first two are androgynous. The third is the heavenly Seth. In other systems the female aspect of the androgynous image of God appears as the second member of the triad and the Son of man occupies the third position. The lower world is organized by the Mother/ Spirit and her offspring, Wisdom/Prunicos. Wisdom descends to the waters, where she gives birth to Ialdabaoth. A second descent into the lower world is attached to the creation of humans according to the divine image. This creation follows the arrogant claim of Ialdabaoth to be the one true god. The third descent is the actual coming of the gnostic revealer to rescue the elect. In the Sethian Ophite version, Christ, the third Man, puts on Sophia and rescues Jesus from the cross.

Hymnic or formulaic recitals about Wisdom's descent are among the most persistent literary forms associated with the early versions of the myth. References to baptism, awakening to gnosis, and sealing that are linked to these hymnic passages suggest that they may have been used in a ritual context. Turner prefers to see the hymn in the long version of *Apocryphon of John* as a composite piece. He thinks that the original version lacked the gloss in 31,4 on the body as the prison in Hades and the concluding references to the awakening of the one who is asleep.[33] The Naasene Hymn (Hippolytus, *Ref.* 5.10.2; Foerster, *Gnosis,* 1:282) also depicts the descent of the revealer bearing the seals. In Hippolytus's version, the descent has become the fall of the soul and the Savior is identified with Jesus. The descent hymn provides the framework for a longer treatise in *Trimorphic Protennoia*. The trimorphic form of the divine Protennoia speaks first as Father/ voice, then as Mother/speech, and finally as Son/Word. This material has passed through several literary stages. The basis for the whole treatise is found in the "I Am" material that follows the introduction. Doctrinal excurses, three "mysteries," have been added: how bonds of flesh are loosened (XIII 36,27—40,29; *NHLE*, 514–16); on the end of the age (41,1—42,2; *NHLE*, 516–17); on the descent of Pronoia as Word (46,7—47,1; 49,1—50,9; *NHLE*, 519–21).

The first stage of Christianizing the text simply identified the heavenly Autogenes with Christ (37,31; 38,2; 39,6-7; *NHLE*, 513–15).[34] But *Trimorphic Protennoia* develops its own christological perspective in reaction to the emergence of Christology among orthodox Christians. Its major titles—Christ, Beloved, Son of the Archigenetor (= Son of God), and Son of Man—are interpreted in a docetic fashion. The Word revealed itself to the rulers of the lower world in their tents (47,14-15; *NHLE*, 520; cf. John 1:14).[35] The rulers are wrong to think that the Protennoia/Word is their Christ, because she is everywhere (49,7-8; *NHLE*, 521). Protennoia identifies herself as the Beloved of the rulers and clothes herself as Son of the Archigenetor until the end of the Archigenetor's ignorant rule (49,11-15; *NHLE*, 521). Though the Father of all, the Protennoia reveals herself as a Son of Man among the sons of men.[36] The cross has no redeeming value. Instead Protennoia has to rescue Jesus and take him along with the elect to the Father's dwelling (50,6-16; *NHLE*, 521). According to this account, the rulers of the lower world falsely believe Jesus to be their Christ. Because they are ignorant of Protennoia's presence, they do not know the true meaning of the christological titles they employ.[37]

The descent of the revealer is associated with baptism and the divine voice (*Trim. Prot.* 40,8-9; *NHLE*, 516; 44,29-32; *NHLE*, 518; cf. *Apoc. Adam* 84,4; *NHLE*, 286). The Word's first descent conveys the spirit through the initiation in the waters of life (41,20-25; *NHLE*, 516–17). According to *Gospel of the Egyptians* Seth's descent as the Word bestows Holy Baptism. His descents into the world are initiated by Barbelo/Sophia, who communicates with the elect by her word/voice (III 63,4—65,26; *NHLE*, 216–17).[38] Baptismal traditions could also become the focus of conflict between different groups, because only the true seed of Seth possesses Holy Baptism.

This reconstruction suggests a line of development for the gnostic materials that share a common set of mythemes. In the second century, Christian gnostic teachers would use these mythemes to interpret the story of Jesus. As already mentioned, in christological speculation the Valentinians engaged problems similar to those confronting other Christian teachers in the second century. Sethianism describes a coherent set of mythemes shared by a number of sects, but it does not represent the only form of speculation in the early period. In the mid-third century, Mani's call to be the founder of a new religion is mediated by identification with a heavenly twin. The gnosticizing Thomas tradition as it is reflected in the collection of Jesus' sayings, the *Gospel of Thomas*, is not associated with the mythologizing of Genesis that is characteristic of Sethianism. Bentley Layton prefers to exclude these materials from the category "gnostic" altogether.[39] Nonetheless, their emphasis on internal enlightenment and discovery of the true self, the real divine image, is certainly open to mythic elaboration. Their ascetic practice lends itself to the ascetic rejection of the passions and the demonizing of sexuality that recur in early Sethian speculation. The gnostic teachers and systematizers of the second century could draw on material from this tradition as well as that from earlier mythologizing in the Sethian tradition and material from the New Testament itself.[40]

Summary

Jewish traditions that gnostic mythologizers took over differ from those commonly appropriated in the New Testament. Wisdom's fall into a hostile universe departs from the commonplace Hellenistic account of divine order as well as from the more sophisticated philosophy of Philo. The gnostic wisdom tradition reflects a skeptical philosophy that intensified the gulf between the human realm of disorder and the divine. Students of early Christianity have come to recognize that the simple division between "Jewish" and "non-Jewish" fails to represent the social phenomena of personal identity in a pluralistic environment. The history of both Gnosticism and Christianity begins in the margins of Judaism, among persons who might be called "Jews" by some and "non-Jews" by others. Even Gnostics refer to themselves as the true descendants of Seth.

The Apologists of the second century identify their opposition as a deviant "school tradition." The great gnostic synthesizers belong to this century. But some hints of schools of interpretation are also

detected in the first century. Both the Johannine and Pauline traditions developed distinctive forms of Christianity that rival teachers
contested by the end of the first century. As noted in chapter 3, a new
cultic movement with its legitimating mythic patterns can emerge without the synthesizing efforts of an individual teacher. First-century
gnostic *mythologoumena* emerged in the context of a baptismal cult.
Second-century teachers drew on that tradition as well as on available
Christian materials.

John Turner's tradition history of the writings that share structural
elements associated with the figure of Seth attempts to trace the movement from the first to the fourth centuries. He demonstrates the com-
plexity of baptismal sectarianism and schools of interpretation that
have produced the surviving texts. There is clear evidence for diverse
levels of Christianizing from the superficial insertion of Christ to structural changes in the mythological system itself.

The Thomas tradition points to yet another line of development.
The early sayings tradition has been developed as the source of hidden
wisdom. The later gnostic thinkers could draw from this material
as well as from the mythological schemata that emerged in Sethian
circles.

PART TWO ————————————————————————

GNOSTIC AND
NEW TESTAMENT TRADITIONS

5

Jesus as Teacher of Wisdom:
Sayings and Revelation

Gospel of Thomas
and the Sayings Tradition

Variants of sayings and parables of Jesus, some of which appear to be independent of the Synoptic versions, have made *Gospel of Thomas* an important witness in studies of the Gospel tradition.[1] In addition to the Coptic version found at Nag Hammadi, Greek fragments of at least one different rescension of the *Gospel of Thomas* collection were found among the Oxyrhynchus papyri.[2] Studies of the Synoptic sayings collection (= Q) have suggested that Matthew and Luke used different versions of that collection.[3] Even more complex hypotheses about the development of Q are being proposed by scholars who specialize in studying that collection.[4] Given the fluidity of sayings material in the oral tradition, it is not possible to use the claim that one version of a collection is chronologically prior to another as evidence that certain sayings are later variants.[5]

The judgments involved in analyzing individual sayings are complex. Some depend on claims about the plausibility of attributing particular themes to the teaching of Jesus. *Gospel of Thomas* does not contain any of the apocalyptic Son of man sayings found in the Synoptics. Some scholars have argued that the apocalyptic sayings are an addition to the original Q collection. This claim is advanced on the grounds that Jesus' own teaching focused on the presence and future coming of the kingdom of God.[6] The Son of man material is also missing from the Q material underlying the Sermon on the Mount. The collections of Jesus' sayings are wisdom collections, not apocalyptic revelation. Helmut Koester has identified several types of sayings in the early tradition: catechetical sayings based on Jewish "two ways" teaching; sayings attributed to heavenly wisdom,[7] and sayings that express hidden wisdom, as in the parables. Because a sayings collection does not contextualize its material, the general takes precedence over particular application. Interpretation requires hypotheses about how to apply particular sayings. The parables provide extensive examples of the overlap between *Gospel of Thomas* and the Synoptic material. Those which the Synoptic evangelists use as indications of the coming kingdom of God appear in *Gospel of Thomas* as evidence for the eternal presence of the kingdom.

Comparative studies of *Gospel of Thomas* and Q have also played an important role in determining the communal setting for the sayings collections. The wandering preachers, who are without home or family, carry the message in towns and villages. Their mission is patterned on that of Jesus and his disciples. Explanatory glosses and allegorical applications of the parables are missing from *Gospel of Thomas*. In some cases, this may be the result of abbreviating a well-known story.[8] In others, the situation of the wandering preachers who transmitted the sayings does not require that the sayings be reinterpreted in order to apply them to the community. When the evangelists set sayings material in a life of Jesus, they must also suggest how they are applied. In some instances the gap between a settled community and the wandering, ascetic radicalism of the inherited tradition requires adaptation.[9]

Dialogue of the Savior

The variations in the transmission of Jesus' sayings do not end with written collections of sayings or with the incorporation of sayings material in Gospels. Other collections of sayings may have informed early discourses such as those found in the Fourth Gospel or in gnostic dialogues, like the *Dialogue of the Savior* (III,5).[10] Studies of the use of gospel traditions in the second-century writers show that free citation or oral repetition seems to have been the norm. The Gospel of Matthew appears to be the basis for most identifiable Gospel citations. Looking at the proposed parallels from *Dialogue of the Savior*, one finds the characteristic distribution shown in table 1.[11] The fragmentary state of the manuscript makes it impossible to determine whether *Dialogue of the Savior* depends on a particular version of a saying. But

TABLE 1

Dialogue of the Savior	*Gospel Parallels*
125,18ff.	Matt 6:22-23//Luke 11:34-36
126,6-10	Matt 7:7-8//Luke 11:9-10; *Gos. Thom.* 2, 92, 94 (seeking and finding)
126,17ff.	Matt 5:4//Luke 6:21b; John 16:20, 22 (mourning now)
127,2ff.	Matt 5:14; John 8:12; *Gos. Thom.* 24 (light)
127,16ff.	Matt 8:12b; 13:42b; 24; 51b; 25:30b; Luke 13:28a
128,2ff.	Luke 17:20b, 23; *Gos. Thom.* 3, 113
132,4ff.	John 14:2-12 (request to see where Jesus goes)
132,15ff.	*Gos. Thom.* 3 (one who has known himself)
134,8-10	John 3:8 (a wisdom saying on the source of the wind?)
138,15ff.	*Gos. Thom.* 37 (remove garments)
139,9	Matt 6:34b (*Dial. Sav.* refers to the Matthew saying by name)
139,10	Matt 10:10b//Luke 10:7b; 1 Cor 9:14; 1 Tim 5:18b; *Didache* 13:1-2
139,11	Matt 10:24-25//Luke 6:40; John 13:6; 15:20a
140,3ff.	1 Cor 2:9a; *Gos. Thom.* 17 (eye has not seen)
140,11ff.	John 1:13; 3:3, 5 (birth from above); *Gos. Eg.* in Clement of Alexandria, *Strom.* 3.6.45.3 (death reigns as long as women bear children)
141,5ff.	Matt 11:28-30; *Gos. Thom.* 90 (burden, rest)
144,15ff.	*Gos. Eg.* in Clement of Alexandria, *Strom.* 3.9.63.1-2; 64.1; 66.1-2 (to pray, destroy the works of femaleness; cf. *Gos. Thom.* 114)

one passage refers to a group of sayings of Jesus by "titles," which suggests that the author assumed that his readers could identify the references with appropriate sayings:

Mary said, "Thus with respect to 'the wickedness of each day,' and 'the laborer is worthy of his food,' and 'the disciple resembles his teacher.'" She uttered this as a woman who had understood perfectly. (III 139,8-13; *NHLE*, 252)[12]

Although the second two sayings appear in several variants, the first appears only in Matthew's version of the pericope on anxiety (contrast Luke 12:32). Because the other two sayings appear in close proximity in Matthew 10, one could argue that the group of titles indicates familiarity with the Matthean tradition of Jesus' sayings.

Sayings in *Gospel of Truth*

Second-century Valentinian teachers often echo New Testament language in tracts intended for a Christian audience. The fact that they do not cite clearly identifiable passages does not mean that they depend on precanonical sources for their allusions.[13] Sayings collections serve as "hidden wisdom" when their proper interpretation is known only to the elect. The catalog of sayings in *Dialogue of the Savior* serves as such a test. In the Gospel of Mark, the parables are presented as serving the function of marking off insider from outsider (Mark 4:10-12).[14] The Valentinian tract *Gospel of Truth* provides striking examples of how a gnostic teacher might decontextualize familiar New Testament language in order to convey to the Christian reader the conviction that the sect teaches the spiritual truth of a tradition with which he or she is already familiar.[15]

One image that the author uses for the Savior is the familiar parable of the Lost Sheep (cf. Matt 18:12-13//Luke 15:3-6; *Gos. Thom.* 107; *NHLE*, 137). It incorporates other sheep references, such as the Sabbath controversy (Matt 12:1-12)[16] and the shepherd giving his life for the sheep (e.g., John 10:11b):

He is the shepherd who left behind the ninety-nine sheep which were not lost. He went searching for the one which had gone astray. He rejoiced when he found it, for ninety-nine is a number that is in the left hand which holds it. But when the one is found, the entire number passes to the right (hand). As that which lacks the one—that is, the entire right (hand)—draws what was deficient and takes it from the left-hand side and brings (it) to the right, so too the number becomes one hundred. It is the sign of the one who is their sound; it is the Father. Even on the Sabbath, he labored for the sheep which he found fallen into the pit. He gave life to the sheep, having brought it up from the pit in order that you might know interiorly—you, the sons of interior knowledge—what is the Sabbath, on which it is not fitting for salvation to be idle, in order that you may speak from the day from above, which has no night, and from the light which does not sink because it is perfect. (I 31,35—32,30; *NHLE*, 46)

A series of commands exhorts those who have received this salvation to spread the message and not to return to what they have abandoned (*Gos. Truth* 32,31—33,32; *NHLE*, 47)

The sayings about the sheep, the shepherd, and the true light are combined with a numerical interpretation of the one, the ninety-nine, and the one hundred. The gnostic reader would recognize "left" and "right" as references to the left and right of the Demiurge or of the enthroned Jesus.[17] Souls on the right will ascend to the light of the divine world. Souls to the left return to earth/Hades. But the Christian reader can also interpret "right" and "left" as an allusion to yet another Gospel passage, the Matthean parable of the Sheep and the Goats (Matt 25:31-46). This association is strengthened by the commands that follow the passage in *Gospel of Truth*. Matthew 25:35-36 sets a list of works of mercy shown to the "little ones" as the criterion distinguishing the sheep, who are at the king's right, from the goats at his left. Although *Gospel of Truth* makes the primary obligation teaching the truth to others, assisting others is included in the list. The reader/disciple is urged to:

Make firm the foot of those who have stumbled and stretch out your hands to those who are ill. Feed those who are hungry and give repose to those who are weary. (I 33,1-5; *NHLE*, 47)

Interpretation becomes an index of the enlightenment of the reader. Although this section echoes sayings and parables of Jesus that are presumably familiar to any Christian reader, none of the allusions can be pegged to any particular New Testament passage. Expanding the search to images of true light and giving life by laboring on the Sabbath would add Johannine texts to the mix as well. John 5:19 resolves a Sabbath controversy by insisting that Jesus merely continues the work that he sees the Father doing on the Sabbath—giving life and judging.

Those who are accustomed to think of the sayings of Jesus set within the narrative realism of the Synoptic Gospels might be inclined to think that the acontextual sayings in *Gospel of Thomas*, *Gospel of Truth*, and *Dialogue of the Savior* have been stripped of that realistic context by gnostic authors. This is also Irenaeus's view of the gnostic handling of the New Testament.[18] But the existence of variant sayings collections into the second century, like *Gospel of Thomas*, indicates that narrative contextualization of the sayings and parables of Jesus was not considered necessary to understand the wisdom that comes from the Savior. Second, the Pauline epistles proclaim a gospel of salvation through faith in the crucified and risen Lord that has no stake in the particulars of Jesus' teaching.

For the Valentinian author of *Gospel of Truth*, for the author of *Dialogue of the Savior*, as well as for the compiler of the Coptic *Gospel of Thomas*, however, understanding the true teaching of the Savior is the key to salvation (cf. *Gos. Thom.* 1; *NHLE*, 126). Finding the true meaning of the sayings is equivalent to finding Wisdom embodied in the Savior. Several sayings in Q refer to Jesus as Wisdom's spokesperson. The clearest examples are the sayings about Wisdom's children (Luke 7:35; cf. Matt 11:19b) and Wisdom's oracle (Luke 11:49-51; cf. Matt 23:34-36). Matthew treats both sayings as words by and about Jesus himself. The lament in Luke 13:34-35 (cf. Matt 23:37-39) may have originally been attributed to divine Wisdom. The hen gathering her brood appears as an image for God (4 Ezra 1:30; *2 Bar* 41:3-4) and for Wisdom (Sir 1:15). The speaker is a divine figure who comes to save but will withdraw, as Wisdom is forced to do when she seeks a dwelling place among humans (*1 Enoch* 42; Sirach 24).[19] The rejection motif has been recast as a Son of man saying in Q (Luke 9:58//Matt 8:20).[20] An indirect link between Jesus and the messenger of Wisdom, which may be intended to imply that Jesus is the last such messenger, appears in the judgment oracle against Jesus' own generation. The queen of the South came to hear the wisdom of Solomon; now something even greater is present yet rejected (Luke 11:31//Matt 12:42). In an apocalyptic context, Wisdom's withdrawal from the world is the prelude to the end of the age. Wisdom and righteousness cannot be found on earth during the last days, when the wicked flourish (cf. 4 Ezra 5:9-13).

The few who obtain Wisdom can expect to be persecuted. Another Q saying observes that God has revealed to children (Jesus' disciples) what is hidden from the wise and intelligent (Luke 10:21-22//Matt 11:25-27). John 1:10-13 depicts Jesus as rejected Wisdom who gives life to the few who receive it. The gnostic sayings collections preserve further examples of this identification with Wisdom.

Wisdom comes into the world in hiding and speaks only to those who are her true children. Most people will not receive her revelation:

> Jesus said, "I took my place in the midst of the world, and I appeared
> to them in flesh. I found all of them intoxicated; I found none of
> them thirsty. And my soul became afflicted for the sons of men,
> because they are blind in their hearts and do not have sight; for
> empty they came into the world, and empty too they seek to leave
> the world. But for the moment they are intoxicated. When they shake
> off their wine, then they will repent." (*Gos. Thom.* 28; *NHLE*, 130)

This saying identifies Jesus with Wisdom seeking a home in the souls
of an intoxicated and blind humanity.

The apocalyptic traditions of Wisdom's rejection found in *1 Enoch*
and 4 Ezra identify possession of Wisdom with the righteousness of
the Law.[21] Neither Q nor *Gospel of Thomas* makes that identification.
Instead, Jesus' message is a challenge to those who claim to know
what the will of God is. When salvation is identified with judgment
based on works, as in the Matthean parable of the Sheep and the
Goats, what is at stake remains doing righteousness. When salvation is
identified with understanding or insight, as in the *Gospel of Truth*
treatment of the sheep parables and images, then salvation is associated with possessing insight.

Kingdom Parables and Gnosis

The end-time separation of the wicked and the righteous appears in a
number of Matthean parables while it is missing in the *Gospel of
Thomas* parallels. For Matthew, the presence of the kingdom requires
such an eschatological judgment. Where the kingdom is understood as
possession of Wisdom, the parables of Jesus are not understood in this
apocalyptic sense. Matthew 13:44-50 contains three kingdom parables:
the Treasure, the Pearl Merchant, and the Fishnet. Each has a variant
in *Gospel of Thomas*. The parable of the Fishnet is treated as a judgment saying:

> Again, the kingdom of heaven is like a net that was thrown into the
> sea and caught fish of every kind; when it was full, they drew it
> ashore, sat down, and put the good into baskets but threw out the
> bad. So it will be at the end of the age. The angels will come out and
> separate the evil from the righteous and throw them into the furnace
> of fire, where there will be weeping and gnashing of teeth. (Matt
> 13:47-50)

The secondary character of the judgment application is evident. What might the parable have meant without that application? *Gospel of Thomas* directs attention to the wisdom by which the fisherman selects the fish:

> And he said, "The man is like a wise fisherman who cast his net into the sea and drew it up from the sea full of small fish. Among them the wise fisherman found a fine large fish. He threw all the small fish back into the sea and chose the large fish without difficulty. Whoever has ears to hear, let him hear." (*Gos. Thom.* 8; *NHLE*, 127)

In structure, this version of the parable is like that of the Pearl Merchant. It focuses on the activity of an individual in acquiring the large fish while throwing back all the small ones.

Scholars who interpret this parable against a gnostic background note the shift in the opening from the "kingdom is like . . ." to "the man is like . . . ." They assume that "the man" refers to the one who has discovered the gnostic identity of his inner self. The large fish that he selects corresponds to the Gnostic's true nature.[22] But the text itself contains no clues that demand such an interpretation.[23] The point appears to be the fisherman's ability to find the big fish in the net full of small ones. The obvious need to toss the small ones back contributes to the point being made in using the image. People know how to conduct the business of fishing prudently. They should also be able to recognize God's Wisdom when it appears.

Matthew groups the three parables together. The Fishnet's conclusion gives an apocalyptic cast to the parables of the Treasure and the Pearl Merchant as well. *Gospel of Thomas* preserves parallels to all the parables in Matthew 13 but in a different order (see table 2). Matthew has expanded the parable collection in Mark 4 by substituting the Wheat and the Weeds for the Seed Growing Secretly (Mark 4:26-29), substituting the combined Mustard Seed/Leaven from Q (cf. Luke 13:18-20), and adding the final group of three parables. The apocalyptic allegories attached to the Wheat and the Weeds (Matt 13:36-43) and the Fishnet (13:49) are the evangelist's application of the parables.

Gospel of Thomas draws upon a collection in which the parables were not grouped as they are in Matthew or Q. Its parables lack the allegorical applications found in Matthew's collection. But some interpretive expansion has taken place. The Pearl Merchant concludes with an exhortation to apply the parable to one's life:

TABLE 2

Matthew	Gospel of Thomas
Sower (13:1-9)	9
Wheat and Weeds (13:24-30)	57
Mustard Seed (13:31-32)	20
Leaven (13:33)	96
Treasure (13:44)	109
Pearl Merchant (13:45-46)	76
Fishnet (13:47-50)	8

> Jesus said, "The kingdom of the Father is like a merchant who had a consignment of merchandise and who discovered a pearl. That merchant was shrewd. He sold the merchandise and bought the pearl alone for himself. You too, seek his unfailing and enduring treasure where no moth comes near to devour and no worm destroys." (*Gos. Thom.* 76; *NHLE*, 135)

This variant is slightly more expansive that Matthew's. By making the central character a general merchant rather than a pearl dealer, it explains the extraordinary nature of the man's action differently. He is not simply an expert in pearls who sells all to obtain the particularly valuable pearl. He is a general merchant who knows enough to trade what he usually sells in order to gain the pearl. This version must be early. Neither the parable nor its application shows any traces of the popular gnostic allegory that makes the pearl a symbol of the gnostic soul.[24] The application in *Gospel of Thomas* has been created by attaching a second saying of Jesus on enduring treasure, which had a more expanded form in Q:

> Do not store up for yourselves treasures on earth, where moth and rust consume and where thieves break in and steal; but store up for yourselves treasures in heaven, where neither moth nor rust consumes and where thieves do not break in and steal. For where your treasure is, there your heart will be also. (Matt 6:19-21)

The Lucan version was expanded with instructions characteristic of the evangelist. Christians are to use earthly wealth in almsgiving in order to gain the heavenly treasure:[25]

> Sell your possessions, and give alms. Make purses for yourselves that
> do not wear out, an unfailing treasure in heaven, where no thief
> comes near and no moth destroys. For where your treasure is, there
> your heart will be also. (Luke 12:33-34)

A variant of this tradition may underlie the *Gospel of Thomas* version,
which lacks thieves and refers instead to the destruction caused by
moths and worms.

The third parable in Matthew's group of three, the Treasure, shows
the most divergence. Matthew's laconic version says little about the
circumstances under which the man came to be digging in the field or
what he does after he actually gains possession of the field. Formally,
it is structured like the Pearl Merchant. The protagonist finds something valuable, sells all, and obtains what he has found. John Dominic
Crossan's extensive study of treasure parables and the legislation associated with cases in which a person finds such treasure shows that the
motif was widespread in folklore and in the legal tradition. Folklore
commonly has deserving peasants as the beneficiaries of such hidden
treasure. Legal traditions provide for the claims against such treasure
by the original owners of a house or field.[26] The version in *Gospel of
Thomas* is much closer to common Jewish parallels than the Matthean
text:

> The kingdom is like a man who had a [hidden] treasure in his field
> without knowing it. And [after] he died, he left it to his [son]. The
> son [did] not know (about the treasure). He inherited the field and
> sold [it]. And the one who bought it went plowing and [found] the
> treasure. He began to lend money at interest to whomever he wished.
> (*Gos. Thom.* 109; *NHLE*, 137)

This variant parallels a Jewish story in which a lazy heir sells a piece
of land, which had been used as a dunghill, for a small amount. The
buyer digs up the dunghill and discovers a treasure that enables him
to build a palace and go about in public as a wealthy person. The
seller comes to lament what he tossed away.[27] Because *Gospel of
Thomas* follows a conventional Jewish treasure story pattern, Crossan
considers it inauthentic. His criterion for authentic Jesus material
emphasizes the amoral and shocking character of the kingdom's
presence.[28]

Charles Hedrick has argued against the assumption that *Gospel of
Thomas* represents a late tradition that substituted the conventional
form of the story for the original Jesus tradition.[29] Because Matthew

and *Gospel of Thomas* have derived their parables collection from different sources, either version might reflect the earlier tradition. The shockingly amoral story that Crossan finds as the criterion of authenticity in Matthew's variant is not necessarily supported by the evidence. Matthew's version is simply an abbreviated story that leaves the reader to fill in the gaps. It follows the parable of the Pearl Merchant very closely. In contrast, *Gospel of Thomas* has a version of the Pearl Merchant that is very close to Matthew as well as a version of the Fishnet that has suffered less allegorical elaboration than Matthew's version.[30] In fact, the Treasure parable is the only one in which the Matthean and *Gospel of Thomas* versions differ radically in their structure. Consequently, it is equally possible that Matthew recast the Treasure parable to fit the pattern of the Pearl Merchant. By emphasizing the hiddenness of the Treasure, Matthew reminds readers that they have received the secrets of the kingdom of God (Matt 13:10-11).[31]

The parable in *Gospel of Thomas* also poses difficulties for the interpreter. Its conclusion is far from clear. The Jewish parallel makes the ostentatious display of the finder an occasion to teach the original heir a moral lesson about sloth. Taken as a whole, the collection of sayings in *Gospel of Thomas* is opposed to wealth and the activities by which human beings generate it. *Gos. Thom.* 95 prohibits usury as does the Torah (e.g., Exod 22:25-27; Deut 23:19-20). If the reader is to attach moral opprobrium to the finder's activity, then the parable would appear to be of a type with the Unjust Steward (Luke 16:1-8a). The protagonist is one of the "children of this age" who knows how to deal with the unexpected windfall.[32] A similar certainty of response should be found among those who discover the wisdom about the rule of God in Jesus' teaching.

Matthew's variant also emphasizes the immediate reception of the treasure. The evangelist may have abbreviated the ending of the parable, because subsequent actions of the finder were of no concern. I have already noted a common motif of Wisdom's coming into the world, seeking those who would receive her, and returning to heaven rejected by most of humanity. In contrast to the flawed understanding of Jesus' disciples in Mark 4, Matthew 13 emphasizes that the disciples have received the secrets of the kingdom conveyed by the parables. Indeed, they know what many prophets and righteous people of old sought but could not find (13:17). Allegorical explanations are provided for three of the parables: the Sower (13:18-23; cf. Mark 4:13-20), the Weeds and the Wheat (Matt 13:36-43), and the Fishnet (13:49-50).

In addition, the disciples state that they have understood Jesus' teaching (13:51). The chapter concludes with another reference to treasure, this time the wisdom of the scribe trained for the kingdom who can bring both old and new out of his storehouse (13:52). But the success Jesus has in explaining his words to the disciples is not matched with the people at large. Their failure to understand Jesus' parables demonstrates a hard-heartedness that cannot be cured (13:10-17, 34-35). Matthew has also shifted the rejection of Jesus at Nazareth from its Markan location so that it follows immediately upon this discourse (13:53-58). Thus Jesus both speaks about and enacts the fate of divine Wisdom when she attempts to dwell among human beings.

This example makes it evident that it is impossible to treat all the sayings in *Gospel of Thomas* as though they were modified versions of the Synoptic tradition designed to advocate a gnostic mythology. Many of the *Gospel of Thomas* parables preserve a nonallegorical variant that was modified when a parable was incorporated into the written framework of a Gospel.[33] The Sower appears without its allegory or any of the internal alterations that the Synoptic versions introduce into the story as a result of the allegorizing process.[34] Although derived from Q, the Great Supper has been extensively altered and allegorized by both Matthew (Matt 22:1-10) and Luke (Luke 14:15-24). By contrast, the version in *Gospel of Thomas* is relatively straightforward:

> A man had received visitors. And when he had prepared the dinner, he sent his servants to invite the guests. He went to the first one and said to him: "My master invites you." He said: "I have claims against some merchants. They are coming to me this evening. I must go and give them my orders. I ask to be excused from the dinner." He went to another and said to him, "My master has invited you." He said to him, "I have just bought a house and am required for the day. I shall not have any spare time." He went to another and said to him, "My master invites you." He said to him, "My friend is going to get married, and I am to prepare the banquet. I shall not be able to come. I ask to be excused from the dinner." He went to another and said to him, "My master invites you." He said to him, "I have just bought a farm, and I am on my way to collect the rent. I shall not be able to come. I ask to be excused." The servant returned and said to his master, "Those whom you have invited to the dinner have asked to be excused." The master said to his servant, "Go outside to the streets and bring back those whom you happen to meet, so that they may dine." Businessmen and merchants will not enter the places of my father. (*Gos. Thom.* 64; *NHLE*, 133-34)

The introduction to the parable makes the reason for the dinner unexpected guests, not a long-anticipated event that the host's friends should have been able to accommodate, as in the Synoptics. Consequently, the host displays hostility and anger in the Synoptic versions. In *Gospel of Thomas*, the unexpected guests interrupt business as usual. Although the host's friends might have been expected to readjust their affairs to show hospitality toward his guests, their refusal to do so is not as shocking as in the other versions.

The expansions in *Gospel of Thomas* are relatively minor. The list of excuses has been expanded from three to four, probably to include the additional example of the merchant. The final saying condemning the merchants reflects a hostility toward those preoccupied with money that is typical of *Gospel of Thomas*. But similar sayings appear elsewhere in the New Testament (e.g., Jas 5:1-6).[35] There is nothing peculiarly gnostic about this condemnation. It indicates a common suspicion of the rising merchant class and its activities in a traditional society. This group cannot be tied down to the traditional demands of friendship and hospitality.

Matthew's version of the Great Supper is particularly blatant in its allegorical condemnation of the Jews for failing to accept Jesus. The king interrupts the wedding feast that he is supposedly giving for his son to gather an army and destroy the city because the people mistreated and killed his servants (Matt 22:6-7). The destruction of Jerusalem is understood as divine punishment for the death of Jesus. A similar allegorical interpretation is given the parable of the Wicked Tenants (Mark 12:1-12; Matt 21:33-46; Luke 20:9-19). Both *Gospel of Thomas* and Matthew have this parable attached to the parable about the Great Supper, although in a different order. *Gospel of Thomas* 65 (*NHLE*, 134) is considerably shorter than the Synoptic versions. The opening lacks the allusion to Isa 5:1-7 that establishes a link between the owner as God and the vineyard as Israel. The servants have not been allegorized so that they represent the prophets and the Baptist as they do in the Synoptics. Instead, one finds a simple example of an absentee landlord sending his servants to collect the rent from unwilling tenants. The narrator characterizes the owner as "good," thus removing the possibility that the tenants might be resisting some form of injustice on the owner's part. The tenants should have respected the son even if they rebuffed the servants; instead, they kill the son. The conclusion makes no reference to what the owner will do in retaliation.

Helmut Koester rejects the possibility that *Gospel of Thomas* has dropped the allegorical elements in the Synoptic versions. This variant is devoid of any of the allegorical details that have been added in the Synoptics. Nor are there any hints in the narrative that this is a tale about the descents of the gnostic revealer.[36] Rather than supply a gnostic framework that the parable lacks or assume that *Gospel of Thomas* rewrote the Synoptic version, it is simplest to assume that *Gospel of Thomas* has preserved a version of this parable that does not have an allegory of salvation history behind it. The episode's proximity to daily life suggests that an example has been created by intensifying a commonplace occurrence. The parable shows how people can come to reject Jesus as God's spokesperson.

Recovering the Divine Image

Although the extant versions of *Gospel of Thomas* have been compiled and preserved among gnostic ascetics, individual sayings and parables assist in recovering variants of the tradition prior to their incorporation into the Synoptic Gospels. Later gnostic writings show that the Gnostics were as ready to allegorize parables as the next person. *Gospel of Thomas* is relatively free of the elaborate allegories that typify gnostic interpretation. The variants in the *Gospel of Thomas* are evidence for interpretations of the kingdom of God that do not depend on expectations of apocalyptic judgment. The kingdom of God is not a dynamic manifestation of God's eschatological power as it is in the teaching of Jesus. Rather the kingdom is a primordial reality that also becomes present when individuals discover their true identity.

Gospel of Thomas opens with the affirmation that finding the meaning of Jesus' sayings is the key to immortality. The clue to the quest lies in the self-knowledge that comes when the Kingdom is discovered within:

> Jesus said, "If those who lead you say to you, 'See, the kingdom is in the sky,' then the birds of the sky will precede you. If they say to you, 'It is in the sea,' then the fish will precede you. Rather, the kingdom is inside of you, and it is outside of you. When you come to know yourselves, then you will become known, you will realize that it is you who are the sons of the living father. But if you will not know yourselves, you dwell in poverty and it is you who are that poverty."
> (*Gos. Thom.* 3; *NHLE*, 126)

Like Luke 17:20-21, this saying establishes the absurdity of identifying the kingdom with earthly places or signs. The assumption that Jesus' teaching is deliberately enigmatic appears in the exchange between Jesus and the disciples over speaking in parables (Mark 4:10-12). Only those privileged to hear and understand Jesus will be saved. *Gospel of Thomas* 62 associates this view with the injunction not to let the left hand know what the right hand is doing:

> Jesus said, "It is to those who are worthy of my mysteries that I tell my mysteries. Do not let your [sg.] left hand know what your right is doing." (my trans.)

Matt 6:3 uses the expression about the right and left hand in a parenetic context to describe Christian almsgiving as hidden. Such diverse applications are characteristic of a sayings tradition that is circulating in various forms and can be constantly reapplied by its users.

The enigmatic and incomplete character of a collection of sayings and parables of Jesus posed the problem of authoritative interpretation within the community. The evangelists frequently shift the audience from the crowds to persons close to Jesus. I have already mentioned that Matthew has constructed chapter 13 so that readers know that Jesus' disciples were able to transmit not only the words of Jesus but also the meaning of those words.

John 16:25-28 acknowledges that Jesus' teaching remained incomplete. Guidance from the Paraclete after Jesus' return to the Father was required. *Gospel of Thomas* refers to its contents as words of the "Living Jesus" (*Gos. Thom.* 1)—words whose authority lies with the risen Lord. Other sayings designate James (*Gos. Thom.* 12) and Thomas (*Gos. Thom.* 13) as authoritative interpeters of Jesus' message. Paul claims for himself the authority to interpret and apply a traditional saying that came from Jesus in dealing with questions about divorce (1 Cor 7:10-16, 40). Paul insists that the ability to understand and interpret the gospel is a gift of the Spirit (1 Cor 2:11-16). This passage includes an important axiom: in order to interpret the Spirit, one must possess the Spirit.

Gospel of Thomas 108 makes likeness to the Savior a spiritual gift by which the individual comes to understand the "hidden things":

> Jesus said, "He who will drink from my mouth will become like me. I myself shall become he, and the things that are hidden will be revealed to him." (*Gos. Thom.* 108; *NHLE*, 137)

These persons are those who have discovered that the kingdom is both their origin and the goal of their quest to discover the true divine self (cf. *Gos. Thom.* 18, 49, 50). *Gospel of Thomas* treats Jesus' sayings about children as examples of true discipleship. They point out the need to recover the true image of humanity—the image of God. This image existed before association with the passions and the material body brought about the separation of humans into male and female and their subjection to death:

> Jesus saw infants being suckled. He said to his disciples, "These infants being suckled are like those who enter the kingdom."
>
> They said to him, "Shall we then, as children, enter the kingdom?"
>
> Jesus said to them, "When you make the two one, and when you make the inside like the outside and the outside like the inside, and the above like the below, and when you make the male and the female one and the same, so that the male not be male nor the female female; and when you fashion eyes in place of an eye, and a hand in place of a hand, and a foot in place of a foot, and a likeness in place of a likeness; then will you enter [the kingdom]."
> (*Gos. Thom.* 22; *NHLE*, 129)

This tradition was widely attested. A variant appears in the formula cited by Paul in Gal 3:27-28.[37] It was easily assimilated to gnostic myths that described the separation of the androgynous Adam/Eve as the fall into death. Wisdom appears as the vehicle by which the soul is assimilated to the divine image and so attains immortality. A version of this tradition also appears in the philosophical speculation of Philo of Alexandria.[38]

In the first century C.E. this saying about returning to the primordial divine image is already being employed in three different contexts: a cultic, baptismal context, as in Galatians; the Genesis interpretation of early Sethian Gnostics; and philosophical speculation, as in Philo. The ascetic context of *Gospel of Thomas* was amenable to the rejection of the passions and of social ties which typifies Sethian use of this tradition. Scholars have proposed that sayings collections like Q and the early versions of *Gospel of Thomas* developed among wandering Christian prophets who were dependent on the hospitality of similarly impoverished villagers in Galilee and Syria.[39] Because these wandering teachers depended on communal support, the radical detachment from social constraints and the ascetic posture of *Gospel of Thomas* do not mean that the "elect and solitary ones" were as detached from society as has often been assumed.[40]

Praxis in *Gospel of Thomas*

Although knowledge rather than behavior is the focus of salvation in *Gospel of Thomas*, one should not assume that all references to way of life are to be spiritualized as in *Gospel of Thomas* 3. There "poverty" clearly refers to those who dwell in the world without knowledge of Wisdom. *Gospel of Thomas* 29 uses "poverty" to refer to the soul's association with the body, which deprives the soul of its direct access to the divine. But other sayings are cast as community rules. Wealth and the economic activities of merchants and landowners that produced it are presented as an obstacle to salvation. Jesus' saying about John the Baptist (Luke 7:24-30//Matt 11:7-15) condemns the wealthy aristocracy:

> Jesus said, "Why have you come out into the desert? To see a reed shaken by the wind? And to see a man clothed in fine garments [like your] kings and your great men? Upon them are the fine garments, and they are unable to discern the truth." (*Gos. Thom.* 78; *NHLE*, 135)

Luke has also expanded the conclusion of the Q tradition to make a social comment. He consistently attacks the Pharisees as examples of those whose desire for money makes them hostile to Jesus' message:[41]

> And all the people who heard this, including the tax collectors, acknowledged the justice of God, because they had been baptized with John's baptism. But by refusing to be baptized by him, the Pharisees and the lawyers rejected God's purpose for themselves. (Luke 7:29-30)

Both *Gospel of Thomas* and Luke see the contrast between the ascetic Baptist and those in positions of authority as an opportunity to comment on the failure of the latter to accept Jesus.

As already mentioned, the conclusion to the parable of the Great Supper in *Gospel of Thomas* categorically excludes businessmen and merchants from the kingdom (*Gos. Thom.* 64). Another saying prohibits usury:

> [Jesus said], "If you have money, do not lend it at interest, but give [it] to one from whom you will not get it back." (*Gos. Thom.* 95; *NHLE*: 136)

This saying is closer to Luke 6:34-35 than to Matt 5:42 but takes a more radical position than either. The prohibition of usury is understood to require that assistance be given to one who cannot or will not repay. The Synoptic variants prohibit demanding repayment or considering the likelihood of repayment when responding to a request.

Other sayings in *Gospel of Thomas* develop another ascetic theme: renunciation of family ties. Several Synoptic sayings relativize the significance of family ties. Jesus' true relatives are those who hear and keep the Word of God (Mark 3:35//Matt 12:50//Luke 8:21). Jesus brings division within the family by setting its members against one another (Matt 10:34-37//Luke 12:51-53). He instructs followers to leave the dead to bury the dead (Luke 9:59-60//Matt 8:21-22), and not to say farewell to those at home (Luke 9:61-62). For *Gospel of Thomas* the motivation for such renunciation has shifted. The elect know that like Jesus their origins are heavenly, not earthly:

> Jesus said, "When you see the one who was not born of woman, prostrate yourselves on your faces and worship him. That one is your father." (*Gos. Thom.* 15; *NHLE*, 128)

> Jesus said, "Whoever does not hate his father and his mother cannot become a disciple to me. And whoever does not hate his brothers and sisters and take up his cross in my way will not be worthy of me." (*Gos. Thom.* 55; *NHLE*, 132; cf. Matt 10:37-39; Luke 14:26-27)

> [Jesus said,] "Whoever does not hate his [father] and his mother as I do cannot become a [disciple] to me. And whoever does [not] love his [father and] his mother as I do cannot become a [disciple to] me. For my mother [. . .], but [my] true [mother] gave me life." (*Gos. Thom.* 101; *NHLE*, 137)

Renunciation of family ties, social status, and wealth removes those impediments to discovering the divine image that Jesus reveals to his disciples.

I have already noted that this stripping away of earthly distinctions also applied to divisions of gender. Jesus points to infants prior to the time when characteristics of gender or personality separate them from one another. The final collection of sayings includes two women disciples among those who receive its revelation. Both Mary Magdalene (*Gos. Thom.* 22; *NHLE*, 129) and Salome (*Gos. Thom.* 61; *NHLE*, 133) demonstrate perfect understanding of the Savior's message. The final saying in the collection returns to the question of what the image of God is. Peter demands that Mary be driven out from the ranks o the disciples, claiming that women are not capable of salvation. In Philo's philosophical reading of Genesis, this assertion would be obvious. The female represents that part of the soul that is attached to the material world through sense perception. Only by turning away from the sensible world and the passions it engenders can the soul discover the divine.[42] *Gospel of Thomas* agrees that Mary is not saved by fulfilling the normal social roles that society imposed on women.[43] But she can follow Jesus and become a living spirit like Jesus' male disciples:

> Simon Peter said to them, "Let Mary leave us, for women are not worthy of life."
>
> Jesus said, "I myself shall lead her in order to make her male, so that she too may become a living spirit resembling you males. For every woman who will make herself male will enter the kingdom of heaven." (*Gos. Thom.* 114; *NHLE*, 138, my trans.)[44]

Echoes of sayings collections occur in other gnostic writings, especially *Dialogue of the Savior* (III,5) and the *Apocryphon of James* (I,2).[45] Similes, prophecies, and wisdom sayings can be found among the discourses in these writings. Unlike *Gospel of Thomas*, both writings shift away from the genre of a mere collection of Jesus' sayings to that of a revelation dialogue in which the Lord instructs select disciples concerning the mysteries of salvation. Although these sayings may preserve some early traditions about Jesus, they are much further removed from the first-century variants than those in *Gospel of Thomas*. Consider the image of the Sower from *Apocryphon of James*:

> Become zealous about the word. For the word's first characteristic is faith; its second is love; the third is works. Now from these comes life. For the word is like a grain of wheat; when someone sowed it, he believed in it; and when it sprouted, he loved it because he looked (forward to) many grains in place of the one; and when he worked (it), he was saved because he prepared it for food. Again he left (some grains) to sow. Thus it is also possible for you [pl.] to receive for yourselves the kingdom of heaven. (*Ap. Jas.* 8,10-27; *NHLE*, 33)[46]

This simile belongs to the tradition of Jesus' seed parables. Because its primary focus is sowing, cultivating, and then a harvest that sustains life, its closest canonical relative is the Seed Growing Secretly in Mark 4:26-29:

> The kingdom of God is as if someone would scatter seed on the ground, and would sleep and rise night and day, and the seed would sprout and grow, he does not know how. The earth produces of itself, first the stalk, then the head, then the full grain in the head. But when the grain is ripe, at once he goes in with his sickle, because the harvest has come.

The author of *Apocryphon of James* has provided the parable with an introduction and concluding exhortation. He has also attached it to a list of parables in which the risen Lord complains that he has had to stay with the disciples another eighteen days to expound. They are all familiar parables: the Shepherds, the Seed, the Building, the Lamps of the Virgins, the Didrachmae, and the Woman. The Shepherds probably refers to the Lost Sheep (Luke 15:3-7//Matt 18:12-13). The Seed could refer to any of the seed parables, although the Sower (Mark 4:2-8//Matt 13:3-8//Luke 8:4-8; *Gos. Thom.* 9) is the most famous. In addition to the parable just quoted, *Apocryphon of James* has another seed parable (*Ap. Jas.* 12,20-30; *NHLE*, 35). The Building may refer either to the Building on Foundations of Stone or Sand (Matt 7:24-27//Luke 6:48-49) or to the Tower Builder (Luke 14:28-30). The Lamps of the Virgins may refer to the Wise and Foolish Virgins (Matt 25:1-12), the Didrachmae to the Lost Coin (Luke 15:8-9), and the Woman to the Leaven (Luke 13:20-21//Matt 13:33; *Gos. Thom.* 96; *NHLE*, 136). *Apocryphon of James* intends to invoke the authority of the canonical Gospels to bolster the esoteric, gnostic teaching presented in the treatise.[47] Many of its other sayings echo passages from the Gospel of John. But all cases are modified versions of Jesus' teaching about the kingdom. They suggest that collections of sayings and parables may have been more common than we often suppose. But *Apocryphon of James* does not make a major contribution to our understanding of the earliest stages of the sayings tradition.

Summary

Gospel of Thomas collects sayings material that is closely related to that in the Synoptic sayings tradition. Its variants play an important role in reconstructing the tradition history of material in the Synoptic Gospels. Some scholars use the results as evidence that Jesus' original teaching emphasized the presence of salvation through wisdom, not apocalyptic judgment. By the time of the second-century redaction of the collection, some of its sayings have also been taken from or influenced by the canonical versions. But variants of some of the sayings and parables are closer to the oral forms than the material that the Synoptic evangelists have reworked. Jesus is understood as the embodiment of primordial divine Wisdom rather than as the end-time judge of the righteous. The kingdom is a dynamic presence that the disciple must discover as he or she recovers the divine image within.

Sayings and parables in *Gospel of Thomas* are not heavily allegorized. Emphasis on the recovery of the true, divine image within does provide the entry points for gnostic mythemes. Individual sayings are more characteristically interpreted by the addition of other sayings than by allegorization. The development of the sayings collection genre can be examined in *Dialogue of the Savior* and *Apocryphon of James*. Such collections preserve sayings as keys to a hidden wisdom that separates insiders from outsiders. They lack the narrative context that the canonical Gospels use to limit the speculative possibilities of such a collection.

Contrary to the main Jewish tradition of Wisdom as a guide to righteousness according to the Torah, both Christian and gnostic collections show only passing interest in issues connected with the Law. However, some of the sayings in *Gospel of Thomas* take the form of community rules. They encourage ascetic detachment and separation from family, and show a hostility toward wealth. Such separation from the common concerns of humanity is evidence of a new heavenly identity. This identity even crosses the conventional gender distinctions between male and female.

6

Gnosis and the Pauline Tradition

Studies of the Pauline tradition sometimes infer that Paul's opponents were a single group of Judaizing Gnostics.[1] This hypothesis is difficult to confirm from the textual evidence of the Pauline letters. Schmithals has contended that those who use this argument against his hypothesis neglect an important feature of the evidence: only at Corinth does Paul confront an opposition about which he has direct information. Therefore Paul's own formulations are unreliable indices of the language or supporting evidence used by the opponents. The author of the Pastorals responded to the heretics by distancing himself as much as possible from their language.[2] It is also necessary to ask a different question. Did Paul himself appropriate exegetical traditions, mythemes, or images of salvation from the gnosticizing interpretations of Genesis that are associated with Jewish circles in the first century C.E.?[3]

Pauline Opponents (Schmithals)

Schmithals insists that the best understanding of the opponents in Galatians, Colossians, Ephesians, and the Pastorals is in terms of a gnosticizing Jewish group. This group insisted on ascetic detachment from the world. It rejected the value of many external religious practices but accommodated circumcision and other Judaizing customs in order to remain within the synagogue. *Gospel of Thomas* 53 reflects the understanding of circumcision prevalent in such circles:[4]

His disciples said to him, "Is circumcision beneficial or not?"

> He said to them, "If it were beneficial, their father would beget
> them already circumcised from their mother. Rather, the true cir-
> cumcision in spirit has become completely profitable." (*NHLE*, 132)

These Jewish Christians allege that Paul himself still preaches circumcision (Gal 5:11).[5] According to this reading, it is Paul, not his opponents, who creates the scenario of salvation by works of the Law in
opposition to salvation through Christ. The real debate is about Paul's
authority as an apostle and his "gospel."

Because Galatians has been the centerpiece of the argument against
continuing the original Tübingen school's project of identifying a uni-
fied opposition to the apostle, it intrudes into any discussion of Pauline
opponents.[6] If Judaizing among the Galatians implies acceptance of
the authority of a conventional form of adherence to the Jewish law
(or at least that part of it essential for claiming to be among the
children of Abraham) and the authority of its apparent claims about
God, then the opposition cannot come from gnosticizing Jews. As
already discussed, the basic structure of early gnostic mythology establishes the gnostic elect as a "seed" superior to the authority of the
creator and his ordinances.

Schmithals takes a different approach. He understands Gal 3:1—
5:12 as Paul's attempt to portray the opponents as Judaizers enslaved
to the Law. They claimed to be spiritual persons with superior insight
into the gospel. Both ascetic emancipation and devaluing of the created order are characteristic of this gnosticizing movement.[7] Scholars
are constantly thrown back on their own reconstructions of the debate
in Galatians. If the argument concerned a spiritualized reading of the
gospel, perhaps even attached to the authority of James as in several
Nag Hammadi texts from the second and third centuries,[8] then a gnosticizing version of the opponents might be plausible. But most scholars
assume that Paul's charges of Judaizing have some substance. Whether
the opponents are actually ethnic Jews or Gentiles who seek to assim-
ilate, they advocate a real—not nominal—adherence to a constellation
of Jewish identity markers that would permit them to claim to be
physical children of Abraham in some contexts.[9]

In Schmithals's understanding of the Pauline opponents, however,
the evidence should not be drawn from a single letter. The pattern
barely visible in Galatians surfaces in the deutero-Pauline letters. The
opponents of the Pastoral Epistles grounded their knowledge of God
in Jewish tradition (1 Tim 1:7-10; Titus 1:10-16; 3:9). Their claim that
resurrection has already occurred (2 Tim 2:18) is typical of gnostic

understanding of resurrection. The ascetic rejection of marriage and of some foods also implies a sectarian use of knowledge to overcome the limitations of the material world (1 Tim 4:3; 5:23). Ascetic Christian women may have also insisted on their freedom from the obligations of marriage and childbearing. Consequently, 1 Timothy resists all attempts to change the conventional position of women in the family or in the community (1 Tim 2:9-15; 5:3-16). Where gnostic interpreters saw sexuality as the curse that the lower creator used to gain control over humankind, the author of the Pastorals alleges that the Christian woman can be saved through childbearing (1 Tim 2:15). Against a docetic understanding of Jesus as revealer, the Pastorals stress his humanity (1 Tim 2:5; 3:16; 2 Tim 2:8). Against the elitism of the opponents, the Pastorals make it clear that salvation is extended to all people (1 Tim 2:4, 6; 4:10; 2 Tim 4:1; Titus 2:11; 3:3).[10]

Colossians and Ephesians present more difficulties for the interpreter than the Pastorals. Schmithals holds the somewhat idiosyncratic view that Colossians was redacted by the author of Ephesians.[11] But this view produces an unnecessarily complex account of the relationship between the two letters. Ephesians is clearly a creative adaptation of material from Colossians and other Pauline letters to the new situation of its author.[12] While Colossians is directed against the cosmic speculation and associated piety of a group of opponents, Ephesians has shifted its focus to the church.[13]

Colossians 2:16-23 rejects a number of precepts that would appear to be derived from some form of Jewish ritualism: food rules (v. 16); festivals, new moons, and sabbaths (v. 16);[14] and things used according to human teaching (vv. 21-23). They are attached to some form of ascetic and visionary practice aimed at inducting the worshiper into the realm of angelic worship (v. 18).[15] This description does not fit conventional Jewish piety but might be associated with an apocalyptic quest for insight into the heavenly realms. A gnosticizing reading depends upon interpreting the *stoicheia* (2:8, 20) as the demonic rulers of the lower spheres. I have noted that early gnostic mythology held that their power over humanity was based in the creation of the material world and the human body. The rituals and ascetic practices mentioned would provide the required means to overcome their hold on human beings. By the third century C.E., the Manicheans had an elaborate system of dietary and ascetic restrictions for elect members of the sect to promote just such detachment.[16]

Schmithals attaches the warnings against Jewish ritual to a Pauline letter that has been redacted to produce the canonical epistle. He sees the dualist conquest of the powers by Christ (2:15) as a gnosticizing element in Colossians. The final editor shifted the imagery of Christ and the powers to make Christ their head and the one who reconciles all things to God (2:1, 18).[17] The final editor also rejects the conventional gnostic description of persons as members of the elect race for the traditional early Christian emphasis on forgiveness of sins (1:13-14, 20; 2:13-14). Sinners are redeemed, not spiritual persons as in gnostic systems.[18] At the same time, they are also recreated according to the original image of the creator (3:10). The question of images in which humans are created—that of a divine heavenly figure, whether Wisdom or the Son of man, and that of the rulers of the lower world who formed the material human being—plays an important role in early gnostic mythologizing. Colossians has embedded this passage from an apparent baptismal formula (3:10-11) in a section of traditional ethical parenesis. This catalog has been interpreted according to the common Hellenistic medical view that linked some vices to the predominance of different elements in the body.[19]

Schmithals's theory separates the two elements that most interpreters assume must be related in any reconstruction of the opponents in Colossae: Judaizing and gnostic speculation that had the effect of reducing Christ to one of the heavenly powers. He may be right to claim that the diverse evidence is difficult to encompass within any single group. Yet it is even more difficult to establish persuasive criteria for redaction criticism in the epistle as a whole.[20] I have previously noted that analysis of the gnostic texts themselves suggests that their earliest traditions took shape in the context of baptismal sects familiar with traditions found in Jewish Pseudepigrapha. I have also pointed out that there is no single line of development from the first century into the sociologically identifiable gnostic groups of the second century.

Where does Colossians fall on this spectrum? Yates has suggested that the origins of the movement being opposed lie in Jewish mysticism. The ascetic regulations and cultic practices of the opponents were aimed at securing visions of the heavenly world. The cosmic powers are not understood as agents of a demonic creator but as beings surrounding the divine throne.[21] Of course, it is a very small step from this picture of the cosmos to a gnosticizing mythology. Early gnostic mythemes account for the exclusion of humans from the divine presence, the need for ascetic conquest of the powers that are at work in the material body and its soul, and how the divine image is restored. They also provide for the conquest of those powers by a heavenly redeemer who is superior to them in the created order.

The soteriological imagery of Col 2:14-15 finds its way into a second-century Valentinian meditation on salvation, the *Gospel of Truth*.[22] The author has combined this image of Christ's victory over the powers on the cross with the Lamb and the scroll of Rev 5:9 and the familiar image of the book of life said to contain the names of the elect (Rev 20:12-15).[23] The names in this book are the elect, written in the heart of the Father from the beginning. Jesus' death is the passage into imperishability by which the material body is stripped off. Thus the cross refers to the saving revelation received by the elect, not to forgiveness of sin as in the canonical version of Colossians. The second-century author of *Gospel of Truth* may not have been the first to attach a different weight to the crucifixion. The opponents of Colossians might have understood it in a similar way as the triumphant victory over the flesh and the cosmic powers who work through its agency.

Because Schmithals holds that the author of Ephesians was the final editor of Colossians, he treats the two together. But he constructs a very different sociological situation for the writing of the two letters. He surmises that Ephesians was written to encourage the gentile churches in the region to accept those Jewish Christians who were being expelled from the synagogue. He also detects this emphasis on harmony in Colossians (e.g., 1:9-23; 2:19; 3:15b—4:1).[24] But the household code material in Ephesians has been much more extensively Christianized than that in Colossians, although it is clearly dependent on Colossians.[25] Therefore it seems more plausible to accept the common view that Ephesians is later than canonical Colossians, which served as the source for some of the traditional material in Ephesians.

Schmithals admits that without the more explicit rejection of false speculation in Colossians, the antignostic themes in Ephesians would not be recognizable. Ephesians seeks to promote the unity of gentile Christians from the Pauline mission with Jewish Christians who have recently been expelled from the synagogue.[26] But the dynamic imagery of Ephesians also leaves room for a gnosticizing interpretation, which second-century gnostic authors would exploit. The epistle emphasizes Christ's heavenly enthronement above all the powers (1:20-23). The elect, who have been predestined by God from all eternity, already receive the blessings from the heavenly places (1:3-4, 18-19; 2:5-6). Christ's appearance establishes the church through which the powers that dwell in the heavens learn of God's plan (3:10-11). The moral struggle of the Christian life is presented as a conflict against the powers (6:12). This passage was picked up by the gnostic author of *Hypostasis of the Archons* to introduce the mythological account of how human beings became subject to the powers (II 86,20-27; *NHLE*, 162).

Both Colossians and Ephesians provide the opening for gnostic mythological explanations. Ephesians depicts Christ as the heavenly Savior who descended into the lower regions, rescued the elect, and then returned above the heavens (4:9-10). These verses have been read as a midrash on the text from Ps 68:19 cited in verse 8. In order to give gifts to humanity, the one who ascends with hosts of captives must have descended from the heavens.[27] The author's primary interest is not in the image of Christ itself but in the claim that the diverse spiritual gifts in the church have been bestowed by its exalted head. The catchword *gift* holds the section together (vv. 7, 8, 11).

The close association between Christ and his body, the church, found in these sections of Ephesians forms the basis for Christianizing the treatment of husband and wife in the household code (Eph 5:22-33; contrast Col 3:18-19). Christians are urged to see the relationship between husband and wife as an image of that which exists between Christ and the church. In the second century, Valentinian exegetes would treat the church as the heavenly counterpart to the Christ (Irenaeus, *Adv. Haer.* 1.8.4).[28] The harmony of the church of the elect in this world reflects that of the preexistent heavenly church.[29] The Christ came for her sake:

> The election shares body and essence with the Savior, since it is like a bridal chamber because of its unity and its agreement with him. For, before every place, the Christ came for her sake. (*Tri. Trac.* I 122,12-18; *NHLE*, 96)[30]

Gnostic exegetes could even accommodate the crucifixion to this imagery. *Gospel of Philip* speaks of Christ laying down his life for his own from the day the world came into being (II 53,1-9; *NHLE*, 142).

These examples do not show that the deceitful human teaching of Eph 4:14 was an early form of gnostic speculation.[31] Ephesians itself is much more concerned with parenesis than with speculative mythologizing. The references to hostile powers occur in parenetic contexts. The gentile converts once lived in subjection to the demonic ruler of the air. That state was reflected in a life according to the bodily passions (2:2-3). Conversion implies putting off the old way of life with its corrupt desires and putting on the new human being created according to God (4:22-24). Arming oneself against the devil (6:11-12) provides the ability to continue to live as children of light (5:6-14). It does not refer to a means of escape from this world into the next. But gnostic mythologizing can easily be used to explicate the cosmic imagery of Ephesians. Consequently, it provides a point of transition between the heterodox Jewish gnosticizing in the first century and the speculative mythologizing of Christian gnostic teachers, especially Valentinians, in the second century.

Gnostic Mythemes
and Pauline Anthropology

I have been dealing with the question of gnostic influence on the Pauline tradition from the outside. The question has always been whether a group or groups of gnosticizing Jewish teachers were distorting the gospel in the Pauline churches. But I have noted that the earliest forms of gnostic mythologizing arose in the context of Jewish speculation during the first century. Therefore one must also ask whether any of the Jewish traditions that were adopted by Sethian Gnostics also appear in Paul's own letters. I have also pointed out that the most obvious ties between Pauline traditions and such speculation are in the areas of anthropology and soteriology. Speculation about the structure of the divine world or the emergence of the lower world does not play a role in the Pauline context.

Paul's perception of the flesh as the entry point for the sinful desires that ultimately bring death to humans unless they receive the Spirit of Christ comes very close to what one finds in gnostic mythologizing. Paul's thought may be an independent development of the type of speculation in the Jewish traditions that gave birth to gnostic mythology. Just as Ephesians is more concerned with parenesis than its later gnostic interpreters are, so Paul is more apt to use the antithesis "flesh/ spirit" in the context of ethical exhortation (e.g., Gal 5:19-25) than his gnostic counterparts would be.

Nonetheless, the mythemes developed in gnostic writers do illuminate elements in Pauline thought that are otherwise opaque. Paul assumes that his readers will accept without argument the view that humanity becomes subject to desire (Gk. *epithymia*) through the flesh. They should also agree that baptism provides entry into the realm of the life-giving Spirit, which is sharply distinguished from the world dominated by sin and death.

Paul traces the enslavement of all humanity under the power of sin and death to the story of Adam. What Paul lacks is the mythic account found in a text like *Apocalypse of Adam* (V,5) to explain how Adam lost his divine glory and fell victim to desire and death. The gnostic writers draw the conclusion that Paul strives to avoid. They insist that if the commandment is an opportunity for sin (so Rom 7:11), then the god responsible for the commandment cannot desire that humanity be saved. Paul's account of the struggle between the good that one knows and the "other law" of sin found in one's members (Rom 7:14-25) is closely related to the "two spirits" tradition found in *Apocryphon of John*. There, in order to render the initial divine spirit that had been breathed into the humans ineffective, the powers created a counterfeit spirit. This spirit enters the body through the defilement of sexuality.[32] The counterfeit spirit is responsible both for the evils that humans do and for their ignorance of the true God. Both Paul and the Gnostics agree that the plight of humanity cannot be corrected by philosophical reason or by the traditional modes of religious practice. Only the final coming of the Savior provides access to the divine Spirit needed to break the bondage in which humans live.

I have previously mentioned that gnostic mythology exploited Jewish interpretations of the dual creation of Adam in Genesis 1-3. A variant of this tradition appears in Paul. According to this tradition, the spiritual Adam was formed directly in God's image and is immortal. The earthly Adam has been molded out of the earth and is endowed only with breath. Consequently, the earthly Adam, who is often said to be the work of angels, is subject to death. All the variants of this tradition also agree that the spiritual Adam is a heavenly being, not an earthly one (e.g., 1 Cor 15:45-48). We have seen that in gnostic mythology this Adam is usually characterized as the Immortal Human or the great Seth. He is only secondarily identified with Christ. For Paul, there is no other heavenly figure who might bear the image of God besides Christ. Because the risen Lord is the one into whose image Christians are transformed (1 Cor 15:49), it appears that Paul is not thinking of Christ as the image of God borne by the preexistent divine Wisdom figure as in the gnostic variants of the tradition. Rather, he refers to the risen and glorified Christ as the one who bears the image of God.[33]

Although Paul speaks in the present tense of the Christian's freedom from bondage to sin, he attaches reservations to the activity of the Spirit. Gnostics claim that the seed of the Immortal Seth is hidden behind the apparent mortality of the elect while they dwell in the human body. Paul insists that death remains a real enemy to be overcome. Only at the parousia when Christ returns all things to God will believers be transformed into the image of the immortal, spiritual Adam (1 Cor 15:50-57). Paul appears to be more pessimistic about the universality of sin than the Gnostics. Gnostic mythology held that an undominated race had been preserved in the pure seed of Seth. Second-century gnostic writers would criticize orthodox Christians for their fruitless attachment to the material body. This attachment was said to lead them to place their confidence in a "dead man," the crucified Christ, rather than in the risen Jesus.

A similar debate about the significance of Jesus' death is clearly evident in Paul's theology. He consistently focuses on the cross, on the suffering and death of Jesus, in polemical contexts.[34] This focus is directly opposed to the Corinthian understanding of the transformation of believers in the Spirit. The Corinthians appear to have adapted a quasi-philosophical spirituality similar to that in Philo. They insisted that "spiritual persons" already participated in the immortality and blessings of the divine realm. They probably understood Gen 2:7 as evidence that human beings contain within themselves the divine Spirit. Therefore, rejecting "resurrection of the dead" as Paul says that they have done (1 Cor 15:12)[35] did not imply that the Corinthians thought the dead perished (15:18-19).

Immortality is a property only of the divine image in the human person. If that image does not include the body or the parts of the soul associated with it, then there would be no reason to assume that resurrection describes the future transformation of the bodily aspects of the person as Paul asserts (1 Cor 15:35-50). By the second century, gnostic teachers were able to read the Pauline texts as though the apostle himself taught that resurrection was a spiritual phenomenon. The *Treatise on Resurrection* from the Nag Hammadi Codex I provides a clear example of this philosophical rendering of the Pauline tradition.[36] Although composed by a Valentinian teacher, *Treatise on Resurrection* is directed to Christians at large. Its argument employs common philosophical assumptions. Immortality is gained through the ascent of the mind to the divine.

The cross and the material world are both illusory. The suffering referred to in the Gospel is only that of the soul that is trapped in matter. When the soul lays aside what is corruptible, then it attains immortality.[37] Release from entrapment in the material world depends on both ascetic practice and faith in the truth revealed by the Savior (I 43,25—44,12; 46,3-9; *NHLE*, 54–55). Consequently, the author of *Treatise on Resurrection* is as opposed to philosophical speculation as Paul is to human wisdom. Nonetheless, the true nature of resurrection is defined in philosophical terms. It entails "standing at rest" (48,33; *NHLE*, 56), a philosophical expression designating the stability of the divine world in contrast to the ever-changing material realm.[38] The latter cannot participate in the former. It is destined to die from the moment it comes into being (49,9-23; *NHLE*, 56).

The philosophical presuppositions for this interpretation of resurrection are already present in Philo of Alexandria. Moses participates in the immutability of God, because his ascent on Sinai was a mystical entry into the realm of the divine forms.[39] The exegesis of Gen 2:7, which distinguished between the "soul" and the immortal "spirit" or "mind," was also readily available in Philo and Wisdom of Solomon. Paul must recast this conventional exegesis by treating the spiritual and mortal Adam as figures in an apocalyptic schema. The inferior Adam comes first. The spiritual Adam and those human beings who will share the divine image come later. Christ's resurrection initiates a transformation that cannot be completed until death is conquered (1 Cor 15:44-57).[40]

Eschatology and Anthropology

Paul's eschatological understanding of the resurrection leads him to depart from the conventional interpretations of the Genesis text whether in Philo or in the traditions that were appropriated in early gnostic mythologizing. There the order of the texts suggests that the heavenly, spiritual Adam and his descendants should precede the earthly Adam, who is the subject of the fall story. Further, as a heavenly reality, the first Adam cannot be subject to mortality or change. Thus the paradigm of the human remains untouched by the imperfections of its material representation.

When this anthropology is set over against Paul's account, the apostle, not his opponents, seems to be the one moving in a more radical direction. Humans are so radically embedded in the constraints of the material world that they cannot be assimilated to the divine image until the end time. Only if the material body is transformed from earthly to spiritual will the faithful share the image of the risen Christ. The apocalyptic elements in Pauline thought contribute to his certainty that salvation cannot be attained in the present order.

This apocalyptic perspective defines the present age as "evil" even though Christians are no longer subject to its ruling powers. As previously mentioned, early gnostic mythology depicts the material order as a place of bondage. Drawing upon Jewish speculation about the fallen angels, gnostic mythologizers are able to explain that humanity is now subject to a counterfeit spirit. That same spirit operates in conjunction with the fates that hold the material world together. This mythological schema is evidently dependent on traditions associated with Enoch. In both *1 Enoch* and *Apocryphon of John* humanity calls out to God for deliverance from its bondage (*1 Enoch* 9:9-11; *Ap. John* II 29,16—30,11; *NHLE*, 121–22). All of creation has been enslaved:

> And thus the whole creation became enslaved forever, from the foundation of the world until now. And they took women and begot children out of the darkness according to the likeness of their spirit. And they closed their hearts, and they hardened themselves through the hardness of the counterfeit spirit until now. (*Ap. John* II 30,5-11; *NHLE*, 122)

The dualism that runs through Paul's description of the redemption of the children of God in Romans 8 touches on similar traditions.[41] The "flesh" that held humans in bondage is replaced by the Spirit of God (8:9-14). Creation itself is in bondage and suffering until the children of God are revealed (8:18-23). Ernst Käsemann is certainly right to argue (against Bultmann) that Paul's language in this section does not imply that the apostle was dependent on gnostic mythologizing, because the presuppositions for Paul's language can be found in Jewish apocalyptic.[42] But those same apocalyptic traditions are being recast in gnostic *mythologoumena* during the first century. Insofar as Paul has adapted them to depict the plight of humanity and a salvation that comes through the Savior's mediation of a new spirit, he belongs to an exegetical tradition that is easily assimilated by gnostic mythologizing.

Paul's own thought remains bound to the material and historical world in a way that is incoherent from both a mythic and a philosophical viewpoint. The views for which second-century C.E. gnostic teachers criticized orthodox Christians are clearly represented in Paul's letters. He does place confidence in a "dead man" to secure the individual's salvation with God (Rom 3:24-26). He does insist that resurrection demands a transformation of the material body (1 Cor 15:34-49). These convictions do not sit well with the more consistent anthropology of Philo or of the gnostic *mythologoumena*. Both distinguish the bodily attachment of humans to the material world from the divine image that makes them part of the divine. Without an apocalyptic vision that included destruction of the world dominated by evil and death as well as the transformation of the righteous, Paul's convictions make no sense.[43] Given this apocalyptic perspective, it was not necessary to remythologize the world of the believer's experience. The inherited descriptions of the world and the patterns of relationship within it still describe the experience of believers, because they are not yet transformed into what faith promises them they will be (Rom 8:18-30).

The Divine Image

The eschatological reservation by which Paul limits the extent to which believers participate in the life of the risen Christ here and now appears when Paul is engaged in combating excessive claims about the present perfection or new status of believers. Other passages suggest that the apostle or his tradition generated some of the misunderstanding by speaking of the transformation of believers in more radical terms. Galatians 3:27-28 has provided an exegetical linchpin for disputes about this aspect of the apostle's anthropology. This formula, set in a larger argument about the adoption of persons as children of Abraham, depicts baptismal transformation as a new identity that eradicates the established divisions: Jew or non-Jew, slave or free, male or female.[44] The variant in Col 3:10-11 refers to transformation effected by a saving knowledge. The baptized are created anew in the image (*eikōn*) of the Creator. Earthly distinctions of Gentile/Jew, geographical origin, or slave/free are all eradicated. Christ is all[45] in all.

This tradition has been reinterpreted by the gnostic author of the *Tripartite Tractate* to argue for the unity of the spiritual and psychic Christians in the Pleroma. The separation between the spiritual, gnostic Christians and the psychics that is a commonplace in Valentinian speculation is a transitional stage in the process of restoring what was lost to the divine world.[46] This application of the formula presumes its authoritative status. The author of *Tripartite Tractate* employs it to establish what may have been an innovation in the Valentinian tradition; at the end no distinction between spiritual and psychic remains. Because the initial appearance of salvation establishes a distinction between the two groups (cf. 118,37—119,8; 119,26-27; *NHLE*, 94–95), the unity envisaged in this passage has an eschatological dimension:

> For it is right that we confess the kingdom in Christ to dissolve all multiplicity and inequality and change. For the end will receive the state of being that is one just as the beginning is one—the place where there is no male and female, nor slave or free, nor circumcised or uncircumcised, nor angel or human, but Christ is all in all. (I,5 132,16-28; *NHLE*, 101, my trans.)

All three examples of this formula make "the beginning" the norm for salvation. Divisions of gender, Gentile/Jew, status, and people are subsequent marks of the separation of humankind from its divine origin. Multiplicity, inequality, and change are characteristics of the material world, not the world of the divine image. Thus Philo distinguished the Adam of Gen 2:7 from the divine image of Gen 1:26:

> There is an immense difference between this molded one and the one made previously according to the image (*eikōn*) of God, for the molded one is an object of sense, partaking already of quality consisting of body and soul, man or woman, mortal by nature, while that which was after the image was an idea or type or seal, an object of thought, incorporeal, neither male nor female, incorruptible by nature. (*Opif. Mund.* 134)

Although he lacks the mythological account found in gnostic sources, Philo blames desire for the division of humans into male and female. This division and the passion to reproduce entangles them in the world of matter. It is ultimately responsible for their subjection to death (*Opif. Mund.* 152).

Those who turn away from the material world to the divine must recover in themselves the unity of the original divine image. Contemporary interest in nonsexist and androgynous imagery of the human person has generated considerable discussion about the development and significance of the tradition underlying Gal 3:27-28.[47] The basic soteriology of the tradition centers on recovering the state of Adam prior to the fall.

Several sayings in *Gospel of Thomas* suggest that the goal of knowledge is to recover the androgynous divine image of the human that existed before the separation of humans into male and female. The addressees are exhorted to seek the primordial unity:

Jesus saw infants being suckled. He said to his disciples, "These infants being suckled are like those who enter the kingdom."

They said to him, "Shall we then, as children, enter the kingdom?"

Jesus said to them, "When you make the two one, and when you make the inside like the outside and the outside like the inside, and the above like the below, and when you make the male and the female one and the same, so that the male not be male nor the female female; and when you fashion eyes in place of an eye, and a hand in place of a hand, and a foot in place of a foot, and a likeness in place of a likeness, then you will enter [the kingdom]." (saying 22; *NHLE*, 129)

His disciples said, "When will you become revealed to us and when shall we see you?"

Jesus said, "When you disrobe without being ashamed and take up your garments and place them under your feet like little children and tread on them, then [will you see] the son of the living one, and you will not be afraid." (saying 37; *NHLE*, 130)

The "garments" to be trampled probably alludes to the body. Most interpreters think that the saying requires an ascetic rejection of the body.

Later patristic writers suggest that "trampling garments" may have been incorporated into the baptismal ritual. Theodore of Mopsuestia describes an exorcism rite that took place prior to baptism. The catechumen removed a garment of sackcloth and stood on it barefoot. By this time, the rite had been reinterpreted to refer to the sins of the catechumen's former life, "from the fact that your feet are pricked and stung by the roughness of the cloth, you may remember your old sins." Augustine also alludes to rites in which the catechumen stood on goatskins as a sign that former sins were being trampled under foot.[48]

Clement of Alexandria preserves a saying that he attributes to the "Gospel of the Egyptians." It combines the "treading garments" with the formula about making the two one and transcending gender:

When Salome asked when the events she inquired about would be known, the Lord said, "When you tread upon the garment of shame and when the two are one, and the male with the female, neither male nor female." (*Strom.* 3.9.64)

Another citation from the same source praises Salome for rejecting childbearing. As already noted, this whole tradition rejects sexuality and childbearing as evidence of bondage to the material world:

Salome said, "How long will people die?" Jesus answered, "As long as people bear children." And Salome said to him, "Then I have done well in not bearing children." Jesus answered, "Eat every plant, but the plant that is bitter you shall not eat." (*Strom.* 3.9.64; *Exc. Theod.* 67)

This tradition of Jesus' sayings holds that salvation mediated through baptismal rites and ascetic practice restores humans to a state that existed before sin and death came to dominate human life. Valentinian sources developed this soteriology into an elaborate doctrine of the androgynous soul that is restored to its primordial unity in a sacrament of the "bridal chamber." The soul returns to her heavenly counterpart.[49]

First-century interpretations of this tradition may not have embodied the elaborate complex of myth and ritual attested in later sources. But elements of the spirituality it engendered are evident in the Pauline epistles. Paul's use of the formula in Gal 3:27-28 suggests that practices he had instituted may have sparked the developments he later rejects. Some Corinthian ascetics expressed their freedom from the bodily constraints of sexuality by renouncing intercourse between spouses or dissolving marriages altogether (1 Cor 7:1-16). Paul's appeal to the authority of the Lord's saying (1 Cor 7:10) may indicate that the Corinthians had appealed to other sayings of the Lord to justify their conclusions.

I have noted that garments play a highly symbolic role in connection with the tradition of baptism as recovery of the primordial divine image. A convoluted argument over the hair of women prophets in 1 Cor 11:3-16 pits a subordinationist tradition grounded in the creation stories of Genesis 2 against an apparently egalitarian practice in which women prophets demonstrated their new identity in Christ by shedding the socially sanctioned public attire for women (vv. 13-16).[50] Verses 7-10 compress an exegetical argument shaped by first-century readings of Genesis. Influenced by the creation account in Genesis 2, Paul presumes that the image of God from Gen 1:26 applies only to Adam.[51] The reference to "glory," which some exegetes take as Paul's modification of Genesis,[52] stems from first-century Adam traditions.

Adam did not forfeit the divine image at his fall. I have mentioned that even gnostic exegesis assumes that some element of the divine image is present in the human formed by the demiurgic powers. What Adam did lose was participation in the glory of God.[53] The Essenes expect to participate in "all the glory of Adam" (1QS 4:23; CD 3:20; 1QH 17:15). Paul himself associates glory with transformation into the image of Christ (2 Cor 3:18; 4:17). The issue of glory, order of creation, and dominion was played out in the tradition of the fallen angels. According to *Life of Adam and Eve*, Satan refused to worship Adam because Adam had been created after the angels (chaps. 13–14). In this context, the angels possessed "glory" but only Adam and Eve were created in God's image. The author assumes that they still possess that image after they have been expelled from paradise (so *Apoc. Mos.* 29:10). The gnostic version of Adam's fall in *Apocalypse of Adam* links loss of glory and the fall into gendered, material existence. Originally, Adam and Eve went about united in glory. As already noted, in other gnostic texts Eve stands in the position of divine wisdom that instructs Adam:

> When god had created me out of the earth along with Eve your mother, I went about with her in a glory which she had seen in the aeon from which we had come forth. She taught me a word of knowledge of the eternal god. And we resembled the great eternal angels, for we were higher than the god who had created us. (V 64,6-18; *NHLE*, 279)

The creator retaliates by dividing Adam and Eve from each other. Their glory leaves them for an aeon that will belong to the children of Seth (64,20—65,9; *NHLE*, 279). They lose their knowledge of the true God and become subject to sexual passion as well as to death (66,25—67,14; *NHLE*, 280).

Other gnostic texts describe the elect as those who are able to "trample the powers." This activity indicates the superiority of the gnostic seed to those powers that claim to rule the world. It also refers to the eschatological destruction of the demonic forces:

> Then they will be freed of blind thought: And they will trample under foot death, which is of the authorities. And they will ascend into the limitless light, where this sown element [= the seed of Seth] belongs. (*Hyp. Arch.* II 97,6-9; *NHLE*, 169)

In *Hypostasis of the Archons* the revelation is set in the primordial history. Seth's sister, Norea, who has resisted the attempts of the powers, asks the rescuing angel about her offspring. Consequently, their destruction of the powers repeats the resistance shown by their mother. From the perspective of the revelation, the victory over the powers is set in the future.

From the perspective of the gnostic reader, "trampling the powers" may not be an eschatological event but a present reality, just as resurrection is a present reality. This temporal orientation is evident in the *Sophia of Jesus Christ*. Jesus describes his own coming from the true God in order to give believers the authority to trample the powers:

> I came [from First] Who Was Sent, that I might reveal to you Him Who Is from the Beginning, because of the arrogance of Arch-Begetter and his angels, since they say about themselves that they are gods. And I came to remove them from their blindness that I might tell everyone about the God who is above the universe. Therefore, tread upon their graves, humiliate their malicious intent and break their yoke and arouse my own. I have given you authority over all things as Sons of Light, that you might tread upon their power with [your] feet. (*Soph. Jes. Chr.* III 118,15—119,17; *NHLE*, 242–43)

"Trampling the powers" could have a number of meanings. The association of the body and its passions with garments to be trampled suggested an ascetic discipline that freed individuals from control by the counterfeit spirit. Because the Law and the commandments served as the means by which the Demiurge enslaved humans in some texts,[54] "trampling the powers" might imply rejecting the authority of the Law in other contexts.

Both ritual or ascetic conquest of the imprisoning passions and rejection of the Law as an agent of bondage have echoes in the Pauline epistles. Yet Paul cites a formula suggesting that baptism implies ritual transcendence of the fundamental distinctions that characterize humans in their mortal, sociohistorical existence. How does he apparently accept the formula of Gal 3:27-28 and yet avoid the radicalized interpretations of the formula that are evident elsewhere in Gnosticism and early Christianity?

Dennis MacDonald argues that Paul is characteristically hostile to the tradition that the image of God was androgynous. First Cor 11:2-16 insists upon an order of creation in which the hierarchical sequence of gender relationships is retained. Even the women prophets whose inspiration might signify the presence of the Spirit that has negated such relationships at the level of salvation are commanded to remain subject to social conventions.[55] Elsewhere Paul consistently avoids speaking of "putting off" the body, an imagery that suits the imagery of trampled garments. Instead, he persistently speaks of transformation and putting on incorruption (1 Cor 15:53-54; 2 Cor 5:2-4).

But Paul is quite willing to negate the socioreligious barrier between Jew and Gentile. Overcoming that barrier in the new community of salvation is evidence of God's new creation (e.g., Gal 6:15;

1 Cor 12:12-13). Paul apparently considers disunity as a social cate-gory rather than as an anthropological one. The author of Ephesians captures this element in Pauline thought. The commandment is the dividing wall between Jew and Gentile, which the cross has negated (Eph 2:14-18). Marriage and its hierarchical ordering of male and female is not rejected but sacralized by assimilation to the sacrificial love of Christ for the church (Eph 5:22-33).

Paul does insist that social divisions between Jew and Gentile, slave and free, female and male cannot override the unity of the community. That affirmation does not imply that Christians must enact a new ontological or anthropological order in their community. For Paul, at any rate, the Christian's place in the large social order remains rela-tively unchanged. First Corinthians 7 shows the apostle insisting on a conventional order for both married Christians and those who are slaves. Where *Gospel of Thoma*s 114 promises that Mary will be "made male" in order to take her place among the male disciples, Paul insists that Christians retain the marks of the status in which they were called. Slaves should not demand freedom. Gentiles should not seek circumcision. Women prophets in the assembly should not seek to demonstrate their authority (over the angels?) by removing the veil that indicates their place in the order of creation.

Summary

Attempts to demonstrate that an organized group of gnosticizing opponents was responsible for the positions that Paul rejects in a number of his letters have been unsuccessful. Systematic formaliza-tion of gnostic theology does not appear to have existed in the first century. Particular, local cultic practices and the development of the exegetical traditions that fed early gnostic mythologizing are more typical of this period. However, the quest for gnostic elements in the positions that Paul appears to refute highlights those phenomena which would contribute to the development of Pauline tradition in gnostic circles. Gnostics would consider ascetic liberation from the constraints of society a necessary condition of returning to the spiritual unity of the heavenly Adam. The motif of Christ's triumph over the powers of the cosmos, already evident in Colossians, finds a congenial home in *Gospel of Truth*. Both Colossians and Ephesians provide a fruitful beginning for speculation about Christ as the heavenly Savior.

The most striking parallels between the Pauline tradition and first-century gnostic mythemes come in the context of anthropology. Sethian Genesis exegesis provides an explanation for the Pauline observation that humanity is subject to demonic powers because of its existence in the flesh. Such mythologizing also explains why all of humanity is trapped by powers of sin and death, which will work through the flesh unless they are countered by the divine Spirit. Gnostic sources also show that Adam traditions were a fruitful source of speculation about the human situation.

The apocalyptic eschatology in Paul's thought moderates his own treatment of the Adam material. The image of the divine Adam cannot be recovered until all things are returned to God in the end time. Pauline Christology enables the apostle to make a distinction between the earthly Adam and the spiritual Christ. For gnostic speculation, both Adam figures belong to the origins of all things. The heavenly image was briefly glimpsed by the powers of the lower world as they formed the earthly Adam. Paul's apocalyptic eschatology apparently inhibits any direct, complete experience of return to divine perfection by the believer until the end time. Consequently, there is no hidden gnostic race that continues to elude the powers. Paul's apocalyptic eschatology leaves the world as much in the grasp of the powers as gnostic dualism does. Both Pauline and gnostic circles also suggest that peculiar ritual practices of trampling the powers or garments are meant to symbolize the individual's liberation from the power of the lower world.

7

Redeemer Myths and New Testament Hymns

How does a Jewish eschatological prophet, suffering righteous one, or wisdom teacher become the heavenly revealer sent from God to enlighten humanity? The transformation in this picture of Jesus as redeemer is already evident in the New Testament. Adolph von Harnack attributed the change to a Christianity that had lost its Jewish roots. Rudolf Bultmann concluded that in order to understand the preexistent redeemer of some New Testament texts, one had to assume that Jesus had been assimilated to a gnostic myth of the heavenly revealer already existent in the first century C.E. Other exegetes have emphasized the role of Hellenistic Jewish Wisdom or Adam speculation in forging the categories of preexistence Christology.[1] As already mentioned, both Wisdom tradition and speculation about the heavenly and earthly Adam figure prominently in gnostic material. Consequently, the history-of-religions question has not been settled.

The Revealer Appears in the World

Although Bultmann's description of the redeemer as needing redemption in his ascent out of the world of darkness hardly fits the gnostic evidence, the sending of Jesus in the Fourth Gospel is easily transformed into gnostic mythologizing. So are affirmations in some of the hymnic passages of the New Testament. As George MacRae observed, the fact that the Fourth Gospel does not advocate the docetic anthropology of second-century systems hardly decides the issue of whether the evangelist is indebted to gnostic mythologizing.[2] Scholars often jump at one distinguishing characteristic like Docetism or "redeemed redeemer"[3] that can be said to separate New Testament christological expressions from their gnostic counterparts.

But the question of "Docetism" emerges only when there is a well-formulated sense of incarnation to which it might be opposed. The critical point appears to have been the apparent contradiction between the divinity of the redeemer and death on a cross.[4] Contrary to the sources that the early history-of-religions school used to construct a gnostic redeemer myth, the variants that are evident in the Nag Hammadi material do not depict the savior as a "redeemed redeemer." I have already noted that the Genesis speculation out of which gnostic mythologizing develops preserves its heavenly figures from contamination by the material world.

Descent into the lower world as revealer is often depicted as a heavenly manifestation of the Immortal Human just as he had appeared to the powers when they created their material image. Wisdom's appearances use the body only as a disguise at best. The long version of *Apocryphon of John* concludes with a hymnic passage in which the Mother is said to come three times for the sake of her offspring. She is never in the slightest danger of being entrapped there:

> I, therefore, the perfect Pronoia of the all, changed myself into my seed, for I existed first, going on every road. For I am the richness of the light; I am the remembrance of the pleroma.
>
> And I went into the realm of darkness and I endured till I entered the middle of the prison. And the foundations of chaos shook. And I hid myself from them because of their wickedness, and they did not recognize me.
>
> Again I returned for the second time and I went about. I came forth from those who belong to the light, which is I the remembrance of the Pronoia. I entered into the midst of darkness and the inside of Hades, since I was seeking (to accomplish) my task. And the foundations of chaos shook, that they might fall down upon those who are in chaos and might destroy them. And again I ran up to my root of light lest they be destroyed before the time.
>
> Still for a third time I went—I am the light which exists in the light, I am the remembrance of the Pronoia—that I might enter into the midst of darkness and the inside of Hades. And I filled my face with the light of the completion of their aeon. And I entered into the midst of their prison which is the prison of the body. And I said, "He who hears, let him get up from the deep sleep." And he wept and shed tears. Bitter tears he wiped from himself and he said, "Who is it that calls my name, and from where has this hope come to me, while

I am in the chains of the prison?" And I said, "I am the Pronoia of the pure light; I am the thinking of the virginal Spirit, who raised you up to the honored place. Arise and remember that it is you who hearkened, and follow your root, which is I, the merciful one, and guard yourself against the angels of poverty and the demons of chaos and all those who ensnare you, and beware of the deep sleep and the enclosure of the inside of Hades." (II 30,11—31,22; *NHLE*, 122)

The extant passage mixes formulaic phrases, especially the "I Am" statements of the revealer, with a narrative account of the savior's actions on behalf of the seed that is asleep in the midst of Hades. This combination of formulaic sections and narrative also appears in the prologue to the Fourth Gospel.[5] The short version of *Apocryphon of John* lacks this extended treatment but does refer to the coming of the revealer and prior activity of the divine Mother:

> The blessed one—that is, the Father-Mother—whose mercy is great, took form in their seed. First I came up to the perfect aeon. (BG 75,10-15; Foerster, *Gnosis*, 1:120)

> But the Mother came once again before me. These are the things that she has done in the world: she has raised up her seed. (BG 76,1-5; Foerster, *Gnosis*, 1:120)

The Mother or the perfect Pronoia is able to shape or awaken those who belong to her without becoming trapped in the lower world. I have already mentioned that gnostic treatments of the Genesis story developed various strategies by which the spiritual Eve and her descendants escaped the grasp of the rulers of the lower world. As Gnostics were confronted with more realistic claims about Jesus as incarnate revealer they would respond with a Docetism that protected Jesus from any contamination by association with the material body or its passions. Another formulaic passage in *First Apocalypse of James* celebrates the fact that Jesus remained uncontaminated by the world:

> You have come with knowledge,
> that you might rebuke their forgetfulness.
> You have come with recollection,
> that you might rebuke their ignorance.

> But I was concerned because of you.

> For you descended into a great ignorance,
> but you have not been defiled by anything in it.
> For you descended into a great mindlessness,
> and your recollection remained.

You walked in mud,
and your garments were not soiled,
and you have not been buried in their filth,
and you have not been caught. (V 28,7-20; *NHLE,* 263–64)[6]

First Apocalypse of James contrasts Jesus' relationship to the world
with that of James. In both examples, then, neither the redeemer nor
the redeemed is trapped by forgetfulness. Yet some scholars continue
to insist that the "redeemed redeemer" is the core element in gnostic
mythologizing:

> Central to the Gnostic redeemer hymns is the idea of a "saved Sav-
> ior." The Savior himself is somehow enmeshed in chains or impris-
> oned. He is redeemed only when "he comes to himself" (in true
> Gnostic fashion). Then he redeems man.[7]

The Powers React

It is characteristic of these hymns to depict a heavenly figure descending into the world of darkness in order to awaken humanity. The
descent is a theophany; hence it creates upheaval in the lower world
unless the redeemer disguises her or his divinity. The primary drama
presupposed by these passages centers on the awakening of the gnostic seed rather than on the redeemer figure's fate. But the section of
Apocalypse of Adam that precedes a catalog of false explanations about
the origins of the illuminator does appear to describe the fate of the
revealer. As in the tripartite scheme in the long version of *Apocryphon
of John,* the third descent of light establishes the gnostic race:

> Once again, for the third time, the illuminator of knowledge will
> pass by in great glory in order to leave (something) of the seed of
> Noah and the sons of Ham and Japheth—to leave for himself fruit-
> bearing trees. And he will redeem their souls from the day of death.
> For the whole creation that came from the dead earth will be under
> the authority of death. But those who reflect upon the knowledge of
> the eternal God in their heart(s) will not perish. For they have not
> received spirit from this kingdom alone, but they have received (it)
> from an [. . .] eternal angel. (*Apoc. Adam* V 76,8-27; *NHLE,* 282)

I have mentioned that gnostic mythology presumes that the rulers of
the lower world treat the agent(s) of divine knowledge aggressively.
The powers try to rape the spiritual Eve when she comes to enlighten
Adam. They also attack her offspring. So in *Apocalypse of Adam* they
recognize the superiority of the person in whom the illuminator dwells

and attack him. As in the other examples, their attack is futile because the spiritual principle departs, leaving behind a counterfeit image:

> Then the god of the powers will be disturbed, saying, "What is the power of this man who is higher than we?" Then he will arouse a great wrath against that man. And the glory will withdraw and dwell in holy houses which it has chosen for itself. And the powers will not see it with their eyes, nor will they see the illuminator either. Then they will punish the flesh of the man upon whom the holy spirit came. (CG V 77,4-18; *NHLE*, 282)

This section recapitulates elements from the opening presentation of the Adam story. Initially Adam and Eve went about in the great glory of eternal angels. Eve had taught Adam the word of the eternal God (V 64,5-15; *NHLE*, 279). The creator god responds to this superior being by dividing Adam and Eve. Glory and the spirit within departs and enters into the heavenly seed of Seth. Adam and Eve are now subject to death and to the creator (V 64,20—65,21; *NHLE*, 279). Although Adam and Eve are now unable to perceive the divine, Adam does have a dream vision in which angelic powers summon him to awake and learn about the seed of those to whom eternal life has come (V 65,26—66,9; *NHLE*, 279). When the illuminator's coming reverses the fate of some of the offspring of Adam, the powers attack again. Just as they "punished the flesh" of Adam and Eve when Eve was taken out of Adam, so they punish the flesh of the one who has received the spirit. There is no need to identify this later punishment as the crucifixion, which the text does not do, or as the echo of any particular Old Testament passage.[8]

If the surviving version of *Apocalypse of Adam* has been edited by Christian Gnostics,[9] then they might easily understand the third descent and persecution by the powers as a reference to Jesus. The authors of both versions of *Apocryphon of John* clearly understood the final appearance of the revealer as a reference to Jesus.[10] But the persecuted revealer in *Apocalypse of Adam* is not explicitly identified with Jesus. Whether such a conclusion is to be ascribed to the author of the extant work depends on how one resolves the problem of the lengthy, formulaic accounts of the savior's origins that follow this passage (V 77,27—82,19; *NHLE*, 283-85). Thirteen false explanations of the savior's origins are offered by kingdoms associated with the angels and powers that govern the lower world. Replete with mythological echoes, this section constitutes a litany of false explanations. The child is born in an unusual way; raised away from human society, often as protection against attack; receives glory and comes "to/on the water." The concluding expression could be used by gnostic writers for coming into the world.[11]

Heavenly drops, animal guardians, and misplaced desire on the part of the mother all figure in the first twelve explanations,[12] although the twelfth explanation lacks the mythic overtones of the others. It refers only to the child's coming forth from two illuminators and "being nourished there" (82,4-10). It has the appearance of being a piece designed to fill out a catalog that did not contain the requisite number of items.[13] The widespread association between twelve powers and the zodiac, which represents the fate that entraps human beings,[14] suggests that such a list was associated with the claim that the true savior liberates the enlightened from the power of fate.[15] Several Christian gnostic texts take the further step of associating the twelve powers with the tribes of Israel. Christ may represent the thirteenth kingdom to which believers belonged (cf. *Pist. Soph.* 2,86). Or the thirteenth may still be part of the lower world, the final heavenly power from which one must escape (*Gos. Eg.* III 63,10-18).[16]

The thirteenth departs from the birth/nurture scheme even further.[17] It refers to the birth of "their ruler" as a word (*logos*) that "received a mandate there," presumably in heaven (82,10-19). Curiously, desire is dislocated from the birth section and attached to his "coming to the waters." Echoes of John 1:1, 9-13 could be responsible for the shift. The entire section presumes that the powers are unable to perceive the savior when he comes (77,18-29; *NHLE*, 282; cf. John 1:9-10). Where Johannine Christians had been promised a new birth that did not involve blood, the will of the flesh, or the will of humans (John 1:13), this "word" actually leads to acceptance of the desire ($\epsilon\pi\iota\theta\upsilon\mu\acute{\iota}\alpha$) of the powers. Consequently, some scholars insist that the explanation given of the thirteenth kingdom shows an anti-Christian or even antignostic Christian cast.[18] This explanation does not belong to the catalog of mythological opinions that formed the original source for the section on the divine child. It alludes to the savior figure of a group with which the Sethians themselves might be confused.

The polemic over which group has the true rite of baptism (84,4-22; *NHLE*, 286) suggests sectarian conflict. Because those represented as the true seed of Seth (82,28—83,23; 85,22-31; *NHLE*, 285–86) are nowhere explicitly associated with Christ, I remain unconvinced by those who argue that *Apocalypse of Adam* is a late, Christian gnostic work. Gedaliahu Stroumsa has suggested that *Apocalypse of Adam* is a reaction against the movement to Christianize the Sethian gnostic tradition which is evident in works like *Gospel of the Egyptians*.[19] The thirteenth explanation of the savior is directed against those who claim that the earthly appearance of Jesus was the beginning of redemption. This group constitutes the kingdom of "another people" into which Ham and Japheth are said to enter after forming the twelve kingdoms (73,28-29; *NHLE*, 281).[20]

Although Stroumsa uses his understanding of the divine child catalog to argue against the view that *Apocalypse of Adam* represents an early, pre-Christian stage of gnostic mythologizing, the case is not closed. The catalog of explanations does appear to have been edited by the author of the existing version of *Apocalypse of Adam* in order to create the schema of twelve plus one false accounts followed by the true version.[21] If Stroumsa is right about the anti-Christianizing intent of the author of *Apocalypse of Adam*, then the sources from which the author drew the true account of Sethian mythology are not likely to have been the Christian gnostic accounts of the revealer in use among his opponents. Instead, the author has used an earlier Sethian account or created one derived from several sources, as other scholars have suggested.[22]

Apocalypse of Adam shows that gnostic redeemer myths developed on the basis of a common pattern. The revealer comes forth from the heavenly world in order to bring light to or to awaken those trapped by the rulers of the lower world. Although the gnostic race, the seed of Seth, is clearly distinguished from those who reject knowledge, these early texts do not presume an ontological dualism between humans. Their reaction to revelation and the extent to which they are free from the desire by which the powers control humans distinguish the immortal elect from those who will die.[23] But the redeemer/revealer is never contaminated by the lower world. In some instances, as in the long version of *Apocryphon of John*, revelation and concealment are the categories used to describe the appearances of the redeemer in the lower world. Thus the redeemer remains more closely associated with the heavenly realm than the lower. Sophia, the Immortal Human, or the heavenly Seth descend only so far as is necessary to awaken Adam.

A Christianized version of this gnostic pattern is clearly preserved in the Naasene Hymn. Kurt Rudolph observes that in this hymnic fragment Christ is the incarnation of the call to the soul.[24] Wandering amidst the evils, ignorance, and death of the lower world, the soul cannot escape. Jesus asks the Father to send him to impart redeeming knowledge by revealing the forms of the gods and the hidden things of the way (Hippolytus, *Ref.* 5.10.2; Foerster, *Gnosis*, 1:282). This example indicates a crucial divergence between the gnostic redeemer figures and the New Testament Christ: whether pre-Christian, Christianized, or anti-Christian, gnostic redeemers are not human subjects. Any relationship between the redeemer and humanity is at the level of the heavenly Adam, the archetype of Gen 1:27. It does not encompass the mortal Adam of Gen 2:7. Nor can it embrace the Gospels if they are read in the modern fashion as realist narrative.[25]

Those elements in the New Testament that diverge from the realist account of the life of Jesus or the redemptive death of Jesus on the cross come closer to gnostic imagery. The sending of the Son from heaven (e.g., Gal 4:4) need not imply incarnation or atonement. Even the expression "in the likeness of sinful flesh" (Rom 8:3) could be read with an emphasis on "likeness"—the redeemer only appeared in the body that belongs to the lower powers. Revelation language in which Jesus is said to transmit to the believer wisdom unknown to outsiders also fits this pattern (e.g., Matt 11:25-27). As already mentioned, speculation about the heavenly and earthly Adam in which Christ transforms the believer into the image of the heavenly or spiritual Adam draws on Jewish traditions also reflected in gnostic sources.

Passages in the New Testament traditionally identified as hymnic often refer to the descent of an exalted, heavenly figure. In their canonical form, these hymns have all been recast to accommodate either the narrative form of the gospel[26] or the kerygma of the cross and resurrection. The question cannot be posed as though such passages (e.g., Phil 2:6-11; Col 1:15-20; John 1:1-5, 9-14; Eph 1:20-23; 2:14-16; Heb 1:2-4; 1 Tim 3:16) are direct appropriations of gnostic redeemer mythology. They have all been formulated with a very different soteriological agenda in view. The preexistent Christ is identified with rather than dissociated from the world into which he comes. This identification is evident in the emphasis on the exchange of divine status for a slave's death (Phil 2:6-11), or in an emphasis on the cross as atonement for sin or as a source of reconciliation in focusing the account of the earthly activity of the one who is God's image (e.g., Col 1:20; Eph 2:14-16; Heb 1:3b). The question is whether the depiction of the crucified as the image of God or as the one who has come into the world from God and returns there is a natural development of the exaltation inherent in the early resurrection kerygma. Or does the mythological speculation about heavenly revealers found in early gnostic traditions shape the cosmological images of Christ found in these New Testament traditions?

By asking whether one must presume the milieu of emerging gnostic mythology in order to understand the history-of-religions context of developments in the New Testament, I am not assuming that New Testament examples will share the conceptual framework of gnostic cosmogony. Some of the root metaphors of the two traditions are quite different, as Andrew Helmbold has insisted.[27] Root metaphors from the gnostic traditions, like "seed," "pleroma," "drunkenness," or "sleep and awakening," as well as the demonic opposition to the revealer and the enlightenment of the elect, are either absent from or only sparsely represented in the New Testament.

Christianizing
the Gnostic Redeemer

One can also turn to the gnostic examples of redeemer mythology for another set of clues about the development of early forms of Christology. Because several Nag Hammadi tractates provide examples for the Christianization of stories about the redeemer, one can see how that process took place.[28] The first-century Jewish traditions that gave rise to the gnostic speculation sometimes reflect a parallel but independent use of traditions, such as those concerning Adam or Wisdom, that were appropriated in the New Testament.

In some of the simplest examples of Christianization, the name Christ has simply been attached to the figure of Wisdom or of the Immortal Human. Details of the Jesus story were completely irrelevant. The revealer happens to be the one whom Christians know as Jesus. The *Letter of Peter to Philip* provides an example of this process:

> Concerning the pleroma, it is I. I was sent to the body because of the seed which had fallen. I came to their dead creation, and they thought I was a mortal man. I spoke with him who belongs to me. And he listened to me, just as you yourselves are listening to me. I gave him the power to enter the inheritance of his fatherhood. (VIII 136,16-28; *NHLE*, 435, my trans.)

The speaker is the risen Jesus instructing the apostles.[29] This response to one of a series of gnostic questions treats the conventional story of the incarnation as the misperception of the powers. The heavenly revealer descends to bring his own the knowledge that will enable the "seed" to return to its heavenly origins. Descent of the revealer belongs to the gnostic myth because it is a requirement for communicating with those in the lower world. This feature appears in the true explanation of the illuminator given in *Apocalypse of Adam:*

> God chose him from all the aeons. He caused knowledge of the undefiled one of truth to come to be [in] him. [He] said, "[Out of] a foreign air [from a] great aeon [the great] illuminator came forth." [And he made] the generation of those men whom he had chosen for himself shine, so that they could shine upon the whole aeon. (V 82,21—83,4; *NHLE*, 285)

The Revealer in *Zostrianos*

A more complex example of the development of gnostic speculation about the redeemer/revealer occurs in *Zostrianos*.[30] Its author is indebted to the ascent of the apocalyptic seer. Maddalena Scopello detects several parallels between *Zostrianos* and *2 Enoch*.[31] The seer is transformed into the heavenly glories that he beholds during the ascent to heaven (VIII 5,15-17; *NHLE*, 405; cf. *2 Enoch* 22:10). In *2 Enoch* the glories represent the highest order of archangel. They stand before the face of the Lord forever. Enoch's identification with the glories occurs after he has passed through the seven lower heavens. The hostility of the angels must be overcome if he is to enter God's presence. God commands Michael to remove Enoch from his garments (earthly clothing), anoint him, and clothe him with divine glory (*2 Enoch* 22:8-10). In *Zostrianos* the glories are the positive counterparts to each of the aeons through which the seer ascends. They save the initiate, who seeks to withdraw into the self and separate from the divisions formed by matter. They do this by providing the initiate with the perfect, immortal thoughts necessary to pass out of this world (VIII 45,12—46,31; *NHLE*, 415–16). Both the idea of the seer's unnoticed ascent and the opposition of angelic powers to the glorification of humans go back to early apocalyptic traditions. The particularly Sethian element in the *Zostrianos* material comes in depicting the seer as the savior who communicates the necessary revelation to the elect upon returning from this heavenly journey.[32]

Several other minor themes suggest that the original story about the seer Zostrianos may have been formulated in Jewish apocalyptic circles before Gnostics adapted it. The seer engages in daily meditation and fasting in order to gain access to divine wisdom, which in the apocalyptic visions is mediated by an angelic figure (cf. Tob 4:5, 19;

12:17-19; Jdt 11:17; 4 Ezra 5:19-21). Zostrianos seeks to understand the heavenly world by following the ancestral practice of meditation. He even withdraws to the desert intent upon dying there if an angel does not come to him (VIII 3,14-28; *NHLE,* 404). In a Jewish apocalypse the ancestors would have been the patriarchs or figures like Enoch from the primordial history. Gnostic tradition has transformed them into the three heavenly ancestors from which the gnostic seed has come: Autogenes, Adam who is "the perfect man," and Seth (30,5-10; *NHLE,* 412). In *2 Enoch,* the seer attains wisdom concerning the whole realm of God's creation from the invisible down to the visible. These secrets are not even known to any of the angels (*2 Enoch* 24:3). A similar revelation formula appears in *Zostrianos* (128,15-18; *NHLE,* 429).

The extant text of *Zostrianos* contains fragmentary remains of a lengthy apocalypse. The surviving angel names and baptisms in the various heavenly regions suggest that it represents a considerably developed variant of traditions taken from Sethian Gnosticism. As it stands, however, the work is not devoted to elaborating the mythological account of origins and redemption that had developed in those circles. Nor is Zostrianos engaged in the heavenly journey to discover the secrets of God's rule over the invisible and visible cosmos, as in *2 Enoch.* Instead, *Zostrianos* employs a Middle Platonic scheme. The seer must abandon all involvement with the material world so that he can penetrate the realms of the divine triad. His goal is to stand at rest in the presence of God. Porphyry reports that an apocalypse of Zostrianos was used among the Gnostics who frequented Plotinus's school in Rome.[33] The philosophical terminology in the work has no clear ties to the reformulation of Platonism by Plotinus. Therefore it was probably composed by a gnostic teacher in the Middle Platonic tradition in the late second or early third century c.e.[34] The author apparently adapts the Middle Platonic theory of demons as different types of soul (43,1-20; *NHLE,* 414–15).[35]

Unlike *Apocryphon of John* and the gnostic Christians opposed in *Apocalypse of Adam,* there is no clear evidence of Christianized Gnosticism in *Zostrianos.*[36] Christ has not been attached to any of the heavenly aeons in the places in which such modifications occur in other works, like *Apocryphon of John* and *Gospel of the Egyptians.* Even the cryptic reference to the "one who suffers but is unable to suffer" (48,27-29; *NHLE,* 416, my trans.) may not be a reference to the crucifixion but to the paradox of the heavenly images of human beings and other entities in the lower world.[37]

Zostrianos seeks to establish its revelation as more ancient than the philosophical mysticism of its environment. To do so, its author has adopted the pseudonym of a reputed magus, who was thought to belong to the lineage of Zoroaster.[38] John Turner situates *Zostrianos* in a later stage of Sethian development, when the Sethians had begun to turn away from Christianity toward Platonic mysticism.[39] Although the work itself does not show signs of Christianization, Turner treats the numerous parallels between its heavenly aeons and *Gospel of the Egyptians* as evidence that *Zostrianos* depends on the latter. But *Zostrianos* may have developed independently of the Christianized Gnosticism evident in *Gospel of the Egyptians*. Its soteriology emphasizes the ascent of the soul, able to separate itself from the somatic darkness in the material realm, to stand in the presence of the divine.[40] Porphyry's notice indicates a sect that drew on a wide range of holy books. It was probably not committed to a single revealer. Michael Williams suggests that we hypothesize a sociological distinction between the relatively open, philosophical sect of *Zostrianos* and the Christian gnostic groups that developed Sethian themes. The latter are sects that have adopted the common Christian view that all revelation is mediated by Christ (e.g., *Soph. Jes. Chr.* CG III 93,24—94,4; *NHLE*, 224).[41]

The Revealer in
Gospel of the Egyptians

Gospel of the Egyptians provides a striking example of how an older holy book was adapted or Christianized by a gnostic sect that held the view that Christ was the Savior.[42] These developments do not appear to have been prompted by polemical relationships with orthodox Christianity. Christ has been inserted into a prior account so awkwardly that it seems evident that the underlying redeemer myth did not contain these elements. In some cases Christ has been added to interpret a figure in the text. The addition has confused the references of verbs.[43] Christ's relationship with the "thrice-male child" shifts in the course of the document (cf. IV 55,11-17 = III 44,22-26; *NHLE*, 210, with IV 59,16-17; *NHLE*, 211). The great Seth, rather than the Christ, is said to put on Jesus and condemn the powers by nailing them to the cross (III 63,25—64,3 = IV 75,13-17; *NHLE*, 216–17). Seth's real garment is the "logos-begotten body." A Christian gnostic redactor has assumed that Christ put on Jesus, as in Col 2:14-17. This motif is more clearly elaborated in works composed by Christian Gnostics.[44]

The *Gospel of the Egyptians* passage on nailing the powers to the tree has been set in a baptismal context. Revelation to the offspring of Seth is said to conquer the thirteen aeons by fixing them to the cross (III 64,3-5 = IV 75,18-20; *NHLE,* 217). A comparable image appears in Col 2:14-15. Colossians has interpreted the defeat of the powers as canceling the debt against sinners. Christ's atoning death on the cross, which the believers appropriate in baptism, has rendered the claims of divine judgment against Christians for past sins null and void (Col 2:12-14).[45] After the author describes the atonement as the source of salvation in contrast to Judaizing rituals, the reference to the defeat of the powers in Col 2:15 introduces a decidedly mythological note.[46] Although it clarifies the way in which the atonement resolves the deceptive philosophy of submission to heavenly powers against which Colossians is written (2:8-10, 16, 20),[47] the participle *apekdusamenos* implies that Christ has first stripped off the powers (cf. 3:9) before making a public exhibition of their defeat.[48] In order to avoid the implication that Christ was somehow first subject to the powers before defeating them, most interpreters translate the verb "disarm" (so NRSV) in this context and "strip off" in Col 3:9, where it refers to the Christian abandoning his or her old way of life.

The gnostic tradition developed in *Gospel of the Egyptians* provides an explanation for this peculiar expression in Col 2:15. I have already mentioned that the gnostic versions of the redeemer myth never make the association that so troubles modern commentators. The revealer can "put on" the powers—the garments they have used to entrap Adam—without becoming subject to the powers. Stripping off the garments is required for the revealer to make his divine identity known to the elect, who will repeat the process in their own ritual experience. I have also mentioned that the agitation which grips the powers when the revealer comes into the lower world indicates that they recognize their defeat.

Gnostic mythology associated the effectiveness of the powers with the rule of fate in the cosmos.[49] This rule creates sins in humanity, because the passions are activated through the movements of the planetary beings. The hymn in Col 1:15-20 affirms the cosmological primacy of Christ as the image of God. As in this section, the interpretation of the death of Christ as an atoning sacrifice for sin is introduced only in the conclusion. It is part of the Christian reading of what is largely a cosmological reflection on salvation and redemption. Within the common Hellenistic cosmological framework, even references to "making peace" do not refer to atonement for sin. They address the pervasive concern with stabilization in the universe.[50] Eduard Schweizer has observed another peculiarity of the Colossians hymn, which links it to the conceptual world of the heavenly revealer as the tradition was developed in gnostic circles:

> Since the community lives in the sphere both of creation and redemption, it praises Christ simultaneously as creator and redeemer. So strong is the concentration on him as present with the community in his *exaltation*, that absolutely nothing is said anywhere at all about his appearing on earth.[51]

Only the references to the Christ as firstborn "from the dead" (v. 18) and to the "blood of his cross" (v. 20) point away from the cosmological functions of the redeemer toward his physical existence.

Colossians has adapted a version of the cosmological understanding of the redeemer's mission to suit the Christian understanding of Jesus. Resurrection as exaltation to the right hand of God and death as atoning sacrifice for sin link the redeemer to the Jesus known by Christians. *Gospel of the Egyptians* depicts a different pattern of development. The cosmological instability of the powers is primarily evident in the external events of the world rather than in the individual's experience of the imprisoning passions.[52] The race of Seth has proved itself immovable because the forces released against it have failed. These attacks are described in the biblical disasters of the flood and the burning of Sodom and Gomorrah as well as other persecutions and deception. The great Seth has rescued his seed from the flood, the destruction of Sodom, and now in his appearance as Jesus (III 64,3-9 = IV 75,17-24; *NHLE*, 217).

Nailing the powers to the cross apparently means causing them to become motionless. If they no longer engage in motion, then the Sethians who receive knowledge of truth and incorruptibility are no longer subject to the astrological forces or to mortality.[53] *Gospel of the Egyptians* may refer to Col 2:14, when it associates the crucifixion with destruction of the Law (III 65,12-22; *NHLE*, 217). Like the other attributes of the Jewish God, the Law is part of the attempt to destroy the invulnerable race of Seth. Baptism arms the believer so that he or she is now invulnerable. *Gospel of the Egyptians* concludes with a hymnic claim to have mixed with the light of the immutable world (III 66,2— 68,1; *NHLE*, 218).[54] Although Christianization of the Sethian tradition led *Gospel of the Egyptians* to find a place for Jesus as the final redemptive appearance of Seth and for the cross, these motifs have not reshaped its redemptive soteriology.

Valentinian gnostic teachers like Ptolemy have converted the Christianized traditions of Sethian Gnosticism into a full-fledged speculative system that associates higher and lower Christs with the higher and lower Wisdom figures. The demonic powers have been largely demythologized. Wisdom's desire to know the true God was inappropriate but not culpable. The creator is an ignorant administrator of the lower world. Wisdom has secretly sown the seeds of the gnostic race in that world. Power was not stolen from the heavenly world. The social location of Valentinians as a sectarian movement within early Christianity is also evident. There are two groups of the "saved": Valentinians and ordinary Christians.[55]

Summary

The Nag Hammadi texts provide a more complex picture of the gnostic redeemer than scholars originally proposed. The primary mythic elements include a manifestation of the divine revealer in the lower world. The revealer's call to awaken the gnostic race forms the decisive turning point in the narrative. The revealer may employ a body as the means to enter the world without the knowledge of its rulers. A person's response to the call indicates whether the individual will possess gnosis or remain under the sway of the demonic powers that rule the universe. This cosmological picture of the redeemer's activity forms an important element in some New Testament writings, like Colossians. But gnostic writings developed the basic soteriological pattern in distinct ways. Some, like *Apocalypse of Adam*, may have intended to defend the earlier non-Christian tradition against Christian claims. Some, like *Zostrianos*, are indebted to an ascetic mystical tradition. Some, like *Gospel of the Egyptians*, have Christianized the redeemer figure.

The gnostic evidence has not provided a sequential pattern of development from heterodox Jewish speculation through gnosticizing Sethianism and its assimilation of Christian motifs to Valentinianism. Gnostic sects Christianized the Sethian traditions in different ways. Some resisted the influences of orthodox Christianity. It is not possible to show from the literary details of gnostic and early Christian texts that influences have proceeded in a single direction. As Jack T. Sanders observes after a study of the Johannine prologue, the *Odes of Solomon,* and *Trimorphic Protennoia,* the best evidence is for independent reorchestrating of shared motifs or traditions:

> The New Testament christological hymns have not directly influenced the *Trimorphic Protennoia* and the Odes of Solomon; we do not have a parental relationship in that direction. That is clear from the clusters of redeemer attributes in the New Testament christological hymns that are then distributed in different ways in the *Trimorphic Protennoia* and in the Odes of Solomon. Yet the parental relationships cannot have proceeded in the other direction either, because the New Testament is much earlier than the other works. What we have is rather different branches on a bush, growing from a root or a trunk that originated in allopatric speciation—parallel developments demonstrating several close similarities.[56]

8

Jesus as Word

The Fourth Gospel opens with an unusual prologue (John 1:1-18), which most exegetes agree employs an early hymn.[1] It has been linked with the life of Jesus by the evangelist's comments about the mission of John the Baptist (vv. 6-8, 15). Other characteristics of the evangelist's style, such as the use of the adjective *alēthinos* to modify a symbolic term (v. 9),[2] or theological concerns, such as the contrast between Moses and Christ (v. 17), suggest that the evangelist has also edited an earlier source. Consequently scholars disagree over which verses represent the pre-Johannine hymn. They also differ over which sections of the hymn refer to activities of the Word in the cosmos prior to its appearance in Jesus and which refer to the incarnation. The insertion of verses 6-8 would lead the reader of the Gospel to assume that everything which follows refers to Jesus.[3] But this conclusion does not follow for the source as an isolated hymn.[4]

Wisdom and Myth in John's Prologue

One can find Jewish sources that depict creation and revelation as activities of a personified divine Wisdom, which gives life and enlightens humans. Philo of Alexandria turns more frequently to the divine Word as the archetype of creation and the source of virtue in the soul than to Wisdom. Because he sometimes merges the Word with Wisdom, many exegetes assume that the prologue to the Fourth Gospel arose in a similar context.[5] Rudolf Bultmann was unimpressed by such arguments, because they did not address the distinctive charac-

teristics of the Word and its activity depicted in the Johannine prologue. The Fourth Gospel has no interest in the philosophical links
between the Word and the cosmos or between the Word and the power
that transforms the souls of the wise in Philo. Nor does the Fourth
Gospel show any interest in the sin-judgment-repentance schema of
Israel's salvation history that informs many of the Old Testament passages depicting God's word or Wisdom as Law. Although some echo of
Gen 1:1 in John 1:1 is unavoidable, the prologue does not follow the
Genesis schema. The Word is initially depicted in its divine eternity,
not as the agent of the temporal creation.[6]

Throughout the hymnic sections of the prologue, one moves at the
level of symbolism and myth. A primordial process of revelation is
identified with the historical activity of a specific person, Jesus, only
by the evangelist's redactional insertions. There is no doubt that he
intended to challenge the original understanding behind the hymn and
associated revelation discourse material later in the Gospel. Jesus is
the one in whom those who had originally sought access to heavenly
knowledge through other figures now find truth. Thus the evangelist's
own agenda is decidedly against the redeemer figures of the early
gnostic groups. Bultmann's hypothesis was that Logos speculation and
early Jewish mythologizing of the Wisdom figure were parallel developments within the context of pre-Christian gnostic speculation. He
also presumed that the apocalyptic parallels to gnostic concepts
showed that the Jewish apocalyptic depended on a pre-Christian Gnosticism.[7] Today scholars more commonly argue that the links between
early gnostic speculation and Jewish apocalyptic demonstrate the emergence of a gnosticizing mythology out of heterodox Judaism.[8]

This new direction does not resolve the question raised by Bultmann about the source of the Johannine prologue or the religious
background of its Christology. Has the evangelist forged the imagery
of Jesus as Word and "man from heaven" out of earlier Synopticlike
traditions about the risen and exalted Son of man and diverse Jewish
wisdom motifs? This interpretation is the one commentators most
commonly advance, although they may be forced to inject the external
catalyst of Samaritan speculation about Moses to complete the transition.[9] Or is Bultmann's intuition essentially sound? He proposed that
the evangelist had encountered a powerful mythological formulation
of the significance of a heavenly revealer among gnosticizing sectarians. In order to win such believers, who may have come from a

baptismal sect associated with John the Baptist, the fourth evangelist transformed their speculation. He insisted on a genuinely orthodox Christology in which Jesus is the incarnate Word.[10]

The prologue to the Fourth Gospel provides only one example of the transformation of Jewish Wisdom speculation into the mythic pattern of a descending revealer. The mythic overtones of a light recognized only by believers has been shaped in part by the experience of the community.[11] The Jewish community's postexilic experience had already introduced a tension between God's wisdom as present and accessible (e.g., Prov 25–29) and God's wisdom as remote and inaccessible to humans (e.g., Job 28; Bar 3:9–4:1). Wisdom cannot dwell with an unreceptive humanity on earth. She must return to the heavens (*1 Enoch* 42). Early gnostic speculation withdrew Wisdom's activity from the realm of human affairs. The periodized salvation history of the gnostic Sethians depicts angels, the great Seth, or the Mother (heavenly Wisdom) coming to rescue the elect from the creator's attempts to destroy them.[12]

Scholars customarily read the prologue to John as though it paralleled the two-part schema of Col 1:15-20: first creation, then redemption. Instead of the cross and exaltation as the basis for redemption, John substitutes the incarnation of the Word. After the christological controversies of the early centuries, Christians would no longer ask whether incarnation is the focus of redemption. It had displaced the cross/resurrection confession as the symbolic key to the meaning of redemption. But one should be wary of retrojecting the formal christological insights of later centuries back to a pre-Johannine stage in the first century.

I have already observed that the two-part schema, creation and incarnation, works only for the hymn as redacted by the evangelist. His insertion of verses 6-8 makes it clear that from verse 9 on the text is speaking about the incarnation. If one asks about the meaning of the hymn prior to the addition of the material on John the Baptist and prior to the formal christological recognition that incarnation is the key to redemption, then another line of interpretation presents itself. If one assumes that the prologue shares imagery with early gnostic sources, then one might expect more than one salvation sequence. As already mentioned, the redeemer figure in a number of gnostic examples must intervene on behalf of the gnostic seed several times before the definitive coming of gnosis.

A Gnostic Reading of John's Prologue

Read in the light of gnostic parallels, the references to light and life in verse 4 are not allusions to creation but to revelation. Rudolf Schnackenburg also points to a formal parallel between verse 3 and the description of God's providential activity in 1QH: "and through his knowledge everything came to be. He establishes everything that is according to his plan and without him nothing comes to pass."[13] But he treats the link between the Essene hymns and John as merely formal, because the latter is dealing with creation and the former with divine providence in history. Any mythological overtones to the opening verses of the Gospel are to be rejected because of the involvement of the Word in creation.[14] But Schnackenburg should have recognized from the second-century gnostic commentators to whom he refers that the situation is far from clear. The monistic understanding of gnostic mythology, which Valentinian exegetes set on a philosophical basis in the second-century disputes about topological theology,[15] has an earlier foundation in Sethian mythology.

Bultmann's insistence that the Fourth Gospel be read against the cosmological dualism of opposed principles, sometimes referred to as "oriental" or "Iranian" dualism,[16] may be responsible for the assumption that gnostic imagery must be represented by a cosmological dualism.[17] Monistic gnostic systems may assert that "all things came into being through him" (John 1:2) either as a statement about the heavenly Pleroma, also called "the All," or as an affirmation of the mysterious activity of Wisdom in directing her offspring to create one higher than himself, Adam. The emergence of the Mother from the invisible, unknowable Father exemplifies the first possibility:

> This is the first thought, his image; she became the womb of everything for it is she who is prior to them all, the Mother-Father. (II 5,4-7; *NHLE*, 107)

The second possibility is evident in the narrative of Adam's creation. A beneficent decree from the Mother-Father sends five heavenly beings to Ialdabaoth. By instructing him to blow into the face of the molded human, Wisdom's power passes into Adam (II 19,15-33; *NHLE*, 116). The luminous Epinoia is hidden within Adam as his helper (II 20,9-28; *NHLE*, 116; 21,14-16; 22,15-18; *NHLE*, 117).

Christian gnostic writers recognize the references to the activity of the Word as indications of God's providential activity. *Gospel of Truth* affirms that nothing happens without the Logos, that is, without the

Father's will (I 37,21; *NHLE*, 49). This assertion appears in a philosophical exposition of the Word as the perfection and revelation of
God's thought. The goal of salvation is perfect knowledge of the Father.
Similarly, the Fourth Gospel insists that Jesus reveals the Father. This
revelation depends on the revelatory function of the Word. The Word
pervades the Pleroma as God's creative activity so that those in the
divine realm come to know the Father (I 23,33—24,24; *NHLE*, 43).[18]

Read as the providential activity of God, the problematic phrase *ho
gegonen* ("what came to be"), which can belong either to the end of
John 1:3 or to the beginning of verse 4, must refer to the "light and
life" of verse 4. The revealer's function is to bring light and life into
existence. Verses 5 and 10-11 constitute parallel expressions of the
Word's activity. The evangelist historicizes the generalized reference of
"his own things." Within the context of a narrative about the life and
crucifixion of Jesus, the expression must refer to "his own people"—
"the Jews." Then the problem of when the hymn refers to incarnation
arises. As a revealer hymn, no such difficulty presents itself. As the
gnostic parallels already indicate, the culminating manifestation of the
revealer requires human embodiment, although not identification with
the negative aspects of human existence. The revealer's body is not
under the control of the powers, the counterfeit spirit that operates
through the passions or mortality. First John 1:1-4 counters the docetic
reading of the Johannine prologue with a thoroughly historical understanding of incarnation.[19]

By insisting on the historical interpretation of its redeemer hymn,
the Johannine tradition cut off its gnosticizing possibilities. Later christological controversies would specify the full human and divine natures
of the incarnate Word. The Johannine prologue focuses on the unique-
ness of the revelation mediated by the Word, not on the details of
incarnational theology. Verses 17-18 contain polemical references that
are acknowledged as both anti-Torah (v. 17) and a rejection of other
visionary and mystical traditions, perhaps Jewish claims for Moses
(v. 18).[20] Verse 18 applies to all claims to possess knowledge of God,
whether in visionary, cultic, or oracle form. Schnackenburg notes that
the term *exegeisthai* used of Christ's revealing activity applies to the
interpretation of oracles.[21] Josephus uses the verb as a technical term
for interpretation of the Law. Its association with vision language in
the Fourth Gospel suggests that it applies to interpreting secrets hidden in God or in the divine world.

This claim follows a contrast between what comes through Moses and through Christ; thus the latter should not be understood as merely bringing the fulfillment of the Law. Rather, one must assert that the Law itself does not know God.[22] In short this polemic reverses the ascent, vision, and enthronement of Moses in first-century Jewish authors like Philo of Alexandria. For Philo, the scene validates Moses' role as founder of the nation and the inspiration of the Law (*Vit. Mos.* 2.11; 2.188-91).[23] *Apocryphon of John* interprets the Genesis story as proper evidence for the gnostic myth. Moses' rendering of the story in the Pentateuch errs because it presents false interpretations of events in that mythology.[24] An unusual episode, the enthronement of the creator's son, Sabaoth, appears in *Hypostasis of the Archons*.[25] Sabaoth occupies the divine throne chariot in the seventh heaven. This development addresses the question of revelation through the Law and the Prophets by providing Sabaoth with Wisdom's daughter. Sabaoth acknowledged the superiority of the divine Wisdom. In turn, he has been exalted as revealer of that distorted wisdom found in the Law and the Prophets.[26]

The Fourth Gospel does not contain any such moderating position. All claims to revelation must be referred to Christ and finally to its own testimony about the revealer. Because "the Jews" and their rejection of the real meaning of Moses represent the cosmic hostility to revelation referred to in the prologue, the attack on other visions, revelations, and oracles does not appear to be directed against Gnostics. Indeed, the community's alienation from Jewish religious authorities provides a plausible impetus for its mythologizing of experience around the symbolism of the heavenly revealer's descent and return to the Father.[27] This observation raises a further question concerning the Johannine prologue. Do verses 1-5 evoke images from the opening of Genesis in order to affirm continuity with that tradition, as most exegetes have supposed since Irenaeus (*Adv. Haer.* 1.22.1)? Or are they intended to replace Genesis with a different account, as Irenaeus's gnostic sources presumed (e.g., *Adv. Haer.* 1.8.5)? If the Law does not reveal God, as verses 17-18 suggest, then the Valentinian exegetes would seem to have a case for their novel interpretation of the prologue.

John's Prologue
and *Trimorphic Protennoia*

The debate over the original form and implications of the Johannine prologue intensified with the publication of a revelation discourse from codex XIII, the *Trimorphic Protennoia*. Like the hymn in the long version of *Apocryphon of John*, *Trimorphic Protennoia* contains the first-person discourses of the perfect Protennoia, who descends into the world of darkness as savior. She appears three times: as the hidden Voice, as the Speech of the First Thought, and finally as the Word.[28] Scholars quickly noticed a striking number of parallels between the imagery of the *Trimorphic Protennoia* and the prologue to John.[29] Wisdom exists before all things and in all. She is light and life (XIII 35,1—36,3; *NHLE*, 513; 47,28-29; *NHLE*, 520). The Son reveals this heavenly Wisdom to those who originated from above (37,3-9; 38,16-18; *NHLE*, 514; 50,15-16; *NHLE*, 521). Only the children of light receive this revelation. The others fail to perceive it (37,18-20; *NHLE*, 514; 41,15-16; *NHLE*, 516; 47,22-25; *NHLE*, 520). On its third descent, the Word appears in human form wearing the "tent" or garment of the archons (47,13-16; *NHLE*, 520).[30]

These observations generated extensive disagreement over the interpretation of such parallels. The docetic account of the crucifixion at the end of *Trimorphic Protennoia* (50,13-17; *NHLE*, 521) includes a Johannine-sounding reference to the "dwelling places" of the Father (50,14). Another Johannine echo introduces the docetic account. The revealer has come to abide in the believers that they may abide in him (50,10-11). Such combinations suggest to many interpreters that *Trimorphic Protennoia* has cast its gnostic revelation discourse in Johannine language. Others have insisted that the sparse Christian references are secondary.[31] Most exegetes recognize that this dilemma cannot be posed in such simple, unidirectional terms. The same redaction-critical analysis that has long been presumed for the Johannine prologue must also be applied to *Trimorphic Protennoia*.[32] Formal analysis of the texts suggests that Wisdom's revelation discourse has been expanded by accounts of gnostic creation mythology, exhortations to believers, and perhaps fragments of a sermon on baptism.[33]

Neither John nor *Trimorphic Protennoia* depends on the other directly. John Turner has observed that the third section, which speaks of the revealer's descent as Word, employs Johannine imagery to establish a Christology that counters the claims of orthodox Christianity.[34] Craig Evans compared the imagery of John 1:1-18 with two pages of this section (46,5—47,28; *NHLE*, 519–20).[35] Although *Trimorphic Protennoia* parallels most of the images in the prologue to John, the prologue does not include much of the rest of the language in these two pages. All historicizing references to John the Baptist, to Moses,

and to the fleshly incarnation of Jesus are missing.[36] The difference
between the two works becomes evident when the sparse "the Word
became flesh and lived among us" (John 1:14) is contrasted with
the elaborate explanation of the revealer wearing the garments of all the
powers in order to bring revelation to his fellows (47,14-27; *NHLE*, 520).

The Fourth Gospel appeals to simpler images for the incarnation,
such as the divine presence at the tabernacle.[37] *Trimorphic Protennoia*
presumes the more elaborate structures of gnostic cosmology. Although
its prologue hints at prior activity of the Word, the Gospel itself presumes that there is only a single manifestation of that Word, its
appearance as the Son of God, Jesus. The use of imagery of light and
darkness in the narrative of the Gospel indicates that the evangelist
does not treat this hymn as though it were modeled on the christological hymns found in the Pauline and deutero-Pauline writings that
speak of the cosmological activity of divine wisdom and then the death
and exaltation of Jesus as Christ (e.g., Col 1:15-20). Instead, the evangelist considers that the whole hymn refers to the redemptive activity
of the Word in Jesus.[38]

Most scholars have recognized that *Trimorphic Protennoia* also presupposes a narrative about redemption. But this narrative consists in
allusions to episodes in gnostic mythologizing of Genesis. Wisdom's
call to awakening raises Adam from his ignorant subjection to the
lower Demiurge and instills the true divine image. During the creation,
heavenly powers inspire Ialdabaoth to create the vessel in which the
divine Epinoia can dwell and so escape the disorder of chaos (XIII
39,13—41,1; *NHLE*, 515–16). The tree of knowledge brought humanity
under the power of lust, death, and chaos. Not even the creator recognized the true heavenly voice, which hidden in her own summons
them back to the perfect light (44,20—45,24; *NHLE*, 518–19). The third
descent, as the Word, details an elaborate ontology by which the children of light strip off the garments that belong to the realm of darkness through the power of the living waters that come from the Word.
They put on Light as part of sectarian baptismal rituals (46,33—50,12;
NHLE, 520–21).

The anthropological references in the third section of *Trimorphic
Protennoia* indicate how the ritual activities of the sect affect the
believer. Such concerns take up questions that the Fourth Gospel's
references to Jesus as "living water," "light of the world," and source of
eternal life raise but never answer.[39] *Trimorphic Protennoia* shows
other evidence of having reworked traditional gnostic language about

the origins of the aeons and the Son to fit philosophical considerations.[40] Alastair Logan bases much of his argument against the suggestion that the hymnic sections of *Apocryphon of John* and *Trimorphic Protennoia* provide evidence for pre-Johannine speculation on the development of the mythological speculation in *Trimorphic Protennoia.* Its author has expanded on the simpler scheme used in *Apocryphon of John.*[41] Logan reconstructs a gnosticized Christian myth behind *Apocryphon of John*, which he claims has been confused by the assimilation of the Johannine prologue into a simpler triadic structure.[42] His proposal creates as many difficulties as it solves, because it presumes a gnosticizing projection of the stories of the virgin birth into the generation of the divine triad.

Both the Fourth Gospel and the gnostic authors of *Apocryphon of John* and *Trimorphic Protennoia* have an established framework within which their affirmations about the revealer are set. As Yvonne Janssens rightly observes, one can find the same vocabulary in John and *Trimorphic Protennoia* without finding the same meaning.[43] This marked difference in meaning makes it difficult to maintain hypotheses about the direct influence of either John or gnostic mythologies in their extant form in *Apocryphon of John* and *Trimorphic Protennoia* on one another.

The Word as Revealer

The arguments on both sides have shown that the use of "Word" for the divine revealer is foreign to the narrative contexts associated with it. The Johannine Jesus boldly appropriates the divine "I Am" (e.g., John 8:24, 58). In *Trimorphic Protennoia* the divine Protennoia uses the identification formula, "I am the Word" (46,5 and 14). For *Trimorphic Protennoia* philosophical considerations make it impossible for the Father to reveal himself. Because the Barbelo is a multiplicity she can reveal herself as the triad of Protennoia, Voice, and Word. The unknowable Father cannot do so. Clement of Alexandria advances a similar argument about the Son. He has a name and a face that the Father cannot have. In some sense, the Son shares in multiplicity that the Father cannot do. Consequently, the Son can reveal God.[44]

By the mid-second century the simple view that the Father is unknowable and that the Son, who is the instrument of divine action, is knowable expressed a theological commonplace. The Son's agency could be characterized as word, power, or Spirit.[45] But the difficulty

of relating these impersonal attributes of God's activity to the person
of the revealer generated a marked preference for speaking of the Son
as revealer rather than of the Word. Origen observes that Christians do
not try to interpret the title "Word," unlike the other names of Christ.[46]
Irenaeus assumes that the Gnostics are the first to incorporate speculation about the Word into their systems (*Adv. Haer.* 1.8.5–14,4). *Gospel
of Truth* begins with an evocation of the Johannine prologue (I 16,32-
36; *NHLE*, 40). The Word designates the perfect knowledge of the
Father that comes through revelation (36,18—37,18; *NHLE*, 48–49).
But the author's real interest is in the name Son as the proper revelation of the Father (38,5—41,3; *NHLE*, 49). The Johannine echoes in
Gospel of Truth include extensive allusions to the life and crucifixion of
Jesus. Consequently, its treatment of the Word has been derived from
the Fourth Gospel itself.

As Bultmann correctly recognized in the case of the Johannine prologue, "Word" appears to function as an agent in a mythological system quite independent of the philosophical traditions of the time.[47]
The relationship between the Word and the female figure of Wisdom,
who is the more common source of revelation, appears to subordinate
the Word to Wisdom in *Trimorphic Protennoia*. Scholars generally agree
that the Word in John performs functions more commonly attributed
to Wisdom. Philo sometimes refers to Wisdom as the source of the
Word (e.g., *Fug.* 109). He may have intended his reader to recognize
that God is the source of the Word in the transcendent sense. The
Word immanent in the world is the offspring of Wisdom and God.[48]
Philo's philosophical concerns have led to this distinction between a
transcendent and immanent Word as well as to a dual picture of Wisdom, both the "mother of All," including the immanent Word, and the
substance of material creation. They have also provided the necessary
cast of characters for a gnostic rendering of the origins of the cosmos.

The early gnostic mythological tradition is decidedly antiphilosoph-
ical. Although Philo may think of the immanent Word as the harmonious operation of divine providence in the material world, gnostic
thinkers do not. Wisdom's offspring did not originate from the union
of Wisdom and her heavenly counterpart. As a result the material
world cannot be a logical or harmonious unfolding of principles
already established in the divine world. Early gnostic dualism depicts
the opposition between the rulers of the lower world and the Light as
a mythological fact, not a dualism of abstract, cosmological principles.
Wisdom personified in the spiritual Eve or in her various manifesta-

tions suffers the attack of the rapacious archons. As already noted, Jewish traditions about the lust of the "sons of God" for the "daughters of men" played a formative role in gnostic accounts of humanity's plight. The lust of the archons has corrupted human life. Only the pure seed of Seth escapes this condition.

It is as easy to read the prologue to the Fourth Gospel as a comment on elements in this mythological schema as it is to find mythological allusions in *Trimorphic Protennoia*. Although most modern commentators reject the cosmological reading, John 1:5 speaks of the attempt made by darkness to grasp the light shining in the world.[49] The children of God have not been begotten through sexual passion or human desire but through receiving the "true light," which was rejected by much of the world (John 1:10-13). In both examples, like his gnostic counterparts the evangelist speaks of light coming into the world. The Word does not function as the subject of these sentences.

This shift suggests that mythological or narrative concerns shaped the formulation of the hymnic material. The gnostic Wisdom figure cannot be replaced by Word without losing the associations with the mythic story. The contrast between a mythic and a philosophical orientation becomes evident in Philo. For him, Word and Wisdom represent philosophical principles, which are to some extent convertible. Wisdom is Logos immanent in the world.[50] Indeed, for Philo Wisdom is not the most suitable revelation of God, for both mythological and philosophical reasons. Mythic associations attached to the feminine Wisdom figure made her a natural counterpart to powerful goddess figures like Isis.[51] Philo's philosophical principles of exegesis made her representative of the material world and its principles rather than the divine.[52] Consequently, "Word" is the preferred term for God's ordering presence in the cosmos and in the soul.

A Hermetic writing, *Poimandres* (C.H. I; Foerster, *Gnosis*, 1: 326–35) illustrates the transition between allusions to Genesis and a mythologized philosophical speculation. The revelation that the highest divine Mind conveys to the seer depicts the Word of Gen 1:2 as the powerful divine warrior who dismembers the coiled chaos monster in order to bring about the emergence of the material world. The Word leaves matter behind to join the demiurgic mind that will govern what has come into being (C.H. I,4-11).[53] When the account turns to the complex process by which the divine image that is the androgynous human appears in the waters, engenders love, and is replicated in the lower world, the Word has no role. Instead life and light are the source of the soul and the mind respectively (C.H. I,17). Immortality consists in returning to the light and life that is the Father of the universe (chap. 21). Cultic activities, which included praise of God, and ascetic practices, which taught the devotee to separate mind from the body and its passions, prepare the believer for a postmortem return to God (chaps. 22–23). The seer's appeal to humanity for conversion adopts the common rhetorical formulae of the philosophers. A drunken humanity must awaken from unreasoning sleep (chap. 27).[54] In this context, the Word plays a role in the cosmogonic myth that accounts for the divided nature of humanity. But the Word does not awaken or transform the soul of those who will be reunited with the divine.

"Word" functions as the principle of divine reason in Philo. As such it could be said to have a soteriological function, because it unites the soul with God. "Word" in *Poimandres* serves solely as a cosmological principle. Neither Philo nor *Poimandres* personifies the Word by associating it with a figure or figures operating in the world of human beings. These examples suggest that "Word" did not carry with it a particular grammar of mythological associations. Personification of the Word requires that it be linked with a powerful narrative story in which such a figure already has a clearly defined role. Both the Gospel of John and *Trimorphic Protennoia* provide such a framework. For the Gospel it is the narrative of Jesus as the one "sent from heaven" to reveal the Father. For *Trimorphic Protennoia* it is the gnostic myth of Wisdom's descents into the world of darkness in order to awaken her offspring to their true destiny. The Gospel invites one to see the revealing Word made concrete in the particular story of Jesus of Nazareth. *Trimorphic Protennoia* invites its reader to step outside all stories, even the narrative mythologies of other gnostic texts, to hear the primordial call of revelation.

Summary

The comparison of the Johannine prologue and gnostic treatments of the Word yields the same results as the study of the other redeemer myths and hymns in chapter 7. Direct dependence of either on the other is excluded. But the personified Word of divine revelation that both traditions have appropriated may point to a common background. The gnostic parallels suggest a context for interpreting John 1:1-18 that differs from the creation/incarnation model established in the christological debates of the third and fourth centuries C.E.

Source analysis suggests that the evangelist historicized a mythic presentation of the coming of divine revelation by identifying the Word with Jesus of Nazareth. Both apocalyptic and gnostic dualism make the presence of divine revelation in the material world problematic. Interpreters should not read the Stoic or Platonic imagery of the Word as a rational ordering of the cosmos into the Fourth Gospel. Gnostic mythologizing provides a monistic account for the origins of the lower world in which the manifestations of the revealer play a crucial role. Read against that background, the Johannine prologue speaks of the manifold appearances of revelation in the cosmos, not singular moments of creation and incarnation.

Comparison with gnostic material raises a further challenge for interpreters. The echoes of Genesis 1 as well as the allusions to a failed Mosaic covenant (John 1:17) should not be read as affirming continuity with the older tradition. The Johannine text replaces that tradition with an exclusive claim to revelation (v. 18) that requires a different story of God's primordial relationship with the world.

All examples in which the term "Word" functions as a designation for the source of divine order or revelation provide evidence that it is a secondary development of some older pattern. By the second century C.E., the philosophical debate over the knowability of God plays a role in both Christian and gnostic speculation. The Fourth Gospel does not reflect the philosophical debate. Its emphasis is soteriological. God is "unknown" because the Father cannot be recognized without the coming of the revealer. Whatever its value as testimony to Jesus (John 5:31-47), only those who have been born again through the Word of the revealer achieve salvation. John, *Trimorphic Protennoia*, and *Poimandres* all use "Word" as an index of divine revelation. The differences among them suggest that "Word" did not carry with it a fixed set of symbolic references. The particular contexts into which it has been incorporated establish the significance of the term. *Poimandres* uses the "Word" in the context of creation; *Trimorphic Protennoia*, to articulate the voice of the heavenly Wisdom of gnostic myth; John, to transform the words of the human figure of Jesus into the Word of revelation.

9

Discourses of the Revealer

The case for a connection between the Fourth Gospel's tradition and gnostic origins does not rest solely on the parallels between its prologue and gnostic texts. The style of revelation discourse in which Jesus speaks constitutes one of the most distinctive elements of the Fourth Gospel. Jesus explicitly identifies himself with the Father. This identification culminates in his use of the divine name, "I Am." Such a claim separates the words of Jesus as revealer from anything that might be spoken or claimed by his human predecessors. Consequently, even within the narrative itself, the Son identifies himself as the one who preexists with God. Because the Son is the only revelation of God, the patriarchs must have seen him as well (John 8:51-58).

Jesus Reveals God

The Fourth Gospel never explains how it is that God is seen in the Son despite repeated assertions that the Father's glory is visible through Jesus (e.g., John 14:8-11). In the Gospel, the form of discourse employed by Jesus is made to carry the weight of sustaining his divine identity. Gnostic writers are more willing to fill in the gap. The opening vision of *Apocryphon of John* reveals the divine nature of Jesus to the grieving and perplexed apostle:

> Behold, the [heavens opened and] the whole creation [which is] below heaven shone and [the world] was shaken. [I was afraid, and behold I] saw in the light [a youth who stood] by me. While I looked [at him he became] like an old man. And he [changed his] likeness

(again) becoming like a servant. There was [not a plurality] before me, but there was a [likeness] with multiple forms in the light, and the [likenesses] appeared through each other, [and] the [likeness] had three forms.

He said to me, "John, John, why do you doubt, or why [are you] afraid? You are not unfamiliar with this image, are you?—that is, do not [be] timid!—I am the one who is [with you (pl.)] always. I [am the Father,] I am the Mother, I am the Son. I am the undefiled and incorruptible one." (II 2,1-15; *NHLE*, 105)

In this example, John's vision of the risen Jesus depicts his identity with the divine triad.

In the canonical Gospels, visions of the risen Lord usually identify the heavenly Lord with the earthly Jesus of the narrative by invoking details from the ministry of Jesus. The Thomas episode in the Fourth Gospel compels the narrator to demonstrate that the risen one is the crucified (20:24-29), even though the Son's return to his preexistent glory (17:1-5) does not require such an identification.[1] *Apocryphon of John* presupposes a different tradition. The manifestation of the risen Lord is not treated as the occasion to affirm his identity with the earthly Jesus. Rather, an ecstatic recognition of Jesus' divinity constitutes the core of the resurrection tradition. Emphasis on the luminous appearance of the revealer appears in most gnostic revelation discourses.[2] Elements of this ecstatic experience of Jesus as divine revealer are evident in the canonical traditions about the transfiguration of Jesus (e.g., Mark 9:2-8 par.; 2 Pet 1:16-18). Some scholars have interpreted the visionary elements in that story as evidence that it was originally an account of the postresurrection appearance of Jesus in Galilee.[3]

Paul's account of his conversion refers to God revealing the Son "in me" (Gal 1:16), which suggests an ecstatic experience more clearly than the "appeared to" of the creedal formula in 1 Cor 15:3b-5.[4] The tale of Paul's miraculous conversion in Acts capitalizes on the light imagery associated with a heavenly commissioning (Acts 9:3-4; 22:6, 11; 26:13). The Fourth Gospel historicizes the visionary tradition by depicting the earthly Jesus as "light of the world." With his departure and return to the Father, that light is no longer directly present (e.g., John 8:12; 9:4-5; 12:35-36, 46).[5] The prologue's image of light coming from God into the world of darkness (1:9-10) invites the reader to envisage the rest of the narrative as the words of the heavenly revealer.

Just as gnostic mythology establishes an ontological dualism that separates this world from the divine, so the dualism of the Fourth

Gospel presumes that God is completely hidden from those who have not seen Jesus. Consequently, the discourses of the revealer must point to himself as the source of knowledge or enlightenment. The Fourth Gospel limits revelation to the incarnate Jesus at the conclusion of the prologue (John 1:18): "No one has ever seen God. But the only begotten God [son][6] who is in the bosom of the Father, he has made him known" (my trans.). The exchange between Jesus and Philip repeats this principle (14:8-11). This limitation makes the Fourth Gospel more restrictive than many of the gnostic revelation dialogues that assume one or more prior descents of the revealer. The exchange with Philip also acknowledges that the identity between Jesus and the Father has not been evident to the disciples at the level of the narrative about events in the life of Jesus. Until they are able to recognize the divine identity of Jesus, the disciples' faith is deficient.

Apocryphon of James opens with a scene of the disciples composing their Gospels. It makes the same point in an argument against the emerging Christian consensus on the gospel canon.[7] James, the fictive author, and Peter receive a special revelation from Jesus. At the beginning of *Apocryphon of John*, the apostle was lamenting the fact that the Savior had not yet taught the disciples necessary truths about his sending into the world, the aeons to which the disciples should go, the Father, or the type of the heavenly aeons (II 1,20-29, *NHLE*, 105). The discourses in the Fourth Gospel respond to all these questions: who is the Father, why was Jesus sent into the world, and even the aeons to which the disciples are to go (John 14:1-4). Yet the riddles Jesus proposes still leave the disciples as perplexed as the other characters in the Gospel. The "I Am" predications by which Jesus identifies himself as the divine revealer and the promised salvation (e.g., John 14:5-6) appear in the narrative as the solution to the paradox of Jesus' claims.

Postresurrection Revelations

The other solution to the contrast between the word of the divine revealer and the words that the disciples of Jesus understood lies outside the narrated time of the Gospel. Understanding of Jesus' teaching is transformed after the resurrection with the coming of the Paraclete. This pattern is similar to an apocalyptic device picked up in gnostic discourses. There the discourse is spoken by some primordial figure. Consequently, the true revelation—that known to the readers of the apocalypse or the gnostic revelation discourse—lies in the future, when the gnostic elect are revealed. The Fourth Gospel defers real understanding of Jesus' teaching to the activity of the Paraclete after Jesus' return to heaven, even referring to the Paraclete as "another" (14:16, 25-26).

The Fourth Gospel limits the Paraclete's activity to what Jesus has taught the disciples. Gnostic revelation discourses, which are associated with the risen Christ, develop this tradition of a postresurrection revelation of Jesus' teaching. In order to establish the authority of its postresurrection revelation, *First Apocalypse of James* begins with a dialogue between Jesus and James prior to the death of Jesus. Jesus promises that he will return after his death/ascent to the Father in order to reveal "your redemption." The content is given by the revelation dialogue that makes up the second half of the work. Jesus reveals a formula for the soul's ascent past the powers, which is also known to have been used by the Marcosians.[8] But James reacts with disbelief:

> James said: "Rabbi, how, after these things, will you appear to us[9] again. After they seize you, and you complete this destiny, you will go up to Him-who-is." (V 29,13-19; *NHLE*, 264)

Jesus responds by insisting that this new revelation is necessary. It will lead others to faith and rebuke the powers. When the Lord returns to James, it will demonstrate that the powers are not able to seize Jesus:

> The Lord said, "James, after these things I shall reveal to you everything, not for your sake alone but for the sake of [the] unbelief of men, so that [faith] may exist in them. For [a] multitude will [attain] to faith [and] they will increase [in. . .]. After this I shall appear for a reproof to the archons. And I shall reveal to them that he cannot be seized. If they seize him, then he will overpower each of them. But now I shall go. Remember the things I have spoken and let them go up before you." (29,19—30,9; *NHLE*, 264)

This section affirms the position of James as successor to Jesus and mediator of the tradition that comes from him.[10]

This exchange contains several echoes of the farewell discourses in the Fourth Gospel. Jesus' departure is a return to God (*1 Apoc. Jas.* V 29,19 "Him-who-is"; cf. John 14:12, 28; 16:10, 17, 28; 20:17). The question of how Jesus will return to his disciples again is posed in John 14:22-23. Rather than refer to future revelation and judgment of the powers, themes that appear in the farewell discourses, John 14:23 treats the "return" as a divine presence of Father and Son abiding with the believer.

Jesus looks beyond the disciple(s) to future believers (John 17:20). *First Apocalypse of James* has attached that motif to the revelation of Jesus' true teaching that James is to receive. After "these things"—the impending passion and return to God—Jesus promises to reveal to James "all things," an echo of the Paraclete saying in John 14:26.[11] The variant of this saying in John 16:13-15 appears designed to eliminate the possibility that the future revelations by the Spirit would depart from what Jesus has already taught, although it does have a prophetic character.[12] The rebuke of the archons echoes another Paraclete saying (John 16:8). When the Paraclete comes, he will convict the world concerning sin, righteousness, and judgment. The explanation in John 16:9-11 identifies "sin" as not believing in Jesus, righteousness as Jesus' departure to the Father,[13] and judgment because the ruler (archon) of this world is judged. Although the break in the text makes it difficult to reconstruct the transition, this section of *First Apocalypse of James* depicts Jesus as the postresurrection revealer in terms closely related to those that informed the Paraclete sayings of the Fourth Gospel. This form of the tradition lacks the awkward juggling of Jesus and the Paraclete/Spirit, because Jesus alone is the one who returns.

The Fourth Gospel separates the Son, who has returned to the Father, from the Paraclete/Spirit, who has replaced Jesus as the guiding presence in the community. This separation causes the evangelist some difficulty when he comes to narrate the resurrection appearances of Christ. Instead of following the primitive Christian tradition that resurrection is exaltation, one also implied in his own language about the cross as glorification and lifting up, he must introduce a narrative pause. Jesus is temporarily risen but not yet glorified. Mary Magdalene's encounter with the risen Lord catches him in the act—not yet ascended but about to return to the Father (John 20:17).

In *First Apocalypse of James* salvation seems to imply that even the believer attains identity with "Him-who-is." After casting off the flesh and escaping the cosmological powers, James will reach the divine, from which he originally came (27,1-10; *NHLE*, 263).[14] James asks how he could possibly reach God with all the cosmic powers ranged against him. In response, Jesus insists that it is the revealer whom the powers seek to destroy (27,11—28,1; *NHLE*, 263).[15] Use of a philosophical epithet for God, "Him-who-is," links *First Apocalypse of James*

to the developing tradition of philosophical mysticism. The Fourth
Gospel remains closer to the apocalyptic roots of this tradition. Jesus
must return to the heavens in order to prepare a place for his followers
(John 14:3). Asked about how the disciples can find the way to these
dwellings, Jesus uses the divine "I Am" to identify himself as the way
(14:4-6). The prayer in John 17:24 repeats the image of Jesus' disciples
coming to the place of glory that Jesus has had with the Father since
the beginning of the cosmos.

The Johannine formulation picks up a common apocalyptic schema
in which the seer ascends into the heavens and views the places prepared for the righteous. But John never refers to the cosmological
structure presupposed in such traditions, even though such speculation appears in Jewish apocalyptic writings.[16] The Gospel does not
clarify what the status of the disciples is when they attain this heavenly destiny or whether the return of Jesus plays a role in facilitating
their ascent to the Father. *First Apocalypse of James* uses common
gnostic traditions to respond to each of these questions. In these
respects, the Fourth Gospel appears caught between apocalyptic
visionary traditions and gnostic mythologizing. It is no wonder that
the list of questions puzzling the disciple at the beginning of *Apocryphon of John* reflects common gnostic themes: the savior's relation to
the Father, his descent, and the aeon to which the disciples will go (II
1,17-29; *NHLE*, 105). When pressed for answers to similar questions in
the farewell discourses, the best the Johannine Jesus can do is to
retreat to expressions of communal solidarity, the indwelling presence
of the Father and Son, and its confessional tradition that Jesus is
indeed Son of the Father and the only revelation of the divine.

The Style of
the Revelation Discourse

The discourse style of the Fourth Gospel is distinctly different from
that in the Synoptic Gospels but shares significant features with gnostic discourses of the revealer. A dualism separates this world from the
divine world. Revelation is possible only when the revealer descends
from the divine world. Belief in the word of the revealer is required of
the elect, who will ascend to the divine. The revealer must also answer
the perplexing questions of the disciples. Short dialogue exchanges
pose those questions of doctrine or teaching that are unknown to the
disciples. Often they state a paradox or resolve an apparent contradic-

tion between the Savior's claims and the world as humans experience it. The revealer must also commission disciples to transmit the hidden or esoteric teaching to the elect.

Two linguistic forms are as typical of the revelation discourses as the kingdom sayings are of the Synoptics. The first is a prayer form that blesses the Father for the presence of salvation (e.g., *1 Apoc. Jas.* 42,5-19; *NHLE*, 267; John 17:1-26). The second is the "I Am" saying. Gnostic mythological texts make a surprising use of the universalist declarations from Isaiah (e.g., Isa 43:10-11), which apparently underlie the absolute "I Am" sayings in John 8:24:[17] they treat the claim to be the only God as an arrogant boast of the Demiurge.[18] But the boast leads heavenly Wisdom to respond by rebuking her aborted offspring and manifesting the Immortal Human in the heavens, thus providing the impulse for the creation of Adam. Contrary to Ialdabaoth's intentions, knowledge of the true God will become possible. This ironic use of the "I Am" predications is not the only one found in gnostic sources.

As is well-known from Isis inscriptions,[19] self-predications in the "I Am" style served cultic purposes by announcing the universal powers and beneficence of the deity. They may serve to identify the goddess as the true divine presence behind other deities, the blessings of culture, and the cosmic order. The Fourth Gospel uses these predications to identify Jesus with the great symbols of salvation as well as to assert his identity with the Father. Consequently, the response to the question about the "way" the disciples are to follow to reach their heavenly destiny is formulated as an "I Am" predication, "I am the way, and the truth, and the life" (John 14:6). *First Apocalypse of James* uses the "I Am" style to introduce Jesus' identity with the divine (V 24,26-28; *NHLE*, 262).[20] The style of "I Am" predication is well developed in gnostic sources, which prominently associate it with the female revealer, Wisdom, or the spiritual Eve.[21] When found in the context of gnostic mythology, Wisdom/Eve refers to the paradox of her origins in relationship to the earthly Adam:[22]

> Now, Eve is the first virgin, the one who without a husband bore her first offspring. It is she who served as her own midwife.
> For this reason she is held to have said:
> "It is I who am part of my mother;
> And it is I who am the wife;
> It is I who am the virgin;
> It is I who am pregnant;
> It is I who am the midwife;

It is I who am the one that comforts pains of travail;
It is my husband who bore me;
And it is I who am his mother,
And it is he who is my father and my lord.
It is he who is my force;
What he desires, he says with reason.
I am in the process of becoming.
Yet I have borne a man as lord." (*Orig. World*, II 114,4-15; *NHLE*, 181)

A variant form appears in the second person when Adam sees Eve for the first time:

And the spirit-endowed woman came to him and spoke with him, saying, "Arise, Adam." And when he saw her, he said, "It is you who have given me life; you will be called 'Mother of the living.'—For it is she who is my mother. It is she who is the physician, and the woman, and she who has given birth." (*Hyp. Arch.* II 89,11-17; *NHLE*, 164)

The form is not limited to the mythic settings. The revelation discourses of Protennoia begin with "I Am" sayings that assert the identity of the speaker as a manifestation of the highest divine reality:

[I] am [Protennoia, the] Thought that [dwells] in [the Light. I] am the movement that dwells in the [All, she in whom the] All takes its stand [the first]-born among those who [came to be, she who exists] before the All. (*Trim. Prot.* XIII 35,1-6; *NHLE*, 513)

The "I Am" sayings exhibit other features of discourse style, which are common in the Fourth Gospel but lacking in the Synoptics. Although the riddles of the Fourth Gospel are not as paradoxical as those derived from the gnostic cosmological mythology, Jesus does present a series of "riddles" that the reader must decipher. When they occur in the narrative, the reader in the know is a Christian who can tell what "born from above" (John 3:3, 5), "living water" (4:10-13), and "eat my flesh and drink my blood" (6:56) refer to because he or she is familiar with the Christian sacramental system. The protagonists in the narrative remain either baffled or become hostile at what they fail to understand.[23] Even Jesus' disciples are left with "riddles" (NRSV "figures of speech") until after Jesus' resurrection (16:25).

As in the example of Eve's call to Adam cited previously, the call to awakening by gnostic revealers provides a parallel to another feature of Johannine discourse that has often troubled exegetes. The narrative suddenly breaks off and Jesus begins to speak with an almost disem-

bodied voice to an indefinite audience. The core symbol of light provides the occasion for such a statement in John 8:12 and a fragment of
discourse in 12:44-50, where "light" announces its imminent departure
from the world. The "living water" reappears in a disembodied fragment in 7:37-39.[24] How are such Johannine discourse traditions related
to the primitive traditions of Jesus' sayings? When contrasted with the
Synoptic Gospels or Q, they seem quite foreign. Bultmann originally
assumed that John had taken over blocks of discourse material from a
gnostic source similar to what is found in later Mandaean literature.[25]

Johannine Discourse and
the Sayings Tradition (Koester)

Helmut Koester has endeavored to recast the Bultmannian hypothesis
to accommodate the newly discovered gnostic evidence. Nonapocalyp-
tic sayings material in *Gospel of Thomas* contains a wisdom tradition
with an emphasis on realizing the kingdom within what has often been
paralleled with Johannine realized eschatology. The revelation dialogue
in *Dialogue of the Savior* also contains shorter units of Jesus material.
Koester has argued that by breaking segments of the Fourth Gospel's
dialogue into formally discrete units, the parallels with such gnostic
traditions become evident.[26] Sayings about light and darkness occur in
gnostic materials, although they are missing in the Synoptic tradition:

> His disciples said to him, "Show us the place where you are, since it
> is necessary for us to seek it."
>   He said to them, "Whoever has ears, let him hear. There is light
> within a man of light, and he lights up the whole world. If he does
> not shine, he is darkness." (*Gos. Thom.* 24; *NHLE*, 129)

Koester also refers to an extremely fragmentary text from *Dialogue
of the Savior* that apparently refers to some form of remaining in light
but cannot be reconstructed.[27] Rather than presume as most exegetes
would that the chronologically later gnostic writers have simply echoed
Johannine themes, Koester insists that John has reformulated traditional material that is better preserved in the gnostic texts. He suggests
parallels for each of the verses in the Johannine discourse along with
redactional elements, such as John 8:20, 21b, 23-24, 28b-29. According
to this proposal, Johannine discourses are built up out of smaller units
of traditional material.

The difficulty with the proposal lies in the fragmentary nature of one of the major texts that Koester uses to support his views of *Dialogue of the Savior* and in the lack of clarity about the formal criteria for dividing units into the various complex layers of tradition that Koester must hypothesize in order to account for even a relatively short section of Johannine discourse material. Koester remains indebted to a paradigm of linear development in the tradition of Jesus' sayings that scholars have widely criticized as they have begun to look for more sophisticated models of how oral and written traditions interacted and developed in the early Christian material.[28] Within an active oral milieu interpreters must reckon with censorship, forgetting, adaptation, condensation, and endless variations.

Koester's proposal attempts to meet some of these objections by proposing form-critical categories for some of the sayings in the Johannine discourse. For example, the saying in John 8:12 is the same as that in 6:35: "I am *x*/ he who . . . / but will . . . / (and he who . . .)."[29] The attack on Jewish opponents opens with a statement about testimony to Jesus (8:14a; cf. 5:31) and then follows with a typical gnostic revealer saying, which refers to the revealer's origin and destiny (8:14b). As in the gnostic parallels, John presumes that the disciples share the same destiny as the Savior (16:28; *Gos. Thom.* 49, 50). But gnosticizing is not simply a shared tradition of Jesus' sayings. Koester argues that the evangelist's redactional work shows that he himself had gnostic proclivities. This tendency is particularly evident when Koester interprets the saying that Jesus' opponents will "die in their sins" as a reference to the origins of two groups of persons, those from above and those from below.[30]

In order to explain how the sayings came to be shaped into dialogues, Koester must postulate a general tendency in both gnostic and Johannine discourses to destroy the integrity of the sayings themselves. Rather than append interpretations to the end of sayings, the interpretations are worked into the sayings themselves. Consequently, this tradition does not really permit the same formal analysis that the Synoptic tradition does. The forms in a particular collection are not felt to be an integral whole. Sayings will attract very diverse material, such as exegesis, wisdom lists, and creedal material, to the general context.[31] Does this departure indicate that the gnostic discourse as well as its Johannine relatives are not grounded in the primitive traditions of Christianity but in the easy manipulations that can take place once material no longer has to be committed to the oral memory of the community but resides in textual form?

"I Am" Predications as
Text and Riddle

This dispute over oral and written forms can also be felt in analyses of the "I Am" predications. The extant Isis aretalogies are written or inscribed texts. Their gnostic counterparts are also written into a mythological narrative. These written or inscribed texts may have played an important role in the propagation of the Isis cult. It had been hellenized and refounded to serve the acculturating and civilizing interests of the Ptolemies. Isis claims to be the true, though not always acknowledged, source of all cultural, legal, and religious institutions in which the human community prides itself. In short, the Ptolemaic dynasty in Egypt could support its ambitions to be the true heirs of Alexander's project by reforming an old Egyptian cult to conquer the new world. Until the disastrous defeat of Mark Anthony, Cleopatra VII clearly pursued a policy of ruling the civilized world that reflected the dynastic ambitions of her forebears.

Isis also claims superiority to "fate," to the power of the universe operating through the stars and planets to determine the course of events in the world and in an individual's life. The pervasiveness of this antiastrological theme in gnostic literature figures prominently in the cosmological myth and its portrayal of the "powers."[32] The Fourth Gospel—unlike some of the hymnic material in the Pauline letters—shows no interest in the question of cosmological powers. But the Gospel's radical dualism, which sets the revealer and the believer over against the world, makes it evident that the world can have no power over the believer.[33] Ioan Couliano asks why exegesis of Genesis played a formative role in gnostic mythologizing.[34] If one rejects the simple answer that they must have been disaffected Jews or Christians for whom Genesis was already a founding text,[35] then the connections among the "I Am" aretalogical predications, emphasis on a divine power superior to the fates, and the cultural availability of such a myth of origins provide another possible explanation. The use of the Septuagint story of Genesis in the non-Jewish speculations of the *Poimandres* shows that the story was culturally available outside Jewish and Christian circles. Because it has an account of the heavens affirming that its governing powers were created in time, it provides a powerful symbolic structure to declare their undoing by exegetical subversion. The later variants of the gnostic myth in which the Genesis foundation is considerably reduced show that the gnostic myth could generate its own system of transformations without retaining the explicit exegetical references to Genesis.[36]

Extended exegetical transformations of myth that depend on word-plays and textual details of a myth that is not directly part of the cultural heritage of those interpreting it suggest a textual rather than an oral basis for the formation of gnostic traditions. Is the "I Am" style of gnostic discourse likewise the creation of persons familiar with epigraphic or literary presentations of such aretalogies? Does Koester's suggested development of the sayings tradition into discourses have any roots in oral traditions, or are the peculiarities of those traditions that he suggests merely evidence of the bricolage of a literary esotericism with no concern for formal structures? If the latter, then the assumption that one can use observations based on a sayings tradition that was preserved, interpreted, and transmitted in quite a different medium becomes problematic.

Werner Kelber suggests that "I Am" formulae were used by early Christian prophets to identify Jesus (or God) as present in their speech.[37] He proposes that the "delayed parousia" of the parables in Mark 4 and the apocalyptic discourse in Mark 13 were directed against such assertions of the presence of the Lord in the words of the Christian prophet.[38] A gap has opened up between the oral world, in which God can suddenly become present through the powerful word of a prophet, and the spatial world of texts and distance, in which the Lord cannot be present directly until his return at the parousia. Read from the perspective of an oral metaphysics of presence, the realized eschatology of Johannine discourse evident in sayings like John 5:22-24; 8:12-15; and the like could be understood as the continuation of the "presence" effected by the prophetic word. The word shapes reality and manifests God's presence, not the world of appearances.

Another oral context for some of the gnostic "I Am" predications has been suggested by Bentley Layton's treatment of *Thunder* and the genre of the "riddle."[39] Where George MacRae's work began with the negative use of the "I Am" in the speech of Ialdabaoth as a parody of divine speech based on Isa 45:5 and Exod 20:5,[40] Layton begins with the formulation of paradoxical "I Am" sayings associated with the Wisdom or Eve figure. These sayings belong to the genre of "riddles." They are based on the gnostic myth of origins, as is evident in the use of the "I Am" paradoxes in *Origin of the World* and *Hypostasis of the Archons*.[41] Gnostic readers recognize that the speaker in *Thunder* is Eve. They are able to solve the riddles posed by her speech. Therefore the gnostic genre is not inherently more paradoxical than the "I Am" sayings of the Isis aretalogy for such readers. Like a type of riddle with which an individual may be unfamiliar, however, they are insoluble for persons unfamiliar with the story to which the allusions are being made or the character of speaker in that story. General parallels to Wisdom figures in Jewish writings, to the Isis figure, or even to early Christian prophetic forms will not elucidate the genre as used in gnostic discourse. That riddle form is grounded in the strong female figures of the Sethian mythological tradition.[42]

If the riddles are grounded in the foundational gnostic story, then they may have circulated in oral form as vehicles by which believers identified their knowledge of that tradition. Layton suggests that gnostic fascination with the riddle points to a concern with the "hidden presence" of the divine. The speaker in *Trimorphic Protennoia* is both identified with the transcendent, unknowable God and is found hidden within all (XIII 35,2-25; *NHLE*, 513).[43] Epiphanius's quotation from the Gospel of Eve reflects the theme of a hidden presence. In this fragment the earthly Eve hears the voice of the divine Thunder.[44] Hearers learn to identify the Eve, "sown in all things," with themselves.

Identification formulae play an important role in the Fourth Gospel as well. The farewell discourses emphasize the identification of the Father and Son with the believer (John 14:18-24). This is the mode in which Jesus "returns" to his followers without manifesting himself to the world. Although the paradoxical formulation of the gnostic "I Am" sayings makes their riddlelike character more evident than the apparently straightforward identification formulae in John (e.g., 8:12), the latter might also be understood as solutions to a "riddle." Riddles of the "what is . . ." plus a list of characteristics whose referent is not immediately evident would fit many Johannine contexts. The "bread of life" discourse (John 6:31-59) plays this game through alternate readings of the Old Testament story about manna in the wilderness. It also highlights a difference between John and the gnostic discourses: the stories one has to use as referents to "solve" the riddle are not the same.

Discourse and the Elect Community

Analysis of the "I Am" sayings suggests that there is a similarity in form and perhaps even in the oral context for such patterns of speech, but that the content is structured by quite different stories. The "voice" that the reader might identify behind the "I Am" is not the same in each case. I have also mentioned that both traditions presume and reinforce a distinction between the believer, who knows what such speech refers to, and outsiders or "the world." In gnostic discourses this distinction is discerned by an individual's response to the word of revelation. A similar emphasis on response to the word and an apparent predestination of some to belief and others to unbelief is evident in the Fourth Gospel.[45] How closely are the two traditions related? One obvious difference lies in the fact that gnostic writers appeal to their rendering of Genesis to explain the origins of the divergent types of humanity. The Fourth Gospel has no such explanations to offer.

In the Gospel, distinctions focusing on differences in "origin" or "paternity" between believers and unbelievers emerge in the polemic against the Jews. Their claim to be descended from Abraham is marked as false. Their deeds, seeking the death of the revealer, show that their true father is the devil (John 8:31-47). Unlike the Jews, those who respond to Jesus' revelation of the Father have been "born from above" (3:3-5). Their heavenly begetting through the Spirit is not mediated by human passion or lust (1:12-13).

The Apologists presumed that because gnostic mythology grounded distinctions between humans in myths of creation, Gnostics held to a materialistic determinism. Gnostics, they alleged, said that "the spiritual ones" could not forfeit salvation; consequently they were free from all moral, ecclesiastical, or social constraints. Modern exegetes frequently use the Apologists' interpretation to distinguish the Johannine presentation from Gnosticism. In John, Jesus addresses his summons to all humans. All are initially capable of believing, even though most will reject the light (e.g., John 12:36b-43). Elaine Pagels has taken the lead in challenging this interpretation.[46] The tripartite divisions employed by the Valentinians make it clear that the Apologists have misconstrued the texts in a polemical fashion. The gnostic understanding of election is no more deterministic than that of the Fourth Gospel. Valentinians constantly appeal to the "psychics"—orthodox Christians—to awaken to divine revelation.

The following comment on baptism from *Gospel of Philip* distinguishes what is received to make the sacrament an effective mediator of enlightenment from the mere ritual of washing with water:

> If one go down into the water and come up without having received anything and says, "I am a Christian," he has borrowed the name at interest. But if he receives the holy spirit, he has the name as a gift.

> He who has received a gift does not have to give it back, but of him
> who has borrowed it at interest, payment is demanded. This is the
> way [it happens to one] when he experiences a mystery. (II 64,22-31;
> *NHLE*, 148)

The emphasis on rebirth through the Spirit in John 3:1-10 makes a
similar point. One who has not been reborn from above cannot enter
the kingdom.

Sethian mythology emphasizes the existence of a pure seed that had
to be preserved by angelic guardians when the evil archon attempted to
wipe it out (e.g., *Apoc. Adam* V 75,22—76,7; *NHLE*, 282). Such
mythological passages could easily be read as evidence for an ontological determinism. Evidence against such a reading appears in some
variants of the myth. Other descendants of Noah are drawn into the
ranks of the elect. In *Apocalypse of Adam* the illuminator returns from
the heavens to leave seed even from the sons of Ham and Japheth. The
characteristic distinction between the gnostic "seed" and other humans
is possession of immortality:

> Once again, for the third time, the illuminator of knowledge will
> pass by in great glory, in order to leave (something) of the seed of
> Noah and the sons of Ham and Japheth—to leave for himself fruit-
> bearing trees. And he will redeem their souls from the day of death.
> For the whole creation that came from the dead earth will be under
> the authority of death. But those who reflect upon the knowledge of
> the eternal God in their heart(s) will not perish. For they have not
> received spirit from this kingdom alone, but they have received (it)
> from an [. . .] eternal angel. (V 76,9-27; *NHLE*, 282)

The Fourth Gospel insists that those who believe Jesus' revelation of
the Father do not taste death, just as they do not come under the
scrutiny of divine judgment. John 12:31 suggests that Jesus' glorification on the cross has made this freedom from death possible by
destroying the "ruler of this world." Belief as an intellectual assent to
the content of the revelation may not be the real referent of such
language. Sethian writings like *Apocalypse of Adam*, Valentinian tracts
like *Gospel of Philip*, and sections of the Fourth Gospel that refer to
baptism all suggest that belief involved ritual practices. Koester's study
of the cult of Palaimon/Melikertes raises an important question for the
study of Greco-Roman religion.[47] In that case a new myth emerged
after the cultic rites to which it was attached. Sometime after the
refounding of Corinth by the Romans, a mystery ceremony in which

athletes and musicians swore oaths was provided with a foundation myth. The foundation myth included traditional elements but was not based on an earlier legend.

One might draw a similar conclusion about some gnostic texts. Sethianism (and later Manicheism) originated in a religious milieu of Jewish and Jewish Christian baptismal sects that had rites of washing and anointing that marked the ritual transformation of persons. The revealer's discourse at the end of the long version of *Apocryphon of John* concludes with references to such ritual practices as raising up and sealing in the light of the water as the conditions of the Gnostic's new immortality (II 31,22-25; *NHLE*, 122). Koester has suggested that the Johannine tradition was reshaped by its communal and cultic history until some form of gnostic mythologizing became a logical explanation of the group's religious experience of alienation and other-worldly salvation.[48] Expulsion from the synagogue precipitated cultic emphasis on baptism and the Eucharist. Just as it is impossible to attain salvation without accepting Jesus as the heavenly revealer, so one cannot possess eternal life without participation in the cultic life of the community.

I have already noted that the Fourth Gospel understands baptism as the heavenly begetting of the children of God. Koester suggests that several sayings which were originally community rules (e.g., John 3:3, 5; 11:9-10) were more developed in the Fourth Gospel. Emphasis was shifted from "born again" to "born from above." Justin Martyr preserves the more primitive form of John 3:3. A traditional saying about walking in light was reshaped in John 11:9-10 so that it referred to recognizing the revealer within.[49] Internalizing light within the believer is closely linked with the Gospel's affirmation that Jesus is the divine I Am, because that predication is the condition for the identity between the believer and the divine.

Koester treats the exchange on entering the places prepared in heaven (John 14:2-12) as a similar development. He considers the Fourth Gospel a typologically more developed form of the exchange concerning the "place of life" found in *Dialogue of the Savior:*[50]

> [Matthew] said, "Lord, I want [to see] that place of life [. . .] where there is no wickedness, [but rather] there is pure [light]!"
> The Lord said, "Brother [Matthew], you will not be able to see it [as long as you are] carrying flesh around."

Matthew said, "Lord, [even if I will] not [be able] to see it, let me [know it]!"

The Lord [said], "[Everyone] who has known himself has seen [it in] everything given to him to do [. . .]." (III 132,6-17; *NHLE*, 249)

The Fourth Gospel has recast the older traditions in the "I Am" form. *Dialogue of the Savior* distinguishes "seeing the place of life," which is impossible in this life, from "knowing it," which is possible for one who discovers the divine origin within the self. The Fourth Gospel collapses "seeing" and "knowing" into the single encounter with the divine Jesus (John 14:8-10).

The full presence of divine revelation in Jesus shapes the dispute over the "bread of life." In the first section (John 6:25-51a), eating the bread is equivalent to believing in Jesus as the one sent from the Father. A protest from the crowd that Jesus cannot be "from heaven" because his earthly parents are known[51] draws the response that faith itself must be taught by God (6:43-51). The manna represents Jesus' revelatory word.[52] Material bread has no significance for those unable to grasp its inner, spiritual significance. The second section (6:51b-58) appears to reaffirm the necessity of physically eating the bread identified with the body of Jesus in order to attain eternal life. Bultmann suggested that this realist approach to the Eucharist had been added to the Gospel in a redaction aimed at bringing its radical theological perspective in line with more orthodox Christianity. First John 5:6 suggests that the dissident Christians rejected the significance of Jesus' death, although they may have accepted baptism. Their docetic Christology (1 John 4:2-3) was based on the Gospel and had to be countered by insertions of more conventional future-oriented eschatology, allusions to the sacrificial death of Jesus (John 19:34b-35), and a realist understanding of the Eucharist.[53]

Although he rejects Bultmann's view that the Fourth Gospel is anti-sacramental, Raymond Brown accepts the conclusion that this material belonged to the final redaction of John and was necessitated by the controversies reflected in 1 John.[54] Schnackenburg takes a more nuanced view. Emphasis on the materialism of the references to "eating flesh" and "drinking blood" as though the Eucharist were perceived as a magic guarantee of immortality misconstrues the language of the passage.[55] That view is represented as the misperception of those who are offended by Jesus' words and cease to follow him.

Like the rest of the discourse in John 6, the final section also affirms the necessity of belief in Jesus as the divine revealer. The ritual cannot be understood apart from its connection with the sending, death as exaltation, and glorification of the Son. John 6:56 is the first example of an immanence formula found in the Gospel. It expresses the unique union between Christians and Christ. From this perspective the elements of the ritual are of no importance in themselves—indeed, they are not even mentioned. The concern of this passage is union with Jesus, the heavenly Son of man, present in the community.

Construed in this way, John 6:51b-58 is another example of the Johannine rejection of literalism and materialistic interpretation of the words of Jesus. Heightening the references to "eating flesh" and "drinking blood" was not meant to introduce a new emphasis on physical reality. Indeed, the very offensiveness of the formulation demands a spiritual interpretation. Like the riddles of the "I Am" sayings, it might even be said to lock out the unbelievers and reinforce the solidarity of the cultic community with its Lord.

Emphasis on Jesus as heavenly revealer and the unity between Jesus and "his own" in a cultic community shapes another peculiarity of Johannine discourse material—its lack of ethical exhortation. The Fourth Gospel contains none of the ethical teaching of Jesus except the command to "love one another." Even that appears only at the last supper (John 13:34-35) and is clearly directed inward, toward those in the cultic community, not outward toward others. Where "walking in light" often carried ethical implications in Jewish apocalyptic, the Fourth Gospel has internalized the "light" so that it points to the revealer himself, not God's righteousness or a way of life.

Although gnostic discourses are not interested in the concrete dimensions of ethics as how persons ought to live with one another in this world, exhortations to flee entanglement with this world or with the passions generated by the flesh are common. They belong in part to the stock of philosophical topoi associated with Platonic mysticism and Stoic teaching on the superiority of the wise man to the passions. A religious framework that found salvation in the revelation of another world could easily adapt these motifs to its own system. For example, *Poimandres* divides humanity between those who identify themselves with the body and those who have learned to identify with the divine intellect within. They will have immortality. Because all humans have a dual nature, even the pious require protection from the power of those passions that originate with the body.[56] When the soul ascends into the heavens after death, everything associated with the body will be stripped away. The soul is transformed into one of the divine powers offering praises in the heavens.

The ethical orientation of *Thunder* follows a similar pattern. From a cosmological perspective the divine Wisdom is present everywhere, in the foolish as well as the wise. But she is despised among humans. The Greeks think she is barbarous. Sayings on childhood and greatness are recast to make this point (VI 17,24-26, 28-30; *NHLE*, 300). Those who hear Wisdom's voice recognize that they must flee the pleasures and passions of the sensible world (21,20-30; *NHLE*, 303). As already mentioned, the gnostic myth provided an account of the passions, their demonic origin, and their association with the material body. Fleeing their grip implied fleeing the domination of the powers.

The Fourth Gospel contains neither the philosophical topos of the soul's liberation from the imprisoning deceits of the sensorially perceptible, nor the Stoic emphasis on conquest of the passions, nor the gnostic variants that provided a mythic rationale for rejecting the sensible world and the passions. Yet it appears as "otherworldly" as any of these traditions. Why this gap? The intense sectarian conflict between the Johannine community and outsiders might be responsible for the single-minded focus on Jesus as revealer to the exclusion of any indications of how the believer sustains that experience in his or her dealings with the world. One of the Nag Hammadi texts, *Second Treatise of the Great Seth*, which has been shaped by conflict with orthodox Christians over the nature of Christ, exhibits a similar reduction. It insists on the docetic interpretation of Christ's crucifixion. The orthodox deceive themselves by thinking that the death of Jesus atones for sin and guarantees them salvation. Only an individual's belief in the revelation brought by Christ can do that. Believers have been prepared before the descent of the heavenly Christ by Wisdom's activity in the world. As in *Thunder,* she is known by the epithet "whore" (VII 50,25—51,20; *NHLE*, 363). The souls of believers are also described as having descended into this world and suffering persecution by those who think that they are advancing the name of Christ (59,19—60,3; *NHLE*, 366–67).

The persecuted gnostic community is exhorted to respond by mutual love and solidarity:

> But you will become victorious in everything, in war and battles, jealous division and wrath. But in the uprightness of our love we are

innocent, pure, (and) good, since we have a mind of the Father in an ineffable mystery. (VII 60,3-12; *NHLE,* 367)

They live in a harmony and perfect love that is established by the heavenly Christ and represents the true nature of the Father (62,8-26; *NHLE,* 367–68; 67,32-35; 68,8-13; *NHLE,* 370). Its allusions to the gnostic myth and the soul's ascent from the body, as well as the vision of Christ's heavenly unity with Wisdom in the bosom of the Father (70,1-10; *NHLE,* 371), provide the possibility of further elaboration. However, *Second Treatise of the Great Seth* focuses its concern on the need for loving unity and solidarity in the face of the hostility of orthodox Christians. The Fourth Gospel demonstrates a similar focus in the face of hostility from the synagogue authorities.

Summary

Gnostic writings provide examples of the peculiar features in Johannine discourse material. Although some gnostic examples, such as the opening of *Apocryphon of John,* echo Johannine tradition, the gnostic material has developed independently of the Fourth Gospel. Reconstruction of the sources and patterns of discourse used in gnostic texts provides important clues about the conventions employed in the Fourth Gospel. The evangelist has not simply edited some first-century gnosticizing discourse. Johannine discourses draw upon a tradition of Jesus' sayings as well as a style of revelation discourse that has been more extensively developed in gnostic circles.

The most striking stylistic parallels between the Fourth Gospel and gnostic material are in the "I Am" sayings and the disembodied call of revelation. Both John and the Gnostics exploit the echoes of the Old Testament divine predications. But the gnostic examples make the associations between this style of speech and the Isis aretalogies as well as the figure of Eve/Wisdom central to resolving its paradoxical riddles. For John, the solution to the riddle of the divine I Am remains tied to the symbolic world of the Old Testament. Similarly, the Fourth Gospel recognizes the need for a postresurrection revelation but limits the activity of the Paraclete/revealer to echoing the revelation speeches attributed to the historical Jesus. Consequently, the Johannine discourses remain awkwardly situated within a narrative account of the historical Jesus that does not anticipate such revelatory language.

Koester's attempts to relate the development of the sayings tradition in *Gospel of Thomas* and *Dialogue of the Savior* to the discourses of the Fourth Gospel raise an important question for Johannine exegesis. What is the connection between the Johannine discourses and the words of Jesus? The narrative setting of the Fourth Gospel makes that question more urgent than it is for gnostic authors, because it imposes temporal limits on the coming of revelation (e.g., John 9:4-5). Once Jesus returns to the Father, the light has departed (John 12:35-36). Gnostic revelation discourses set revelation outside the parameters of such an individual and limited history. One hears either the voice of the primordial Eve/Wisdom or the words of the exalted, divine Savior.

Study of the gnostic discourse material also sharpens the debate over Johannine ecclesiology. The riddles of the divine "I Am" predication as well as the call of revelation establish the readers as a community of insiders. As in the Fourth Gospel, recognition and knowing the true identity of the revealer separate the elect from the rest of humanity. The disputes over baptism and rebirth as well as over Jesus' claim to be the bread of life underline the sociological distinctions established by such speech. Without the knowledge that leads the believer to a spiritual identification with the revealer, cultic actions have no effect. Reinforcing the solidarity of those who hear the word of revelation emerges as the primary ethical function of discourses of the revealer in both the gnostic and the Johannine settings.

PART THREE

GNOSTIC CHRISTIANITY

10

Gnostic Identity: Conversion and Asceticism

I have mentioned that gnostic mythology supported a turning away from the material world with its bodily and social claims on the individual. This form of conversion from the world played a major role in the varied expressions of Christianity that surrounded the Gnostics as well.[1] Interpretation of Genesis and other inherited religious traditions established a gnostic rhetorical pattern that Ioan Couliano has termed "creative misprision."[2] Although susceptible of many variations and permutations, the fundamental principle of this interpretation is that nothing means what it appears to mean on the surface. Gnostics have learned to "see through" the blindness, ignorance, and malice of the powers that rule the cosmos. Established canonical or cultural traditions are fuel for the deconstruction of gnostic interpretation.[3] But unlike modern nihilism, gnostic deconstruction serves the purposes of conversion.[4] The anticosmic stance of gnostic dualism is weighted toward positive identification with the transcendent divine Father.

Interpretation and Antinomianism

Ever since the Apologists accused the Gnostics of libertinism, this hermeneutical position has been suspected of undermining the ethical conventions of society. The ascetic cast of the collection of gnostic writings found at Nag Hammadi forced a reevaluation of the libertine charges against gnostic ethics. Scholars recognized that escaping the traps that the powers had set up for human beings in the Law could be expressed either through ritual enactments of libertine behavior or through a radical asceticism that opposed sexuality, procreation, and any other ties that might bind an individual to the dominant social powers. Gnostic accounts of the creation of Adam's body by the powers provide a map of their control over the passions of human beings.

A similar dilemma appears in New Testament traditions concerning the Law. By abandoning its restrictions on their bodily and social demands, those who lived in the Diaspora among the communities of the Pauline mission appeared to be opening themselves to lawless, demonic influences.[5] The ethical interpretation of the kosher rules in Hellenistic Judaism is merely a rationalized version of the deep-seated connection between such rituals and the order of the cosmos.[6] The links between "Judaizing"—circumcision, observing Jewish festivals and food regulations—and the powers of the cosmos are evident in Galatians, Philippians, and Colossians.[7] H. D. Betz rightly insists that one must understand the Judaizing crisis in Galatia as a response to the anxiety and uncertainty generated by the ethical freedom of the Pauline message, which apparently left the community without boundaries.[8] Even without an underlying gnosticizing mythology, anxiety over the vulnerability of the community to external powers and passions probably extended beyond the sphere of concrete ethical behavior to the threat of invasion by other powers and forces in the universe. Such anxieties were characteristic of the religious sentiments in the first century.[9] Consequently, "Judaizing" might easily be advocated by gentile Christians as a necessary way of protecting the "spirit" that the community had been given in Christ.[10]

Confusion over whether Christianity implied an ascetic or libertine stance toward social conventions emerges repeatedly in the Corinthian correspondence as well. Paul either forbids outright or seeks to restrict what appear to him as radical violations of the social ethos, such as the presence within the community of a man married to his stepmother (1 Cor 5:1-5) and the dress and behavior of women claiming inspiration by the Spirit (11:2-16). Other behavior, acceptable by pagan standards although not among Jews, cannot be said to be a deliberate violation of social convention. Paul insists that the Corinthians must avoid liaisons with prostitutes (6:12-30); the appearance of participation in an idolatrous cult through consuming meat used in an idol sacrifice in the presence of those who would be scandalized (8:1-13; 10:23-30), as well as any actual participation in cult meals (10:1-22).

On the ascetic side, the Corinthians themselves have misunderstood an earlier letter to suggest that they should avoid contact with "the wicked"—nonbelievers (1 Cor 5:9-10). Paul's own example may have been responsible for those who insisted that Christian couples should renounce sexual intercourse (7:1-7). Second Corinthians 6:14—7:1 advocates a policy of purification through separation from the unbeliever that is inconsistent with the toleration of existing pagan/Christian marriages (1 Cor 7:12-16) and of relationships with nonbelievers generally (1 Cor 5:9-10; 14:23) evident in 1 Corinthians. Many interpreters have concluded that this section represents either an interpolation into Paul's original text or the apostle's own use of an independent section of parenetic material.[11] In either case, the passage presumes that holiness requires a sharp separation between the believers, men and women who belong to Christ (2 Cor 6:15-18), and the nonbelievers associated with Beliar (v. 15). But 2 Corinthians gives no indication of either the libertine or the ascetic tendencies debated in 1 Corinthians.

Some New Testament scholars have adopted elements of an anthropological account of the body to explain the relationship between bodily symbolism and social experience.[12] First Corinthians repeatedly treats the community as a "body" whose members must function in harmonious and controlled ways (e.g., 6:15, 19-20; 12:12-30). If bodily boundaries and their control serve as images of social boundaries, then the repeated emphasis on the correlation of community and body suggests anxiety about the constitution of the community. The most evident uses of the imagery to address social tensions appear in 1 Cor 11:2-16 and 11:17-34. In the first instance, Paul insists that Christian prophets, especially women, must not violate conventional, public attire when prophesying in the assembly. Although scholars remain sharply divided over the type of head covering at stake and whether Paul also intends to legislate against gender crossing by male prophets, the general import of the passage is clear.[13] Paul insists on what he perceives to be acceptable attire of males and females. The tortured logic he uses to establish his position indicates a recognition that it conflicts with established practice in the Corinthian church.[14] Although it is impossible to determine what the symbolic practice of the Corinthian prophets was, the "unveiled head" would appear to indicate access to the divine as a "new creation in Christ." Paul himself is quite willing to employ such an example in an exegetical argument that distinguishes the living Spirit of Christian understanding from that of those bound to the Law of Moses in 2 Cor 3:12-18.

The second instance, 1 Cor 11:17-34, also speaks to a situation in which Paul implies that the Corinthians are not observing traditions that he had handed on to them (11:2, 17). Their behavior at the Lord's Supper reinforces common social divisions between rich and poor (vv. 17-22).[15] The Corinthians must learn to discern the "body of Christ" that is being profaned when the wealthy demean the poor members of the community during the supper. Paul warns that the consequences of their failure are already evident in the illness and death of members of the community (vv. 27-34). Paul uses the same verb "humiliate" to describe those Christian prophets who broke with conventional standards (vv. 4-5) that he uses here for those wealthy Christians who "humiliate" their poorer brothers and sisters (v. 22).[16] Although social custom permitted the wealthy to consume richer and more abundant fare in the presence of their poor, humble clients and retainers, Paul treats such behavior at the Lord's Supper as an instance of defilement. As such, it has elicited God's punishment. Consequently, as Gordon Fee rightly observes, this case is the more serious one.[17]

Neither example speaks to the behavior of Christians outside assemblies for worship or celebration of the Lord's Supper. Paul's injunction to eat at home (v. 34a) suggests that he has nothing to say about the behavior of the wealthy and powerful when they are giving a private meal for their friends and clients. Similarly, a Christian prophet "humiliates" his or her head by inappropriate dress only when praying or prophesying. The private behavior of Christian women and men is not at issue. Each section draws on an authoritative tradition to support Paul's position. Verses 7-8 refer to the creation of Adam in God's image and of Eve from Adam to insist upon differentiating the sexes. Verses 23-26 apply the words of institution repeated at the supper to insist that there cannot be divisions among those who celebrate the meal. These words had been transmitted to the Corinthians by the apostle as an authoritative text (v. 23).

The link between the texts and the communal behavior they are said to mandate is established by the apostle's application of the word as an authority in favor of his position. But the association of text and argument depends on obvious readings of the earlier tradition. No deeper meaning or inversions of the story in Genesis 2 or of the words of institution are required. The apostle has not deconstructed either canonical or cultural traditions even in restraining the exhibition of sociocultural divisions during the celebration of the Lord's Supper. Nor has he mythologized the dangers that profaning the body of Christ brings on the community. God's immediate, disciplinary judgment seems to protect the holiness of the community. An awkward argument that the women prophets must have heads veiled "because of the angels" (v. 10) has led some exegetes to suggest a reference to the mythological story of the seduction of the angels by human women (Gen 6:2) or to the weakness of women as a secondary creation, which makes them vulnerable to such powers.[18] The story of the lustful archons and Eve played a crucial role in the formulation of early gnostic mythology. Paul's reference shows no indication of any such development.

The Danger of the Demonic

The apostle consistently speaks of the "demonic" as outside the Christian community. The sinful man who is excommunicated will be "handed over to Satan" (1 Cor 5:1-5). Handing him over may destroy his flesh, but it preserves the Spirit. Christians who think they can participate in feasts at pagan temples—"share the cup of demons" and that of the Lord (10:14-22)—run the risk of a punitive act of God similar to that suffered by Israel's wilderness generation. Christians married to unbelievers may sanctify both spouse and children (7:12-14). For Paul the community may suffer internal divisions, but it does not face an external threat from the demonic. Instead, it appears to be a secure zone of the Spirit. Its holiness is assured by divine action.

Nonetheless, the apostle's convictions were not universally shared. The myth of the creation of Adam in *Apocryphon of John* shows that the bodily sphere can easily be invaded by the demonic. Cosmic powers can incite the passions assigned to its various creator demons. As a result the Gnostic must wage an incessant war against the chaos of the passions and the powers that manipulate those passions to imprison humans.[19] Although the particular mythic explanation for the situation is a gnostic creation, the idea that the demons can manipulate human passions is not. Athenagoras refers to fallen angels producing in souls movements akin to their own desires (*Leg.* 25.1—27.2). Taught to experience the passions in this way, early Christians found that myths of this sort fit their actual experience. Peter Brown observes that the devastating effects of such passions apply to the social realm as well as to the individual. Such myths provided:

> an image of the demonic that made their "earthly power" over the human community responsible, not only for its obvious misfortunes and misdeeds, but also for the anomaly and confusion that was latent in human culture and in human social relations. To the Chris-

tians of the second and third centuries . . . this story of the mating of
the angels with the daughters of men and of its dire consequences
for the peace of society, was not a distant myth: it was a map on
which they plotted the disruptions and tensions around them. When
Tertullian reported the exile of astrologers from Roman cities, he
treated the measure as an attempt to "mop up" anomalous and disruptive elements which directly continued, on earth and in his own
age, the exile of the fallen angels from heaven. The Christian therefore stepped from a world shot through with "loose powers," made
dangerous by incomplete and destructive skills learned from anomalous sources, into the firm and unambivalent protection of a guardian angel.[20]

Anthropologists have attempted to correlate social control in terms
of bodily control. Such studies have also warned against presuming
that a ritual or symbolic reversal of the social order implies an actual
rejection of that order. Within a fixed social context the inverse of the
social order may be enacted in ritual form only to reinforce the established order.[21] Thus one must be cautious about concluding that antinomian expressions in gnostic texts or rituals led to actual reversal in
the customary social behavior of Gnostics.

Jerome Neyrey attempts to apply a typology taken from Mary
Douglas to the revolt language of the Fourth Gospel.[22] One element of
the schema distinguishes societies that locate personal identity in relationships among members of the group from those that find it within
the individual. The latter may emerge as a protest against the former
type of social group, which is seen to be oppressive.[23] The latter may
use bodily symbolism but subordinates it to the spiritual. Both the
lack of concern for the ethical behavior of individuals and the strong
focus on the unity of the Father and Son with individual believers in
the Fourth Gospel fit the typology of a "weak group" that is breaking
away from the social strictures of a dominant cultural system that
fixed identity in reference to the group.[24] Symbolism within the Gospel is undifferentiated so that it does not provide the possibility of
distinguishing one believer from another. Bodily metaphors are practically nonexistent.

Although they share similar discourse patterns with the Fourth Gospel, the gnostic writings present a more differentiated picture. The
body's creation and the savior's relationship to the bodily form in
which he or she appears are a central concern. Even when they share a
common mythological structure, which scholars have designated as
Sethian, gnostic writings differ in their estimate of how vulnerable the

body and its associated psychic/emotive components are to invasion by the powers.[25] *Apocryphon of John* exhibits an emphasis on the internal movements of the passions. The archons have gained power over the human race by creating an "imitation spirit" within humans. By contrast, *Gospel of the Egyptians* focuses on the cosmological evidence for mutability. The ancestral seed of Seth, which consists of those who repented from the error of the archon, was able to keep itself virginal and committed to truth and justice (III 60,2—61,1; *NHLE*, 215).[26] The rituals of the sect are sufficient to arm the Gnostic against hostile attack by the powers:

> This great name of yours is upon me, O Self-Begotten One, without deficiency, you who are not outside me. I see you, who are invisible to everyone. For who will be able to comprehend you in another language? Now therefore, I have known you. I have mixed myself with the immutable. I have armed myself with the armor of light. I have become light. For the Mother was in that place because of the beauty of grace. Because of this, I was formed in the circle of the riches of light which is in my bosom, which forms the numerous begotten ones in the light into which no accusation reaches. I will truly glorify you. (III 66,23—68,12; *NHLE*, 218, my trans.)

Ritual protection and identification with the divine, which cannot be grasped by the noninitiate, belong together. The combination was a commonplace in second- and third-century Christianity, as Peter Brown's observations suggest.

More properly ascetic practices develop when believers discover that the ritual protection afforded by entry into the community has not kept the powers at bay. One strategy, which some gnostic sources apparently shared with early monastic traditions, involved the discipline of "standing," a rigid control of bodily posture that forced it to imitate the stability of the divine world.[27] A rigid posture is correlated with the mind's "standing" in the presence of the divine:

> Having successfully accomplished every form of activity which I had put my mind to, I then came upon another desire, namely, I wanted to spend five days with my mind totally undistracted from its concentration upon God. Having decided this, I shut my cell and its hall so that I might not answer anyone, and I stood still beginning at the second hour. I commanded my mind as follows: "Do not descend from heaven. There you have angels, archangels, the powers above, and the God of the universe. Do not descend from heaven." (Macarius, *Hist. Laus*. 18.170)[28]

There is some evidence for a practice of "standing" in gnostic circles as well. Although one might think that the immense cosmological gulf that separates the lower world governed by hierarchies of demonic powers from the heavenly world as well as the numbers of aeons in the Pleroma would make this practice impossible, the heavenly ascent of the seer in *Zostrianos* as well as the Platonizing mysticism of *Allogenes* suggest that "standing" in the various divine spheres is part of the process of recognizing the divine.

Allogenes refers to the seer standing to receive the revelation of the divine triad (XI 68,16-35; *NHLE*, 500). Michael Williams has raised the possibility that "standing" had become a technical term in Syrian monasticism. The ability to "stand" as evident in the monastic citation probably demonstrated that the individual had obtained angelic status and was a true child of the resurrection. *Gospel of Thomas* points to a particular emphasis on those who "stand solitary" (saying 16), who will not taste death (saying 18).[29] *Zostrianos* emphasizes the connection between the seer's participation in the glories of the angelic realms and the immovable race to which the seer belongs. Standing and withdrawal of the soul into the intelligible, divine world demonstrate the divinity of the Gnostic. Other ascetic practices are presumed by *Zostrianos*. The author refers to the requirement of rejecting "somatic darkness and the psychic chaos in mind and the feminine desire [. . .] in the darkness" (VIII 1,10-13; *NHLE*, 403). Gnostic and other ascetic traditions typically associate femaleness with the body and its passions. Achieving the divine requires separation from its influences. Throughout *Zostrianos* "maleness" is an attribute of the divine. Even Barbelo, traditionally the divine "Mother," is described as "great male, invisible, perfect Mind."[30]

A Call to Conversion

With this appeal to common ascetic traditions and common Platonic topoi in gnostic texts, the possibility of gnostic texts as appeals to those outside the boundaries of the sect can be raised even if the monastic settlements in the vicinity of Nag Hammadi tell little about the provenance of that collection.[31] Recent studies of *Gospel of Truth* have raised a similar issue with regard to that text. The rich intratextuality of its allusions to the New Testament, including intepretations of the cross that employ traditional language, have generated the suggestion that it was intended as an exoteric work, one that would attract the attention of interested outsiders.[32] Clearly, the peculiar mythology of gnostic sects, not evident in writings like *Gospel of Truth* or sayings collections like *Gospel of Thom*as, may have been transmitted within closed circles. Nevertheless, the open-ended categories that are used in Sethian writings to speak about the "immovable race" allow for a process of conversion.

Scholars have long recognized that Valentinian writings moderate their treatment of the Demiurge and operate with a monistic, metaphysical schema that permits the whole cosmos, including the lower world, to be "in the Father."[33] *Gospel of Truth* provides a striking example of this monism. The entirety that receives gnosis exists within the world of error, which was generated by the will of the inconceivable one. The Father withheld perfection in order to lead all to turn to him in knowledge and love when he is revealed.[34]

Zostrianos returns from his visionary ascent into the heavens to call others to gnosis. The extensive series of initiations and baptisms suggest that souls pass through levels of attainment. They do not immediately attain the vision of the immortal Father. *Gospel of the Egyptians* attributes the begetting of members of the elect race to the activity of the Holy Spirit (III 65,26—66,8; *NHLE*, 217). Rites and symbols provide the vehicle for the transformation of individuals (63,14-15; *NHLE*, 216). In *Sophia of Jesus Christ* (III 117,8—118,2; *NHLE*, 242) those who attain the highest level of the divine require both pure knowledge and the ability to produce the proper symbols. These symbols may refer to the "signs" achieved at various stages of initiation. *Sophia of Jesus Christ* presumes that souls will attain differing degrees of perfection.

These suggestions of "degrees of salvation" stand in some tension with the mythological tradition that suggests that one must attain gnosis in order to recover the true image of humanity. In *Apocryphon of John* the seer is told to transmit the revelation to kindred spirits of the "immovable race, the perfect human" (BG 22,10-17).[35] Although Seth is described as the ancestor of the Gnostics, the revelation of the "true human" is the heavenly Adamas (*Ap. John* II 8,28-34; *NHLE*, 109; Irenaeus, *Adv. Haer.* 1.29.3; Foerster, *Gnosis*, 1:105). Adamas is the cosmological revelation of the first human, which appeared to the archons (II 6,2-4; *NHLE*, 108; 14,19—15,3; *NHLE*, 113). In *Three Steles of Seth* all the members of the Sethian race, the immovable race, are identified with Adamas. According to *Zostrianos*, Adamas, Seth, and the immovable race are all members of the Self-Begotten. But Adamas and Seth may represent different levels of gnosis. Seth refers to the individual soul; Adamas refers to the universal image of the human in which individuals participate (VIII 30,4-14; *NHLE*, 412). The order varies in *Gospel of the Egyptians* because Adamas appears to be the image of a prior first human (III 49,1-16; IV 60,30—61,18; *NHLE*, 212).

Gospel of the Egyptians develops a soteriology in which the cross becomes the final stage in salvation history. The race of Seth has been protected from the attacks of the powers by each of the appearances of the redeemer. On the third coming, he puts on Jesus and fixes the thirteen aeons to the cross (III 64,1-9; IV 75,17-24; *NHLE*, 217). The members of the Sethian race can no longer be led back and forth under the influence of the cosmological powers.[36] Freed from the influence of the powers, the gnostic initiate has recovered the image of the divine human (III 67,19-21; *NHLE*, 218). Ritual rather than ascetic practices or internal control of the passions appears to be the key to soteriology in *Gospel of the Egyptians*.

Salvation and Metaphor in
Gospel of Truth

Gospel of Truth presumes a process of transformation that is internal rather than external. Its myth of cosmic conversion and revelation depicts the pattern of individual awakening to gnosis.[37] Although scholars have often thought of Gnosticism as insisting on sharp distinctions between this world and the divine world, between Gnostics and outsiders, *Gospel of Truth* consistently blurs distinctions. The Pleroma that must be awakened is within the world wrapped in ignorance. Those whose own awakening is part of the cosmic process must still address the message to others, because without their conversion the return of the Pleroma to purity, silence, and unity is impossible (I 25, 8-24; *NHLE*, 44). Some have not yet come into being—they have not experienced the redeeming activity of the Son (CG I 27,3—28,24; *NHLE*, 44–45).[38]

"Rest," a crucial soteriological term in *Gospel of Truth*, also blurs the distinction between the revealer and the world. Instead of emphasizing the gulf that separates the revealer from the world when speaking of "rest" as reunification with the soul's angelic partner in the Pleroma, *Gospel of Truth* refers to "rest" as the present state of the individual. Jan Heldermann has categorized the passages in *Gospel of Truth* that speak of "rest." Some passages refer to the period of "preexistence," that is, elements in the myth. Paradise is a place of rest (36,35-39; *NHLE*, 48). Emanations that belong to the Father are at rest (the will, 37,19-21; *NHLE*, 49; the name, 38,25-32; *NHLE*, 49). Rest also refers to eschatology—the future reunification of Gnostics with the Father—which also overcomes the deficiency (41,12—43,1; *NHLE*, 50–51). But Gnostics also find this rest in the present (22,11-12; *NHLE*, 42; 23,29-30; *NHLE*, 43; 24,16-20; *NHLE*, 43; 33,4—34,9; *NHLE*, 47–48; 35,25-27; *NHLE*, 48).[39] The blurred distinctions in *Gospel of Truth* suggest that the cosmological expression of salvation requires the transformation of the arena in which ignorance operates through the continued enlightenment of individuals rather than removing those who are enlightened from this world.

Blurred distinctions typify the use of the New Testament in *Gospel of Truth*. Comparing *Gospel of Truth* with *Testimony of Truth*, C. M. Tuckett found that the latter cites New Testament texts directly, whereas the former refers to the New Testament only indirectly.[40] Scholars who have emphasized the psychological dynamics of *Gospel of Truth* see this literary trait as part of the persuasive rhetoric of the work. B. Standaert observes that *Gospel of Truth* speaks as though its words came from within the divine. It places both the author and hearers in the "Rest."[41] The spoken word of the discourse is to correspond with the effect produced in the hearers, their transformation into "sons of the Father." The motif of the "name" that is ultimately received from the Father applies at all levels of reality: to the Son, to the aeons, and to believers. When the name is spoken, the unknowable Father becomes known. Only the Father can utter it. Only the Father can beget children (I 38,7—41,14; *NHLE*, 49–50).[42] In keeping with its allusions to orthodox Christian *theologoumena*, *Gospel of Truth* insists on the unique moment of "begetting the Son" as central to the process of salvation.[43]

Does the allusive character of gnostic discourse in *Gospel of Truth* serve to establish the ontological reality of the Son in the same sense as the orthodox believer understands the expression "only begotten son"? Joel Fineman approaches *Gospel of Truth* from the perspective of Lacan's understanding of language as a metaphoric process of erasure. The metaphor "erases" its referent in signifying the unconscious. At the level of the unconscious only images exist.[44] Father, Son, and "name" refer to each other in a way that does not permit claiming that the origin, the Father, is somehow prior to the name of the Father, that is, the Son. Divine naming is equivalent to ontological creation both at the level of the Father and Son and as reflected in the determination of the believer's new reality as "named by the Father."[45] Yet the Father is excluded from the very discourse that must speak about him. Irenaeus has correctly discerned the response of the believer to a gnostic perception of language and reality, a continual series of allegories of allegories or "types" of types: "God is the image of another Father" (*Adv. Haer.* 4.19.1).[46] Christianity will fix its referents by appeal to a world of history or events that stand in relation to the one God.

When *Gospel of Truth* affirms that the "name of the Father is the Son," it is not asserting a simple identity in which the Father is the Son. It generates a gap between the Father and the Son that is only partially bridged by naming. This distance corresponds to the absence and presence of God in the world of deficiency. The loss of the "fullness" that is constituted by Sophia's fall has created a fracture in the divine aeons at the same time that what has been lost through her fall brings fullness to the world of emptiness.[47]

Its fixation on image and metaphor leads the Valentinianism of *Gospel of Truth* to reverse the Platonic understanding of the lower world as an image of the real divine world. The lower world is a reversed image of what is itself an image. It creates metaphors through substitution rather than through likeness or analogy.[48] Taken to its logical conclusion the metaphoric process in Valentinianism is radically docetic. All reality is constituted as images of images. As a result, Valentinianism is less ascetic than other gnostic traditions. The body has no significance for identities that are constituted through the metaphoric process of naming. Anthropological descriptions of bodily boundaries and social identity suggest that where the emphasis on guarding the boundaries of the body is lacking, one finds more diffuse group identity. This suggestion confirms the complaints of the Apologists that Valentinians cannot be rooted out of orthodox Christian congregations.

Conflict over Ascetic Practice

Other gnostic groups felt compelled to distinguish themselves from prevailing Christianity. Stephen Gero notes that a libertine gnostic sect, the Borborites, formed in reaction to the ascetic ethos of Syrian Christianity.[49] Sacramental collection, manipulation, and consumption of bodily fluids associated with sexuality formed the distinguishing feature of this sect.[50] The libertinism of this relatively late gnostic sect was the underside of the growing ascetic influence in Christian circles. Yet its policy could hardly be said to be unrestrained license. Rather than renounce sexuality, this sect used ritual means to master its powers.[51]

Another relatively late gnostic text from Nag Hammadi, *Testimony of Truth*, castigates both orthodox Christianity and a number of gnostic groups for their lack of ascetic detachment from the body.[52] Orthodox Christianity represents the "leaven of the scribes and Pharisees." The leaven refers to the passions that are manipulated by the demons and astrological forces (IX 29,10-21; *NHLE*, 450). The Law that commanded humans to marry produces defilement. It is contradicted by the heavenly origin and virgin birth of Jesus (29,22—31,3; *NHLE*, 450). Orthodox Christians are deceived because they think that the name "Christian" constitutes salvation. If mere words could save, then the whole world would have been saved (31,22-33,12; *NHLE*, 450). Other false opinions about salvation assure them that they can conquer death through belief in the death of Christ, through willingness to suffer martyrdom, or through bodily resurrection on the last day (32,18—37,5; *NHLE*, 451).

Testimony of Truth insists on a rigorous asceticism as the only way to know the God of truth (41,4-14; *NHLE*, 453). This process begins with victory over the bodily passions that afflict the soul. That victory causes the true Gnostic to "stand upright within himself" (42,25—43,9; *NHLE*, 453). The ascetic must then discipline the mind so that it contemplates the unbegotten aeons and the light flowing from them (43,22—44,3; *NHLE*, 453). A discipline of silence and separation from others characterizes the daily life of the ascetic:

> He began to keep silent within himself until the day when he should become worthy to be received above. He rejects for himself loquacity and disputations, and he endures the whole place; and he bears up under them, and he endures all of the evil things. And he is patient with every one; he makes himself equal to every one, and he also separates himself from them. (44,3-16; *NHLE*, 453–54)

The knowledge of self and God achieved through ascetic renunciation and meditation is the only way to gain salvation.

Testimony of Truth incorporates extended midrashic traditions that are employed to depict the folly and ignorance of the God of the Old Testament.[53] The first extended passage (45,23—49,10; *NHLE*, 454–55) is inserted into the tractate after the polemic against orthodox Christianity and prior to the attack on other gnostic sects. The midrash itself appears to have originated in a Jewish environment. It serves as a prime example of the revolt against the religious traditions of the Old Testament that typifies early Gnosticism.[54] Its function in this text is less clear due to the fragmentary nature of the document. It appears to be opposed to the spiritual interpretation by which orthodox Christians attached the Old Testament to Christ. Nonetheless, *Testimony of Truth* appears able to find positive examples in some Jewish traditions. The martyrdom of Isaiah demonstrates the need for the soul to be divided from the passions of the body by the Word (40,21—41,4; *NHLE*, 452).[55]

The rejection of water baptism on the authority of Jesus and the disciples at the Jordan could be directed against orthodox Christians as well as gnostic sects that also practiced such rituals (69,7-24; *NHLE*, 457).[56] A very fragmentary section apparently catalogs the errors of the various gnostic teachers who are mentioned by name. They include Valentinus and his disciples (56,2, 5). Klaus Koschorke has suggested that these sects were not sufficiently ascetic for *Testimony of Truth*.[57] The author rejects their baptismal practices (55,8-9) as well as the fact that these sects permit their followers to marry and beget children (58,3-4). The author may also be opposed to these sects because they permit their adherents to acquire wealth (65,10; *NHLE*, 456).

The "image of an image" understanding of language and ritual found among the Valentinians generated fluid boundaries. Members of the sect might be invisible among ordinary believers. *Testimony of Truth* demands a more rigid separation between the Gnostic and the larger social environment. But its author cannot divorce himself from the canonical texts of his orthodox Christian opponents. Despite its derisive treatment of the Old Testament God, mysteries for the edification of the initiate are still to be found through allegorical interpretation of some of its stories (CG IX 45,19-22; *NHLE*, 454). The death of Isaiah serves as a type for the process of division by which the Word separates the rational soul from the body that was created by the archons, light from dark, male from female, incorruptible from corruptible (40,21—41,4; *NHLE*, 452-53).

The fragmentary state of the text makes it impossible to delineate the exegetical distinctions between *Testimony of Truth* and the Valentinianism of *Gospel of Truth*. But some correlation would appear to exist between the hermeneutical stance toward the text and the ascetic practice of the two traditions. The sharp distinctions of the former and the allusive accommodation to orthodox language patterns in the latter represent divergent understandings of the relationship between Gnostics and the larger Christian community.

Fineman's discussion of the process by which *Gospel of Truth* names the deficiency that provides the key to the "sacred" emphasizes the shifting place of metaphor in gnostic texts.[58] The quest for hidden meaning requires continual distortion of any text, including its own, which comes to have normative status. Every statement begins as a reinterpretation or rejection of a prior, foundational meaning.[59] Applied to *Testimony of Truth*, this observation suggests that the gnostic tradition of the midrashic passages that demean the creator god, also the god of the orthodox, has been further turned against itself by new allegorization. Certain gnostic "schools" are now the real "other" against which the author establishes the true tradition. Fineman praises Valentinian hermeneutics for being least anti-Semitic and placing a minimal distance between itself and the other. This closeness requires that the distance separating gnostic hermeneutics from the orthodox Christian variants becomes clearest. For the Valentinian, Fineman suggests, everything is text.[60] Truth cannot be established by comparison of the text with a separable reality said to be represented by it.

The polyvalence of gnostic interpretation raises a dilemma for a work like *Testimony of Truth*, which claims to fix a particular reading of the tradition. As already noted, Paul uses his own authority as apostle to establish both interpretation and practice in disputes with the Corinthians.[61] Gnostic texts give no evidence that a similar "apostolic authority" is fixed in the descendants of particular teachers, although the model of gnostic "schools" suggests such a transmission of authoritative teaching. Gnostic hermeneutics opposes fixing either canonical boundaries of authoritative scripture or normative interpretations of its traditional *mythologoumena*.

The Rhetoric of 1 John and *Gospel of Truth*

A similar dilemma is evident in 1 John. Accustomed to the polemics of orthodoxy and heresy, scholars have tried to fix the position of the secessionists in dogmatic or ethical terms that might reflect an early gnosticizing sect.[62] The evidence for that possibility in the Johannine epistles is rather thin. The opponents refuse to confess that Jesus has "come in the flesh" (1 John 4:3). They apparently accept some form of purification or baptismal initiation but reject the cross as atonement for sin (5:6-7). Their understanding of the perfection of believers leaves no place for acknowledgment of sin by those who believe (1:8—2:2). The author of 1 John comes close to that position when he admits that those who are "born of God" cannot sin because God's "seed" remains in them (3:9). All these positions can be found in second- and third-century gnostic writings. But they could all be derived from particular elements within the Johannine tradition as represented in the Fourth Gospel.[63]

The author of 1 John constructs an authoritative voice to speak for a reading of the Johannine tradition that rejects these options. An echoing and reinterpretation of the prologue to the Gospel that emphasizes both the human reality of Jesus and the testimony of persons associated with the author establishes the reader's interpretation of the epistle (1 John 1:1-4).[64] Although these verses summon the hearer to fellowship with the voice of established witnesses to the human reality of Jesus, the author never claims direct authority over the community's understanding of the tradition. Nor does 1 John cite the Fourth Gospel explicitly. Instead the author uses phrases that echo the Gospel without citing it directly. Despite this indirect speech, much of 1 John would be unintelligible unless its intended audience was familiar with the discourse material in the Fourth Gospel.[65] Readers can confirm the truth of the author's teaching through the Spirit, which they possess (1 John 4:1). Those bound together in this fellowship of mutual love recognize the truth that they have received "from the beginning" (2:21, 24; 3:11).

The emphasis on reassurance, mutual love, and the presence of salvation in the community has led other scholars to reject the heresiological reading of 1 John. Judith Lieu points to the recurring emphasis on eternal life (e.g., 1:2; 5:11, 20) as evidence that 1 John is exhortation, not polemic.[66] The ambiguity of interpretation by allusion in 1 John is similar to the rhetoric of *Gospel of Truth*. The reader must construe the authority to which the writer appeals on the basis of his or her own recollection of the Gospel. Interpretation does not begin with a fixed quotation of the text. But the textual repertoire demanded of the reader of *Gospel of Truth* is considerably more extensive than that in 1 John. Its author presumes much of the New Testament canon as well as other noncanonical works.[67] First John does not require its readers to venture beyond the Johannine tradition as it is reflected in the Fourth Gospel and the more primitive Christian traditions used by the evangelist.

Both authors presume that the reader is enlightened by a divine gift of insight. Outsiders cannot discern the true revelation. The opening section of *Gospel of Truth* also echoes the beginning of the Fourth Gospel, in which the Word comes from the Father (I 16,31—17,4; *NHLE*, 40).[68] But if 1 John turns away from the cosmological implications of the Johannine prologue toward the earthly Jesus, *Gospel of Truth* plunges immediately into the cosmological. The reader is challenged to discover the cosmological myth as the key to the psychological drama by which the "perfect" move from ignorance and oblivion to knowledge of the Father. Thus the mode by which the reader verifies the truth of the author's claims appears both individualized and subjective despite the concluding reference to the fellowship of the perfect seed on whom the Father has poured out his love (*Gos. Truth* 43,2-23; *NHLE*, 51).

Gospel of Truth joins the debate over the significance of the death of Christ precisely at the point where 1 John and its opponents have parted company. The cross is the revelation made to those in darkness. The "tree" of the cross and the "tree of knowledge" are collapsed into a single image (18,22-26; *NHLE*, 41). Salvation is discovered by those who find the fruit of knowledge within. Although *Gospel of Truth* never explicitly denies the death of Jesus on the cross, this interpretation clearly substitutes knowledge and revelation for the death of Christ as atoning sacrifice.[69]

The exhortation in 1 John does not necessarily demonstrate that its author has turned away from the polemic task. Although *Gospel of Truth* is much more speculative than 1 John, it too contains elements of conventional parenesis. Harold Attridge has proposed that the second section of the argument concludes with a remarkable series of exhortations that call for attention to the ordinary physical needs of others (32,32—33,32; *NHLE*, 47). The author has transformed this traditional material by incorporating it into the revelation discourse.[70] The readers are to demonstrate their knowledge of the Father by doing his will. Stengthening the weak, feeding the hungry, enlightening those who are ignorant, giving rest to the weary, defeating the devil, and not returning to one's past ways all reflect general Christian exhortation. The exhortations in 1 John are no more precise than those in *Gospel of Truth*. The elder could not demonstrate that the moral practice of the secessionists deviated from the tradition of the Johannine community. But he can confirm the authenticity of his own discourse by incorporating the expected elements of parenesis.

From a rhetorical standpoint, *Gospel of Truth* provides a striking example of how the deviant Johannine Christianity referred to in 1 John might have developed in second-century Gnosticism. Without an established Christian canon or a strong sense of a fixed and bounded sacred text, the meaning of the tradition can be established only in each instance of interpretation or application. First John has no other recourse than to confront the opposition of its time with a strong voice that claims to speak from the founding days of the tradition. *Gospel of Truth* has combined a more extensive set of Christian images with a psychological rendering of themes that derived from gnostic cosmological myths. Conversion and enlightenment, not asceticism, form the foundation of this reading.[71] Its openness toward Christianity suggests a nonsectarian form of Gnosticism that hoped to win converts through its exoteric teaching[72] or through continuing the revelatory mission of Jesus.[73]

Summary

Interpretation that undermines conventional readings threatens to reshape social relationships. Both Christian and gnostic communities elicited suspicions of dangerous antinomianism. The radical break with the rules evident in gnostic hermeneutics might find expression in either libertine or ascetic practice. The former appears to have been constrained within cultic practices that depict the destruction of the powers. The latter appears in a variety of ascetic forms that were shared with other philosophical and religious groups of this period, such as the ascetic practice of "standing" in the presence of the divine.

Gnostic mythology provided an account that expressed widespread anxiety over the demonic powers of the cosmos. Entry into the ritual community might be sufficient to protect persons from their assault. But the development of ascetic practices to overcome the passions suggests that communal participation was not considered sufficient to ensure the freedom of the believer in all cases. The sense of the body as a map of society suggests that the differences between the various gnostic texts concerning the vulnerability of the body reflect their social situation.

Although the gnostic mythology of a "pure seed of Seth" might suggest a rigid dualism between the gnostic elect and the rest of humanity, many gnostic writings present a more diverse position. Several texts depict degrees of perfection or conversion as a gradual process. They also emphasize the necessity of expanding the call to salvation to those who are not among the elect. The metaphysics of images and naming in *Gospel of Truth* provides an elaborate schema that justifies the gnostic claim to embrace the practices of the larger Christian community while calling its members to a higher knowledge. As Irenaeus recognized, such teaching undermines the fixed boundaries of ontology, text, and community. But other Gnostics, like the author of *Testimony of Truth*, rejected the accommodations of second-century Christian gnostic teachers. This redrawing of sectarian boundaries sees ritual as the means by which others have accommodated themselves to a world that remains under the powers. Only strict ascetic separation leads to knowledge of God.

The gnostic examples also indicate that a hermeneutic that undermines the traditional voices of authority by subverting the literal meanings of a canonical text remains subject to the same process. Neither interpretation nor communal practice can be bounded by an authoritative voice. The developing Christian canon provided *Gospel of Truth* with the echoes of such a voice to make its case for salvation. In 1 John, one can see an earlier variant of such a struggle. The Johannine communities confronted the gnosticizing proclivities of their tradition. The author of 1 John creates an authoritative voice for redrawing communal boundaries against the alleged secessionists by echoing the discourses of the Gospel. Writings like *Gospel of Truth* provide instructive examples of how the opposing readings of John may have been developed in other Christian communities.

11

Women
Disciples and Worshipers

Women in the Marcosian Sect

Irenaeus castigates Marcus and his followers for enticing wealthy women into the sect by permitting them to pronounce the thanksgiving over the eucharistic cup. Various magic tricks enabled him to show that the wine had been transformed by the heavenly aeon, Grace (*Adv. Haer.* 1.13.1-2). Additional rituals enabled the women to prophesy in the name of the divine being, Grace. Irenaeus assures his readers that the women were in such a state of excitement that they said whatever sprang to mind. Marcus was able to use the power he gained over them to obtain both money and sexual favors (*Adv. Haer.* 1.13.3-6; Foerster, *Gnosis,* 1:201–2). Irenaeus clearly expects his readers to be as repelled by this description as we are by a "Sixty Minutes" report on the latest religious scam.

Like modern television journalists, the bishop gained his information about the shocking practices of the sect from women in his own community who had been duped by the Marcosians (*Adv. Haer.* 1.13.7). His comment reflects a significant element in early Christianity: the struggle to recruit and retain wealthy patrons. The conflict of magical powers between Peter and Simon Magus in the *Kerygmata Petrou* also turns on the problem of patronage.[1] Elsewhere Irenaeus accepts the reference to men and women prophets in Corinth at face value. He chides the Montanists for having left the church when the apostle insists that men and women prophesy within the church (*Adv. Haer.*

3.11.9).[2] But those wealthy women who have repented their participation in the Marcosian sect are clearly not being offered an alternative ministry of prophecy within Irenaeus's church. Only those willing to make a humiliating public confession are readmitted to the community. Others remain on the margins of the church or apostatize altogether. Those who did return were doubtless called on to support the Christian churches as patrons.

Although it is not possible to investigate the motives of Marcus and his followers, women seem to have continued to prophesy and teach in smaller, sectarian groups in the second and third centuries. Jewish, pagan, and Christian reports of women prophesying consistently treat such activity as of doubtful authority.[3] Women who belonged to the flourishing artisan and merchant class in the cities of the Pauline mission were not among the extraordinarily wealthy patrons of their community. But they were able to provide facilities for various cultic and social groups. The extent to which such patrons participated in the activities of the groups, molded their opinions, and made other demands on the members is not clear.[4] The apocryphal acts depict a Christianity that refuses to endow its wealthy patrons with the social prestige and influence that they would have expected in other social contexts.[5]

Irenaeus's portrayal of Marcus evidences a departure from established conventions about wealthy patrons in general. Its emphasis on the gullibility of women in particular avoids the issue of how successful the Marcosians had been among males in the churches of the Rhone region.[6] Even Irenaeus admits, however, that the women drawn to the Marcosian cult did not attain their new status because they had become the group's patrons or even because they were permitted to speak words of consecration over the cup. Their new status derived from a ritual in which the cult leader endowed them with the spirit of the heavenly Grace, which he himself had received. This gift of the spirit enabled the women to prophesy.

Women in Pauline Traditions

Much of the conflict between Paul and the Corinthians in 1 Corinthians is also fueled by the claims of those said to be endowed with wisdom or with the Spirit. Paul speaks explicitly of women in connection with (a) the responsibility to remain in an existing marriage (1 Cor 7:10-11, 13-14); (b) the preference given to remaining single for those unmarried women who are able to do so (7:8-9, 28, 34, 39-40); (c) the dress of women prophets (11:3-16); and (d) the turmoil during assemblies at which speaking in tongues was practiced (14:33b-36).[7] Some feminist critics have argued that the rhetorical agenda of 1 Corinthians as a whole constitutes an attack on those household churches in which women patrons like Chloe and women prophets had challenged Pauline authority. Instructed by Prisca and Aquila (Acts 18:24-28), the Alexandrian Jewish convert Apollos may have been responsible for their understanding of wisdom and status in Christ.[8] Antoinette Wire suggests that the social status of females and males was changed by their conversion in different ways. For women, Spirit-filled prophecy and possession of wisdom mean an enhanced social status that they could not otherwise enjoy. For men, with the possible exception of slaves and the poor, the journey was more like that of Paul, from a position of some public esteem to a lesser or despised position. This downward transition for males is particularly marked in Luke's portrayal of the Corinthian community (Acts 18).[9]

Prophecy as inspired speech in a cultic context can be regulated by communal conventions. Paul's rules about the head covering of women prophets (1 Cor 11:3-16), limits on behavior of males and females in tongues speaking and prophecy (14:1-40) begin the process. The Pastorals prohibit women from speaking in the assembly (1 Tim 2:12). Paul's suggestion that the widow may remarry but should prefer to remain unmarried (1 Cor 7:39-40) is rejected by the Pastorals. Only women in their sixties who have led exemplary lives as wives and mothers and have no one else to care for them can be enrolled as widows (1 Tim 5:9-16). Because most women did not live beyond their thirties, this rule effectively depletes the numbers of celibate Christian women who might claim support from the community.

Prophecy, prayer, and other forms of intracommunal speech provide one link between the roles of women in the Pauline churches and reports about women in gnostic sects a century later. The second question concerns the role of women as missionary apostles. Wire insists that the expression "sister woman" (NRSV "believing wife") in 1 Cor 9:5 does not refer merely to the wife of a male apostle but presumes that she is a participant in the missionary task.[10] The Pauline correspondence refers to other women missionaries or wife and husband teams (e.g., Phil 4:2-3; Rom 16:3-4, 6, 7). Prisca and Aquila also appear in Acts 18. The story of the Samaritan woman in John 4:4-42 suggests that women had played an important role in the evangelization of

Samaria, even though Acts 8 attributes the conversion of Samaria to male disciples. The story of Thecla in the third-century *Acts of Paul* preserves the legend of a female missionary who was venerated in Asia Minor.[11]

Paul grounds the authority of his own call to preach the gospel in a vision of the risen Lord (Gal 1:15-17), which he equates with the Easter commissioning of the other apostles (1 Cor 15:5-10). A canonical tradition that Jesus appeared to women near the tomb (Matt 28:9-10; John 20:11-18) does not appear to have been interpreted as legitimating women as apostles.[12] Gnostic revelations invoked the testimony of women disciples, especially Mary Magdalene, as the grounding for their claims (e.g., *1 Apoc. Jas.* V 38,15-23; 40,19-26; *NHLE*, 267; *Gos. Mary* 17,7—18,15; *NHLE*, 526–27).[13] The control of the canonical paradigms makes itself felt in these writings. The fragmentary ending of *First Apocalypse of James* obscures the author's defense of the women disciples of Jesus who are included in the chain of authoritative witnesses. But the author is clearly forced to defend that position.[14] Although Mary's insight into the Lord's teaching is greater than that of the male disciples, *Gospel of Mary* concludes with male apostles going out to preach the gospel.

The Ambiguity of the Feminine

The ascetic stance of many gnostic texts resulted in tensions over the use of feminine images. On the one hand, *Gospel of Thomas*, *First Apocalypse of James*, and *Gospel of Mary* affirm the authority of women disciples over the male apostles said to be the founders of the orthodox tradition. On the other hand, they retain an identification of the feminine with the passions through which the archons gained power over humankind. This ambiguity continues to be evident in gnostic treatments of divine Wisdom.[15] Wisdom appears to have been preferred to the Word as the principle incarnate in the souls of those who were to transmit gnostic wisdom. An early version of this Christology that seems to have circulated in Corinth[16] was superseded by Logos Christology in orthodox Christianity. Irenaeus's account of Marcus points to the ambiguity of this identification with the feminine divine principle. Marcus claims that the divine tetrad could descend into the world only in the form of the feminine principle, Grace. Grace inspired this gnostic founder with the revelation concerning the numerical patterns of the world (*Adv. Haer.* 1.14.1; Foerster, *Gnosis*, 1:203).

The feminine imagery in gnostic cosmology and soteriology depicts an intense experience of the world's ambiguities. Even the blind creator god, Ialdabaoth, incorporates the negative side of the feminine that precipitated Wisdom's falling away from the divine Pleroma.[17] Did women actually formulate such gnostic mythology or interpretation? We do not know. The women disciples of Jesus, especially Mary Magdalene, demonstrate ability to interpret the sayings of Jesus in *Pistis Sophia*. Such activity may have been open to women in some gnostic circles. No women are named as gnostic teachers in the surviving sources, however.

Identification with Wisdom on the part of both male and female worshipers distinguishes gnostic religious experience from the orthodox emphasis on Christ as Son of God and Lord. The gnostic images of Wisdom in myth and ritual provide an alternative to the forms of piety that the orthodox developed around the canonical traditions. Even in gnostic circles, however, one finds the male voice of the Word/Son competing with that of the Mother/Wisdom.

The only sources for asking the question about the place of Wisdom in gnostic myth and ritual are admittedly texts that clearly result from a scribal recording of the tradition. Ritual activities are understood to be governed by specialists able to interpret them to believers in line with the textual orthodoxies of the group. Paul's use of the eucharistic formula to regulate Corinthian behavior at their cultic meal (1 Cor 11:17-34) provides an example of such an interpretation. Christian gnostic teachers who reinterpreted established cultic practices to show that they were vehicles of gnostic enlightenment, as in *Gospel of Philip*, perform a similar function in gnostic circles.[18]

The intellectual syncretism of the Greco-Roman period sought to endow ancient rites and myths with higher meanings. Plutarch recasts the tale of Isis and Osiris to reflect speculation about the dyad and the fate of the soul in the world. The holy rites enabled worshipers to enact and to see representations of philosophical truths (*Isis and Osiris* 27).[19] Plutarch's treatment of the Isis myth parallels Irenaeus's report of Ptolemy's interpretation of the wanderings of Achamoth outside the Pleroma. The parable of the Lost Sheep that the Savior comes to seek reflects the fate of the Mother from which the church has been sown. The woman seeking the lost coin cleaned her house. Therefore the parable refers to the heavenly Wisdom. She found her lost desire after all things had been cleansed by the coming of the Savior and was able to return to the Pleroma (*Adv. Haer.* 1.8.4). As already mentioned, the wandering and suffering of Wisdom in the lower world provided the key to rejecting Moses' literal meanings in Genesis for an exegesis grounded in gnostic mythology (*Ap. John* II 13,5-27; *NHLE*, 112).

The Suffering of Wisdom

Suffering cannot apply to the Christ on the cross, but it does apply to the disciples who suffer through the Mother's transgression (*Ep. Pet. Phil.* VIII 139,23-25; *NHLE*, 536). Repeated use of this mytheme, the wandering and suffering of the divine Wisdom, to interpret a variety of other texts demonstrates its central place in gnostic religious experience. The myth of Wisdom could be pressed into service to explain the origin of elements in the material world. All the passions experienced by human beings because of their material nature are mirrored in the sufferings undergone by Wisdom when she discovers that her entanglement with darkness prohibits her from return to the Pleroma. Matter came into existence out of her passions; the soul, from her repentance (*Adv. Haer.* 1.4.1-2).

When set within a Christianized reading of Genesis, Wisdom's fall into the lower world becomes a fault or disobedience for which she is blamed. She must await the gracious coming of the Spirit and the redeemer in order to be restored. Deirdre Good has argued that the Valentinian tradition has turned the earlier traditions of Wisdom as the supreme self-sufficient goddess into a myth of the fallen, erring aeon. Identifying the female Wisdom with the dyad of material creation makes her ontologically inferior to beings who belong to the world of light.[20] As Wisdom is increasingly submerged in the material world, the healing activity of the male savior becomes the key to her eventual salvation.

Excerpts from Theodotos makes this development in Valentinian exegesis evident.[21] In order to accommodate the Christian tradition (represented by John 1:3), Ptolemy makes the savior the source of the lower world. This creation occurs when Wisdom turns toward the divine and so becomes passionless (*Exc. Theod.* 45,1-2).[22] The passions she sheds become the matter for the lower world. By turning Wisdom toward the divine and separating the passions from her, the Word becomes the source of all things. Another variant of the theme appears in Plutarch. Here Isis must enable Zeus to walk by separating his legs, which had grown together. Thus Zeus is able to leave the wilderness in which he had dwelt out of shame and to move rapidly through all things. This mytheme demonstrates the ability of the divine mind to go through all things (*Isis and Osiris* 376C). Plutarch identifies Isis with both the animate, intelligent movement of the world soul and the "matter" in the receptacle of the *Timaeus* (49A). Consequently, she is both an imperfect being seeking completion by the Word and the cause of creation and the human capacity to know God.[23]

Rather than constrain our perception of salvation along the lines set by orthodox Christianity, which insisted on a sharp distinction between the perfect, divine Savior and fallen beings who could not return to God without his assistance, we should acknowledge the fluidity of the mythic accounts. Isis's own activities are largely responsible for healing her impassioned wanderings. She is also able to come to the aid of her devotees because she is the divine power behind the gods, fate, powers of nature, and human laws and culture.

I have noted that gnostic soteriologies adapted the philosophical motif of passionless immobility. This state demonstrated that the cosmic powers had been conquered. Many gnostic texts suggest that the believers participated in this divine stability by turning toward the divine Father-Mother. They join the praises attributed to the heavenly aeons who stood at rest and glorified the Invisible Spirit and Barbelo.[24] Such activity represents an ongoing process that differs from the rituals of a call of awakening, raising up, washing, anointing, and endowing with new garments that occur in Sethian accounts of enlightenment (e.g., *Ap. John* II 31,3-25; *NHLE*, 122). The triple descent in *Trimorphic Protennoia* concludes with the coming of the Word/Son to complete the mysteries of initiation for the Spirit, which remains in the world after the coming of Wisdom. All traces of darkness and ignorance are removed by the coming of the Word (XIII 49,26-35; *NHLE*, 521). It is his voice, not the Mother's, that the gnostic initiate hears in this tradition.

Repentance Displaces Wisdom

Another development away from the mediation of salvation by Wisdom appears in *Gospel of the Egyptians*. It presupposes Sethian baptismal rites like those in *Apocryphon of John* and *Trimorphic Protennoia*. As Williams has observed, however, conversion of the soul toward an inner practice of stability does not appear to be of primary concern.[25] Both Wisdom and the mytheme of her wanderings as the origin for movement disappear. Wisdom appears in the divine Pleroma with Barbelo (III 69,2-3; *NHLE*, 218). Earlier, four angelic aeons decide that the lower world requires a "material Wisdom" as its ruler (57,1). An established mytheme in the Wisdom tale has the Mother repent when she hears the arrogant boast of her offspring. At this point, *Gospel of the Egyptians* substitutes a hypostatized figure, Repentance. She comes into being through the will of the Father to rescue the seed trapped in this world (III 59,9—60,2; *NHLE*, 215).

Repentance is a heavenly power whose activities are directed both toward the seed of Seth that will be sown in the lower world and the seed that has come from the arrogant archon.[26] Only when Jesus comes is the seed of Seth redeemed from the sway of the astrological powers that lead them back and forth. He nails the powers to the cross and provides the initiates with the armor of true knowledge (III 64,3-9; *NHLE*, 217).[27] In a hymnic passage praising the Self-Begotten for providing this armor, the initiates also speak of the Mother as in the place of light to which they have come (III 66,22—67,16; *NHLE*, 217–18). How the Mother's presence and transforming beauty were represented in the baptismal rites of the sect remains unclear. If this group considered it necessary to be undefiled by the world, "virgins" in whom the seed of Seth could be sown during the initiation process,[28] then perhaps the initiates discovered themselves reborn through the Mother.

The Sethian mythemes of the fall and wandering of Wisdom as well as her heavenly call to the initiate have been displaced in *Gospel of the Egyptians*. The Mother remains part of the divine as Barbelo. She apparently figures in the baptismal regeneration as the place of grace discovered by the initiate as well. But the agent of redemption is the great Seth, whose final, decisive manifestation occurs in Jesus.

Where one might anticipate the mytheme of Wisdom's quest for the divine, one finds the coming of a heavenly power, Repentance. Repentance is part of the process by which the soul turns toward justice and truth in order to enter into the process of initiation. This concern with repentance may reflect the Christian gnostic origins of *Gospel of the Egyptians*. Emphasis on the conversion of the soul and its repentance shapes two other Christian gnostic works from the Nag Hammadi collection, *Exegesis on the Soul* and *Authoritative Teaching*.

Both the myth of the wandering goddess and the popular romances

of separated lovers shape the narrative in *Exegesis on the Soul*.[29] This
work opens with the stages in the repentance that is necessary to
purify the soul:[30]

1. Conscience troubles the soul because of her indecent passions
   (II 128,28-29; *NHLE*, 192).
2. The soul repents of prostitution (128,30).
3. She calls on the name of God (128,31-33).
4. She weeps sincerely (128,33-34).
5. She again pleads with the Father (128,34-35).
6. She confesses and identifies her fault (128,36—129,2; *NHLE*,
   193).
7. She makes a final appeal and promises to return to the Father
   (129,2).

Then the soul, which has been described as a prostitute, is pronounced
worthy of divine mercy because of all the afflictions she has suffered
(129,2-5).

Maddalena Scopello recognizes that the sequence of confession,
plea for mercy, and concluding affirmation that the soul is worthy of
divine help suggests a penitential rite. She turns to Jewish sources,
such as lament psalms, prayer formulae, and the plea of Asenath (*Jos.
Asen.* 12:4-11), as evidence for the piety of repentance. Tears, pleas,
and other outward signs of distress demonstrate the sincerity of the
penitent.[31] The narrative account of Asenath's conversion provides
the closest parallels to *Exegesis on the Soul*. Asenath repents of her idola-
try, asks God to become a father to her, and is redeemed by the visit of
the angel Michael. The angel is the heavenly double of the earthly
Joseph with whom Asenath had fallen in love. In order to be cleansed
from her life of prostitution and defilement, the soul in *Exegesis on the
Soul* must also receive its heavenly counterpart. Both writings understand redemption as a return to the state of undefiled virginity.[32]

Literary parallels to *Joseph and Asenath* do not answer the question
of the religious function of *Exegesis on the Soul*. Scopello has argued
that the quotations used to illustrate the themes of the soul as prostitute, her repentance, and her return to the Father's house were taken
from early Christian collections of citations. Similar groupings occur
in patristic authors.[33] Such material probably developed along with
the ecclesial practices of penance in the late second and third centuries.

Another work in the Nag Hammadi collection, *Authoritative Teaching*, also deals with the conversion of the soul away from its attachments to the material world.

Authoritative Teaching describes the soul's dual nature. Originally, the soul lives in the Pleroma where she can be fed by her heavenly bridegroom (VI 22,1-34; *NHLE*, 305). Her association with the body can lead the soul to bestiality (23,13—24,26; *NHLE*, 306). Material pleasures form an alluring bait. If the soul starts to desire them, then all the other vices come to exist in the heart: pride, love of money, envy, fraud, vanity, ignorance, and desire for pleasure (30,27—31,7; *NHLE*, 308). Once the soul has been trapped, she can be freed only by the Word. Through the healing power of revelation, she comes to despise her former pleasures. She strips them off to put on the true bridal garments and run into the fold guarded by the good shepherd (31,24—32,16; *NHLE*, 309).

In *Authoritative Teaching*, the Word provides the healing medicine that enables the soul to reject the life of worldly pleasure for the ascetic life. The author recognizes that some alleged Christians are worse than pagans because they do not seek God. When the truth is preached to them, they become only more obdurate and even persecute those who truly seek salvation (33,4-25; *NHLE*, 309). *Authoritative Teaching* does not refer to any gnostic mythemes or develop the motif of Wisdom's fate in the world. Had it not been found with other gnostic writings, one might consider it part of the inner-Christian debate over the place of wealth and bodily pleasure in the life of the Christian, such as one finds represented in Clement of Alexandria. In that case, the reference to persecution of the ascetics would appear slightly out of place. *Testimony of Truth* has shown that disputes over the necessity of asceticism also occurred within gnostic sects.

Authoritative Teaching says that the true disciple will persist in seeking God, "enduring distress in the body, wearing out her feet after the evangelists, learning about the Inscrutable One" (35,4-6; *NHLE*, 310). As a reward, the soul finally enters the heavenly rest and partakes of the divine banquet. The reference to "the evangelists" suggests that interpretation of the Gospels may have played a role in the contest between the false shepherds who claimed to be feeding the soul and those who have the true knowledge that comes from the good shepherd (32,31—33,3).[34] The teaching on repentance and the need to turn away from all bodily attachments found in *Exegesis on the Soul* and

Authoritative Teaching seems more at home in third-century disputes about asceticism in the Christian life than in the wide-ranging, mythic syncretism of the second century.

Because the soul is feminine regardless of the gender of the body it inhabits, these treatises do not appear to address the question of women in gnostic sects. But the abstract account of the soul's fall into prostitution and her conversion and return to the heavenly bridegroom found here appears to have been embodied concretely in Simonianism. Simon Magus, the reputed founder of the sect, was said to have been accompanied by a former prostitute, Helena. The couple represented the primal unity of male and female (Irenaeus, *Adv. Haer.* 1.23.2). The female is the thought (Gk. *ennoia*) that the divine mind used to create the universe. The myth of this earlier gnostic sect may have shaped the story of repentance in *Exegesis on the Soul* and *Authoritative Teaching.*[35]

The Helena of Simonian myth may have been an actual person whose close association with the sect's second-century founder may have given her a role in formulating its particular teaching. Just as prominent women are reported to have adopted both Judaism and Christianity in the early centuries, so others patronized gnostic teachers and their disciples. The letter from the Valentinian, Ptolemy, to a wealthy Roman lady, Flora, takes great pains to instruct her in the sect's understanding of the Old Testament. She is promised further teaching if she converts. Her question shows that she must have already been familiar with either Jewish or orthodox Christian teaching. Consequently, she was probably not drawn to the Isis cult, which provided a major vehicle for women's religious experience in the first and second centuries C.E.[36] Ptolemy's *Letter to Flora* as well as the descriptions of repentance in *Authoritative Teaching* and *Exegesis on the Soul* point to a convergence of gnostic and orthodox Christian sects similar to what one finds in *Gospel of Truth*. The elements of revolt and hostility to the creator god that figure more prominently in the Sethian mythological accounts are not the structural principles in such depictions of awakening, repentance, and conversion.

Summary

The essentially private structure of gnostic sects as well as their need for influential patrons may have provided opportunities for women as teachers and leaders that the more public and formally ordered orthodox churches denied them. Such activities could easily become a lightning rod for antignostic polemic. But the available evidence does not indicate whether the figure of Wisdom in gnostic myth and ritual played a significant role in determining the position of women.

Gnostic Wisdom figures mirror the ambiguity of human experience in gnostic mythology. Humans find themselves in a world that is dominated by heavenly (and human) powers that are hostile to Wisdom or gnostic enlightenment. Yet these same powers pretend to possess divine authority for themselves, their rituals, and their scriptures. In the early Sethian mythology, one finds a response of defiance. Norea's rejection of the powers in *Hypostasis of the Archons* repeats the escape of the spiritual Eve from their attempt to rape her and deprive her of spiritual power. It sets the pattern for her offspring. In *Apocryphon of John* the repentant Wisdom receives heavenly assistance. Her turning away from the passions mirrors the freedom of the Gnostic.

Wisdom is not only lost and wandering. Her heavenly embodiment, the divine Mother, descends prior to the coming of the Immortal Human. She constantly foils the plots of the powers so that her offspring remain open to awakening. Wisdom dominates the ritual imagery of some gnostic sects. Her voice issues the call that awakens the soul to its true nature. The story of her wandering, isolation, affliction by the powers, and eventual incorporation into the Pleroma suggests a typical initiation pattern.[37]

This basic pattern of gnostic enlightenment could be reshaped by other forms of religious experience. I have pointed out that some texts focus their understanding on the conversion of the soul along the lines of a Platonizing mysticism. The soul ascends into the divine realm to praise the powers. Myths about the divine Mother are reinterpreted and understood as representations of a philosophical truth about the origins of the world. The female figures in the myths represent the dyad, which underlies the emergence of the material world. Sometimes the dyad (or the Barbelo aeon) also serves as the place from which the soul contemplates the transcendent One.

Assimilation to the ascetic piety of conventional Christianity displaced the focus on Wisdom as the divine Mother. Instead, one meets the soul, lost and wandering in the world until she is rescued. I have noted that in some versions of the gnostic myth, such as that in *Apocryphon of John*, the archons used passions that could be awakened through the body. Consequently, Wisdom's story and the tale of the soul's quest for salvation easily coincided. Repentance and conversion of the soul take center stage. Both the emphasis on contemplation of the One and the refocusing of the story on repentance and conversion lose sight of the myth of Wisdom. Instead of serving as the vehicle by which other traditions are interpreted, an inherited gnostic myth is subordinated to a mystical or ascetical tradition that existed in the larger Christian world without the mythology of Wisdom's fall. The powers in *Origin of the World* express the fear that the Immortal Human will enable even the female creature to conquer the powers (II 118,10-16; *NHLE*, 183–84). In the end, it is not the archons who silence the voice of the Mother but the stronger voice of the divine Son, the Word.[38]

12

Christians: Gnostic and Orthodox

Prior to the publication of the Nag Hammadi materials, church historians had been accustomed to define the problems of orthodox and heretical Christianity much as the Apologists had done. The "heretic" has subverted the true standard of Christian teaching by assimilating it to some alien mythology or system of thought. This approach appears already in the Pastoral Epistles (e.g., 1 Tim 1:3-7). Sometimes modern scholars turn the Apologists' argument upside down. The emerging orthodoxy becomes the foreign element that shut down the liberal, individualist, freethinking Gnostics.[1] Study of the Nag Hammadi codices has forced scholars to reevaluate such simple accounts. How does one define deviation from acceptable Christian teaching? Gnostic writings run the gamut from the mythological speculation that has reformulated Jewish material with only slight Christianization (e.g., *Apocalypse of Adam*; *Hypostasis of the Archons*) to other works that are expositions of Christian ascetic praxis (*Exegesis on the Soul*) or even an adaptation of gnostic themes to third-century, Christian theological speculation (e.g., *Tripartite Tractate*).

Gnostic Christian Writings

Exegesis on the Soul is so conventionally Christian in its teaching about repentance that some scholars question whether it should be considered a gnostic writing at all. J.-M. Sevrin finally bases his treatment of the work as gnostic on the claim that such "hatred of the world" could never be predicated of the God of the New Testament.[2] Although the antignostic polemic in the church fathers would suggest that Gnostics never attended to the doctrinal concerns of orthodox Christianity, those gnostic treatises that are extensively Christianized suggest otherwise. Study of *Tripartite Tractate* shows that its author has reformulated a Valentinian system to bring it more in line with the thought of third-century orthodox Christianity. Harold Attridge and Elaine Pagels have suggested six major areas of revision:

1. There is a single, unique Father who is ultimately the creator of the universe.
2. The Father no longer generates paired aeons. His offspring is the Son. Together they produce the third member of the heavenly triad, the church.
3. The material world resulted from a deficient but providential act of the Word. All elements of the female Wisdom falling into passion or ignorance have disappeared from this system.
4. The Demiurge is not a demonic figure but an instrument used by the Word.
5. The tripartite division of humanity—earthly, psychic, and spiritual—explains differing responses to the coming of the Savior.
6. Both spiritual and psychic persons belong to the same church and will experience the same ultimate salvation.[3]

Its author may even have taken a position on the hotly debated question of how the Father generates the Son. Contrary to the common third-century view that the Father generated the Son from his substance (Gk. *ousia*), *Tripartite Tractate* insists that one cannot say that the Father has a substance from which he engenders anything (I 53, 34-36; *NHLE*, 61).[4]

The gnostic authors of *Apocalypse of Peter* and *Testimony of Truth* present themselves as guardians of the tradition that has been distorted by the heretical opinions of orthodox officials and other gnostic teachers. *Tripartite Tractate* presents itself as a work of Christian theological speculation. After the cosmological section, which describes the origin of all things through the Logos, the treatise refers to those who hold heretical opinions concerning the origin of all things (I 108,13—114,30; *NHLE*, 89–92). The alleged wisdom of the Greek philosophical schools is inferior to the truths about the creator god and the prophecies of the Savior found among Hebrews who have interpreted their tradition in the Greek manner. The teachers of the Law recognized the truth of the one God. They are inferior to the prophets who recognized that true knowledge of the Father would come with the Savior.[5] *Tripartite Tractate's* critique of the materialism of Greek speculation (109,22-23; *NHLE*, 90) echoes the polemic of Wis 13:1-7.[6]

Just as the diverse opinions of Greek philosophers show that their speculation is not based on the truth, so Jewish teachers have derived different opinions from their Scripture. They have not agreed concerning the unity of God or God's relationship to the created order (112,19—113,5; *NHLE*, 91). Because the prophets did not know the origin of the Savior, their testimony was diverse and incomplete (113, 6-32; *NHLE*, 91–92). None of them could conceive of the Savior as the incarnation of the spiritual Logos (113,33—114,30; *NHLE*, 92). Although commentators have treated these lines as variants of Valentinian views of the Old Testament, the arguments stated could easily be advanced by a Christian apologist.

Irenaeus Against the Gnostics

The diversity in the Nag Hammadi material makes it difficult to maintain the categories for gnostic sects inherited from the heresiologists. Irenaeus sets the terms for later orthodox treatment of gnostic sects. The attack may be pursued on philosophical grounds, theological and exegetical grounds, or sociopolitical grounds. The philosophical arguments found in Irenaeus follow well-established rhetorical topoi. The opponents are ridiculous fools whose errors can be traced back to the heresiarch Simon. They mistake psychological processes for real entities and draw conclusions from false analogies.[7]

The philosophical arguments occur in the first book of the *Adversus Haereses*, where Irenaeus establishes the genealogy of gnostic schools; thus they receive much more attention in survey treatments of Gnosticism. But Irenaeus considers the theological and exegetical arguments that are developed in the later books to be more significant (*Adv. Haer.* 2.pref. 2). He accuses the gnostic teachers of patching together a new garment out of the useless old rags of Greek philosophical speculation (*Adv. Haer.* 2.14.1-6). If the philosophers had known the truth, then there would have been no need for the Savior's descent. Against the gnostic reading of the Old Testament prophets, Irenaeus insists that the prophets knew what they were saying (*Adv. Haer.* 2.14.7). Opposing a direct, literal reading of the Gospels to gnostic allegory leads Irenaeus to advocate harmonizing divergent texts. The Gnostics saw symbolic evidence for the thirty heavenly aeons in the fact that the Lord engaged in a ministry of one year when he was thirty. Irenaeus combines the Synoptic notice that Jesus was thirty when baptized with the Johannine references to multiple Jerusalem visits and the claim that Jesus was not yet fifty (John 8:56-57). He concludes that Jesus must have preached until he had passed his fortieth birthday. Like some of his gnostic opponents, Irenaeus then appeals to the testimony of apostolic tradition to confirm this extraordinary claim. It was a tradition taught by the elders of the churches in Asia who had been instructed by John, the disciple of the Lord. John had lived until the time of Trajan. Some of the elders learned the same tradition from other apostles as well (*Adv. Haer.* 2.22.1-6).

Irenaeus's appeal to apostolic testimony shrinks the number of generations necessary to link Jesus' time to his own by extending the age of Christ as well as that of the apostles. Elders in the Asia Minor churches of the early second century C.E. were still able to learn the truth directly from apostles. The gnostic teacher Ptolemy, Irenaeus quips, has not even seen an apostle in his dreams! (*Adv. Haer.* 2.22.6). But apostolic testimony is not only ranged on the side of the orthodox. The Gnostics are quick to counter with their own claims to apostolic tradition.[8] The members of such groups of apostolic testimony vary. Douglas Parrott has attempted to order the material by arguing that a gnostic grouping of Thomas, Philip, Matthias (or Matthew), and Bartholomew has priority over the orthodox list of Peter, James, John, and Andrew.[9] Women followers, especially Mary Magdalene, also figure in the preservation and transmission of gnostic teaching. But the Nag Hammadi material shows that gnostic authors quickly appropriate the canonical figures Peter, James, John, and Andrew. In *Gospel of Thomas* James (saying 12), Matthew (saying 13), and Peter (sayings 13, 114) are shown to be inferior to Thomas. But in *Apocryphon of John, First and Second Apocalypses of James, Apocryphon of James*, and *Apocalypse of Peter*, James and Peter are the sources of gnostic teaching that has been rejected by the larger church.

For most of the second century, the argument for apostolic tradition was conducted on both sides by claiming descent from a single apostolic figure. Irenaeus's appeal to Johannine authority for his own unusual interpretation of the length of Jesus' ministry is similar to that of gnostic authors. He differs from his opponents because he seeks to found all tradition on the ministry of the earthly Jesus, not on revelation by the risen Christ. Irenaeus recognizes the weakness of a one-year chronology for that purpose. Jesus would not have obtained the mature wisdom of a "master" or been able to form his disciples in so short a period. The presumption of an apostolic tradition that goes back to postresurrection experiences of the apostles already appears in the New Testament. The Johannine Paraclete sayings as well as the Lucan narratives of Jesus teaching the disciples to interpret the prophets christologically demonstrate this necessity.

Once Irenaeus has established the possibility of grounding the tradition in the narrative accounts of the earthly Jesus, he then argues for the unity of apostolic teaching. He employs texts from Acts to support the claim that the apostles never taught gnostic tradition (*Adv. Haer.* 3.12.1-7). The framework of some of the gnostic writings has been formulated to address this type of argument. The apostles gather as a group and receive a gnostic revelation that forms the core of their message before they depart to preach throughout the world in *Letter of Peter to Philip* and *Gospel of Mary*.[10]

The success of Irenaeus's argument in pushing gnostic authors to retreat from the earlier second-century views of apostolic authority is due in no small measure to the growing influence of the four-Gospel canon and Acts. Material remains from Egyptian Christianity support this conclusion. Study of surviving manuscripts in Egypt disproves older scholarly claims that Coptic Christianity originated in a primarily gnostic milieu. Instead, one finds concurrent literary production of codices containing both gnostic and orthodox material. Tito Orlandi has made a significant analysis of the workmanship of the codices in each case. The Nag Hammadi manuscripts are much less professional in orthography. They are inconsistent in the use of titles as well as in the personal notations made by scribes. By contrast, orthodox codices display accurate and precise orthography, consistency of language, and careful construction of the codices themselves. The gnostic writings do not enjoy the same status as sacred books. The translators and copyists of the surviving gnostic materials were probably attempting to emulate a tradition that was established in the larger Christian community.[11]

Jesus' Disciples in Gnostic Sources

If the collection of gnostic writings in codices, as well as their translation into Coptic, shows that groups of gnostic Christians sought to emulate the practice of the orthodox communities, the final redaction of these works may exhibit similar concerns. *Apocryphon of James* is conveyed from one esoteric teacher to another. The letter introducing the work insists that the Lord did not wish to make its contents known to "the twelve" (I 1,1-28; *NHLE*, 30). Its author claims that all the apostles wrote what the Savior had said to them whether openly or in private (2,1-15; *NHLE*, 30). The revelation conveyed in the apocryphon was subsequent to those compositions. It represents the only way to salvation.

Scholars have suggested that writings such as *Gospel of Philip* and *Gospel of Mary* were also intended to displace the public revelation contained in the Christian canon. Both distinguish the exoteric teaching of the disciples from the revelation given to those whom the Lord loves. Mary Magdalene figures as a primary example of the private relationship between the believer and the Lord. She enjoys a special place as the companion of the Savior (*Gos. Phil.* II 63,33—64,9; *NHLE*, 148). In *Gospel of Mary* the Savior's love for her demonstrates the union of spirit and mind that is necessary for salvation.[12] The first half consists of a postresurrection dialogue between Jesus and his disciple. Its conclusion deliberately echoes the departing promises of the risen Lord in Luke and John as well as the prophecies of Mark 13 (BG 8,12—9,5; *NHLE*, 525).[13] But this public revelation fails; the disciples are not able to preach the gospel. Instead, they remain afraid to preach the gospel lest they suffer the same fate as the Son of man (9,6-12).

Mary must summon them back to the task at hand, which she does by insisting that "the Lord has made us male" (9,20). The disciples can "become male" only if they overcome the divided soul evident in their fear and despair. The contrast between the "double-minded" and "single-minded" person was a topos of Hellenistic Jewish ethical reflection. The "single-minded" person devotes him- or herself wholeheartedly to the Law. *Gospel of Mary* has the risen Lord proclaim the end of the Law (9,1-4). The terminology must refer to the anthropological speculation in which the feminine, weak elements of the soul that lead it away from the divine are transformed by being united with the Spirit, the Mind, or the Word.[14]

The disciples are not transformed and able to undertake their task of preaching the gospel until the closing lines of *Gospel of Mary* (18,15—19,2; *NHLE*, 527). The author incorporates a visionary account of the soul's purification from passion (15,1—17,7; *NHLE*, 526) as it ascends past the cosmic powers to the realm of the divine, where it attains rest. This vision forms the content of a private revelation that

Jesus had made to Mary. This account of the process by which the soul comes to see the vision of God through the mind provides an interpretation of the Lucan saying that the kingdom is within (Luke 17:21-22), which Jesus had commanded the disciples to preach (8,15-22; *NHLE*, 525). In the exchange with Mary that opens the vision, Jesus refers to the mind as the "heavenly treasure" of Luke 12:34 (10,15).[15]

Because Mary questions Jesus about visions after seeing the Lord and is praised for her ability to view the divine without wavering (10,10-15), the reader knows that she has already attained the inner realization of the kingdom. Her enlightenment contrasts sharply with the fears of the disciples. Their souls have not yet attained the immovable vision of the divine. Andrew and Peter become angry, insisting that the Savior could not have made such a revelation to Mary and not to them (17,10—18,5).[16] As in *Apocryphon of James*, the debate centers on whether Jesus gave teaching in private to some of his followers that differed from his public testimony. Andrew and Peter represent the orthodox position that there can be no such revelation. Levi defends Mary against their charge that she is lying by chiding the other apostles for treating Mary as though she were an adversary. They should instead "become men"—undergo the spiritual transformation that Mary has already achieved. Then they will be able to carry out the command that the Lord gave them (18,5-21; *NHLE*, 526–27).[17]

Although the narrative elements in *Gospel of Mary* depict her as the first to attain gnosis, she is not a recipient of the commission to preach the gospel to the nations. *Gospel of Mary* evidently understands the narrative accounts in which the risen Jesus sends his followers out to preach to refer only to the male disciples. As in *Letter of Peter to Philip*, the male disciples receive gnostic teaching when they are all assembled. Only after that conversion do they go out to teach. In its present form,[18] *Gospel of Mary* has reconciled the gnostic tradition of private revelation with the orthodox claim that all the apostles preached the same gospel. Its incorporation of kingdom sayings of Jesus into the canonical framework of resurrection appearances suggests that the canonical Gospels played a crucial role in determining what could be credibly attributed to the Lord.[19] But the true meaning of the sayings of the Lord contained in the canonical materials cannot be perceived by those who have not attained the vision that is the goal of gnosis.

Gospel of Mary has the risen Lord command his disciples not to lay on others any burden of the law. The Savior's warning that those who

give the law may be imprisoned by it (9,2-4; *NHLE*, 525) has a decidedly Pauline ring.[20] Although scholars are sharply divided over whether
Gospel of Philip can be considered as a single discourse[21] or merely a
collection of Valentinian sayings,[22] it incorporates Pauline material
into its treatment of the ministry and sayings of Jesus.[23] Just as *Gospel
of Mary* insists that there is no true Christianity without gnosis, so
Gospel of Philip claims that the name "Christian" applies only to those
who have received the gnostic initiation that culminates in the reunion
of the soul and its heavenly counterpart in the mystery of the bride
chamber (II 69,1-13; *NHLE*, 151).[24] Like *Tripartite Tractate, Gospel of
Philip* establishes its Christian identity by drawing a sharp contrast
between Christians and Jews.[25] At the same time, doctrinal disputes
over the nature of salvation and of the Eucharist (II 56,26—57,21;
NHLE, 144) show that the author is engaged in inner-Christian theological polemic.[26] Those who have not attained perfection (or "the
resurrection") in this life through sacramental initiation will not escape
punishment after death (66,7—67,30; *NHLE*, 149–50; 76,22—77,1;
NHLE, 155).[27]

This initiation also requires that the Christian overcome the roots
of evil hidden in the heart (82,30—84,13; *NHLE*, 158–59). Knowledge
exposes the sources of evil to the light of truth, which makes a person
free. Faith, hope, and love also nourish the life that the Christian
possesses (79,18-30; *NHLE*, 156). This account of Christian virtues
along with the role attributed to the Spirit in sustaining believers and
operating as the supreme power in the cosmos can scarcely be distinguished from orthodox Christianity.[28] Christian scholars have commonly reacted much as the Apologists did to gnostic writings that
are engaged in interpreting the accepted texts and sacraments. This
engagement with inner-Christian concerns by gnostic writers is taken
to be deceitful rhetoric (cf. *Adv. Haer.* 1.9.1) by which nongnostic Christians are caught off guard.

The gnostic writings that treat specifically Christian topics exhibit a
range of polemic, apologetic, and hortatory features. The bitter opposition to orthodox Christianity that one finds in *Apocalypse of Peter*
and *Testimony of Truth* is not evident in writings like *Gospel of Truth,
Gospel of Philip,* or *Tripartite Tractate.* How one treats the conflict
between Peter and Mary in *Gospel of Mary* depends on whether one
presumes that its author has a hostile Christian majority in view or
one assumes that *Gospel of Mary* has formulated a response to the
kind of objection raised in Irenaeus about esoteric revelation and

the universality of apostolic preaching. In the former case, Peter is the embodiment of orthodox dogmatism. In the latter case, his eventual conversion provides a foundation for a gnostic claim to the inner meaning of Christian teaching.[29]

Some gnostic texts have taken over the emphasis on evangelization typical of much of the canonical understanding of the apostles. Michel Desjardins suggests that *Gospel of Philip* considers it incumbent on Gnostics to help others to attain the same perfection that they enjoy.[30] This concern is also evident in the section of *Tripartite Tractate* that deals with the church. Although humanity is said to be divided into spiritual, psychic, and earthly persons (CG 118,14—119,10; *NHLE*, 94–95), both spiritual and psychic persons participate in the heavenly church. Whatever differences exist among believers as a result of their responses to revelation, all are restored to the heavenly church together (122,12—123,22; *NHLE*, 96–97).[31] Baptism in the name of Father, Son, and Holy Spirit is the prerequisite for salvation (127,28—128,19; *NHLE*, 99). For such gnostic groups the claim to represent the truth of Christianity is supported by participation in evangelization, theological speculation, and sacramental practices typical of most Christian groups.

Christian Gnostics
and Religious Pluralism

Such Christian gnostic writings provide evidence for the influence and extent of the New Testament canon by the late second and early third centuries. What is to count as revelation must be recognizably associated with canonical texts. Irenaeus considers the existence of gnostic sects a danger to the public status of the larger church. People who confuse gnostic preaching with the Christian message will not be receptive to the true message. People who are repelled by the excesses of gnostic practice will assume that all Christians behave in similar ways (*Adv. Haer.* 1.25.3). Consequently, Irenaeus casts his refutation of gnostic systems in dualistic terms. Although he is well aware of monistic developments in second-century Valentinian thought, Irenaeus always interprets the Gnostics as dualists who reject the Creator. Confronted with a monistic system, he argues that the gnostic account of knowledge and ignorance would have to admit ignorance into the Father himself (*Adv. Haer.* 2.17.5).

Analysis of second-century Christianity must not import the understanding of ecclesial identity and dogmatic conformity that emerged only from the Arian crises after Nicea.[32] Jewish, Christian, and gnostic groups of the first three centuries are not defined by sharply articulated doctrinal boundaries. Henry Green has attempted to employ Max Weber's categories to understand the emergence of new religious groups in Jewish Alexandria. A social anomie born of the disenfranchisement of the large Jewish population provided the conditions for the emergence of new salvation religions:

> The rise of religious movements is an expression of both social and psychic experiences. It points to social conflict and the search for social integration, to psychic revolt and the quest for meaning. In Alexandria, in the wake of numerous Greek-Jewish clashes, a segment of the population was experiencing acute social and psychic dislocation. Anomic, they also possessed a social cause. A salvation religion has the best chance of being permanent when a privileged class loses its political power to the bureaucratic, militaristic state. Both Christianity and Gnosticism were new salvation religions. Their development intersected Roman socio-economic development in Egypt.[33]

The intellectual environment of Alexandrian Judaism provided the opportunity for the pluralistic syncretism that is evident in many gnostic writings:

> The Jewish community in Egypt was large and prominent enough to attract "teachers" of many kinds. In the first century C.E. ten to fifteen percent of the Egyptian population was Jewish. . . . The particular consequences of the *laographia*—social stigmatization and legal disenfranchisement—and the resulting status dissonance to a subgroup of the educated within the Jewish mosaic, however, signify a critical juncture in the history of Alexandrian Judaism. According to Weber, the distinctive characteristic of disenfranchisement is that they tend "to work in the direction . . . of seeking salvation through mystical channels." The quest for transcendence implies a search for authority outside the institutionalized offices of normative society.[34]

The pluralistic but otherworldly speculation of Alexandrian teachers, whether they were Jewish, Christian, or gnostic, drew on an intellectual environment that preserved ancient traditions and valued philosophical debate.

The dogmatic hardening of the fourth century reflects a major sociological shift within the Christian community. By the end of the century, the Nag Hammadi codices that had been copied in the mid-century would lie discarded and buried. The late fourth-century church faced the pastoral dilemma of a wide cultural gap between the cosmo-politan, intellectual Christianity of Alexandria and the populist Chris-tianity that had developed in the Nile valley. Charles Kannengiesser sees this gap as an essential element in the theological conflicts of the fourth century:

> Was Christian theology in Alexandrian terms synonymous with a systematic integration of specific beliefs into the cultural, highly sophisticated frame of a philosophical attitude favored by the plural-istic abundance of local traditions? Or was Christian theology in fourth-century Alexandria demanding urgently a philosophically war-ranted but pastorally nontechnical exposition of the basic Christian catechesis?[35]

Although Irenaeus's claim that gnostic teaching violates the "rule of faith" (*Adv. Haer.* 1.10.1-2) might seem to anticipate this demand for a formally uniform doctrine, Irenaeus does engage in speculative refuta-tion of his opponents. The fourth-century conflict in Alexandria pro-ceeded differently. Athenagoras's denunciations were not speculative refutations of Arian thought. They were the fixed, dogmatic catechesis of the nonintellectual majority in the church.

In the earlier period, divergent doctrines did not necessarily sepa-rate persons into different philosophical schools. The earliest extant examples of the use of the Greek term *hairesis* for the teaching of a rival group appear in the medical treatises of Alexandrian writers. But here a *hairesis* did not refer to a uniform doctrine taught by all who belonged to a particular school. Nor did the differences between schools of medicine give rise to separate institutional structures, because doctors were trained by being apprenticed to other physi-cians.[36] Consequently, Heinrich von Staden concludes that writing apol-ogetic and polemic treatises did not create normative self-definition among medical theorists and practitioners.[37]

The early gnostic mythology that contrasted the pure, heavenly seed of Seth and the polluted seed of the other offspring of Adam and Eve emphasized separation. The Gnostics identified themselves as offspring of this pure race, which had been preserved in its own heavenly land. The Sethians dwelt with the angels (cf. *Apoc. Adam* V 72,1-14; *NHLE*, 281). As already noted, the early mythological accounts stressed the danger of polluting the seed through sexual passion. The archons attempt to rape and defile the spiritual Eve so that her light will never be able to return to its heavenly home. Within Judaism the reforms of

Ezra-Nehemiah used purity laws, prohibitions of exogamy, and Sabbath rules to separate Jews from others. Persons of mixed descent were no longer acceptable members of the holy people.[38] The Samaritans were among the groups alienated from the purified race of Jews returning to their sacred land. According to the Apologists, two early gnostic teachers, Simon Magus and Menander, carried on their activities in Samaria.[39] Writings like *Apocalypse of Adam* invert the Jewish traditions about the pure race of Seth. Finding themselves excluded as "impure seed" by those with whom they continued to dwell, gnostic mythologists turned the Jewish tradition against itself.

Second-century Christian gnostic teachers offer a different pattern of social relationships. They present themselves as teachers in schools like those of philosophy or medicine. Individual schools were highly eclectic even though particular slogans or doxographical traditions distinguished one from another. Gerd Lüdemann has insisted that among educated Christians in Alexandria or Rome the role of teachers like Valentinus or Ptolemy was indistinguishable from that of Justin Martyr.[40] Several gnostic treatises use the doctrinal ploy of insisting that their work gives truths about the origins of the cosmos or the soul that philosophical schools have been unable to attain (e.g., *Orig. World* II 97,24—98,10; *NHLE*, 172).[41] As already mentioned, correcting the opinions of previous thinkers does not separate a given author and his followers from competing teachers.

Another example of this speculative development is the tractate *Eugnostos*, which was later incorporated into a Christian revelation dialogue between Jesus and his disciples.[42] *Eugnostos* emphasizes the inability of humans to discover the truth about the transcendent God as well as the standard doxographical list of errors concerning the governance of the world (III 70,1—71,1; *NHLE*, 223). The Christian Gnostic who adapted *Eugnostos* to the revelation dialogue genre has Philip elicit this doxographical introduction from the risen Lord by telling him that the disciples are searching for the underlying reality of the universe (III 92,4-5). The Christian writer of *Sophia of Jesus Christ* treats the divine nature of the revealer as the key to truth. The other thinkers could not discover the nature of the universe. The risen Lord has come from the Light to reveal the truth (93,5-10; *NHLE*, 223).

Both writings accept the philosophical commonplace that those who attain knowledge of God and the things in the divine world become immortal. *Eugnostos* describes the "immortal one" as a person whose knowledge of God has freed him from an empty life, providence, and fate (71,1-13). This description fits the conventional pattern of philosophical conversion in the Greco-Roman period. *Sophia of Jesus Christ* has revised the conventional formula of *Eugnostos* to introduce the mythic theme of a polluted and unclean seed. The only persons who can receive knowledge from the Savior are those who have not been "begotten by the sowing of unclean rubbing but by the First Who Was Sent" (93,12-24). For *Eugnostos* the Immortal Human is the first offspring of the unknown Father. Jewish speculation about the powers of God apparently played a role in identifying the Immortal Human with the powers of God, "divinity, lordship, kingship" (NHC V 6.14-22; "divinity and kingdom" in III 77.9-13; *NHLE*, 229).[43] For *Sophia of Jesus Christ* the Immortal Human is the heavenly Savior. The Savior's offspring are revealed when they accept his revelation. This shift from the Immortal Human as an expression of the powers of God to the Savior as well as the return to speculation about the "pure seed" suggests that *Sophia of Jesus Christ* does not see gnosis as the product of a speculative school tradition. Rather, *Sophia of Jesus Christ* requires identification with a particular sect. The implied conversion may be from a non-Christian gnosis to a sectarian form of Christianity. The disciples are told that they must separate themselves from the sexual passion by which the powers defile human beings (III 108,5-14; *NHLE*, 235). The deficiency of the female must be overcome. Those who attain heavenly rest are a "masculine multitude" (118,6-16; *NHLE*, 242). The ascetic Christian sect envisaged by *Sophia of Jesus Christ* probably included women. The disciples who receive this secret teaching are characterized as "the twelve and seven women" (90,16—91,1; *NHLE*, 222). Mary is included along with several male disciples as persons who ask the Lord questions.

I have pointed out that *Apocalypse of Adam* uses a doxographical catalog of false opinions about the origin of the Savior to attack the claims of a group that alleged that the Savior was a Word sent from heaven (V 82,10-18; *NHLE*, 285). The guardians of baptism speak from the heavens to condemn those who have polluted the baptismal waters by "drawing it within the will of the powers" (84,4-23). Because the same list of guardians appears in *Gospel of the Egyptians*, an account of Christian gnostic baptismal ritual, Gedaliahu Stroumsa has suggested that *Apocalypse of Adam* is directed against a sect of Christianizing Gnostics similar to those represented by *Gospel of the Egyptians*.[44] How this sect permitted the waters of baptism to be controlled by the powers remains unclear. Perhaps the baptized were not required to renounce sexual passion, hence the powers retained control over them. I have mentioned that *Testimony of Truth* attacks both orthodox and gnostic groups for relying on external things like the death of Christ and baptism. These examples of sectarian division demonstrate that some gnostic groups were not content with gnosis as insight into or speculation about the stories of cosmogony and salvation. They insisted on particular rituals and practices that separated members from the larger community.

Christian Gnostics
and the Gospel Canon

Irenaeus is most concerned with those Gnostics who are part of the Christian communities. He not only takes pains to demonstrate the theological absurdity of their mythic speculation but also attacks their treatment of Scripture. They destroy the narrative order of the Gospels and Acts and reject the revealed four-Gospel canon (*Adv. Haer.* 3.11). As already noted, the developing authority of a Christian canon does become evident in gnostic writings. *Sophia of Jesus Christ* sets the content of *Eugnostos* in a dialogue between the risen Jesus and his disciples. The frequent use of such settings in gnostic material demonstrates the authoritative status of the canonical resurrection accounts. A similar polemic use of the canonical appearance tradition occurs in 2 Pet 1:16-19. There the author bolsters the authority of his teaching about the parousia by appealing to a version of the canonical transfiguration account.

But Irenaeus's idea of "gospel" as a closed narrative text embodied in the words of a book was not common in gnostic circles. It may even have been unfamiliar to many Christians. More fundamental senses of scripture as a heavenly book revealed to a seer or as the heavenly book in which the fates or the deeds of humanity are revealed had widespread appeal in gnostic circles.[45] A Valentinian meditation on the senses in which the gospel is a book appears in *Gospel of Truth* (I 19,27—24,9; *NHLE*, 41–43). The book is a heavenly scroll taken by the one who has been slain (19,27—20,14); it is edict and testament (20,15—21,2); it is the book of life (21,2-25), which is itself living (22,38—23,18). The section concludes with a hymnic passage on the coming of the revealing Word (23,18—24,9).[46] Associating the suffering of Jesus with grasping the heavenly book that has been in the mind of the Father from all eternity shows what was the most telling difficulty with the canonical narratives for Gnostics—their presentation of the death of Jesus. *Gospel of Truth* deliberately speaks in terms familiar to orthodox Christianity. It apparently affirms the significance of Jesus' death. But confronted with the canonical Gospels' realism about the death of Jesus, the gnostic reader would have to reject the plain meaning of the text.

Some writings, as already noted, attack the orthodox accounts directly. *Apocalypse of Peter* provides an alternative story of the passion. The "living Jesus" was not nailed to the cross but stood by laughing at the futile efforts of the powers to crucify him (VII 81,4-24; *NHLE*, 377). In this case, the author must appear to accept the canonical narrative at the same time that he rejects it. The author and his audience remain within the larger Christian community, whose blind bishops and deacons (79,23-27) have been granted power over the "little ones" for a time (80,8-11). Peter is told to ignore those who remain blind. As long as they continue to read the Gospels literally, such persons are as deluded as the demons who crucify a body that they falsely think to be the Christ.

As I have suggested, another example of the growing influence of the canonical Gospels appears in the introduction to *Apocryphon of James*. The risen Jesus picks James and Peter out from among the apostles, who are putting everything they had heard from Christ into books (I 1,2—2,17; *NHLE*, 31).[47] Although it claims to be a secret book, *Apocryphon of James* does not contain the type of gnostic mythologizing that Irenaeus found offensive. It appeals to lists of parables well-known from canonical sources (8,5-10; *NHLE* 33) and uses familiar-sounding expressions concerning the "kingdom of God." Suffering is necessary for disciples, who will even accept martyrdom as evidence of their saving belief in the cross (6,1-20; *NHLE*, 32). Faith, love, and works lead to eternal life (8,10-15). The reader of this secret revelation would still recognize its speaker as the Jesus familiar to him or her in the canonical Gospels and the traditions of the orthodox churches. Some modern scholars have read *Apocryphon of James* as the creation of an orthodox Christian writer in the second century C.E. For most of that century, apostolic tradition could be guaranteed by claiming the authority of one or more apostles.[48]

This view overlooks the evident polemic against the apostolic circle of the Twelve that typifies both the opening and closing sections.[49] It shows no hostility toward the orthodox churches. Use of the four-Gospel canon to frame the picture of Jesus and his teaching in *Apocry-*

phon of James demonstrates that the charges of persons like Irenaeus are false. Peter's exclamations of surprise show that the larger Christian community has been wrong to reject gnostic teaching (3,38—4,2; *NHLE*, 31; 13,26-36; *NHLE*, 36).[50] Because the orthodox remain "unenlightened," they will not participate in the kingdom (9,24—10,6; *NHLE*, 34). The gnostic reader will discover familiar elements in turns of phrase, the lengthy period of postresurrection instruction, Jesus' descent to bring revelation to an elect group, and the concluding hints that in the end none of the disciples followed this revelation except James. Paradoxical formulations of sayings material urge the reader to discover a new identity so that he or she will be able to ascend to the Father (13,11-17; *NHLE*, 35). Throughout, the text retains a separation between the "apostolic circle"—Peter and James—and the real addressees of the text, those gnostic believers who received the tradition that had originated with James in Jerusalem (16,4-19; *NHLE*, 37).[51]

Some gnostic teachers were close enough to orthodox Christianity to pen treatises that did respond to objections being raised by the Apologists in the second century. Yet for the most part Gnostics did not create new social forms of religious association. One finds indications of sectarian gatherings, schools of disciples or of esoteric learning that exist within larger movements of the time. In the second half of the third century, the creative period that produced the Nag Hammadi texts and the systems reported in the Apologists was over. But a new synthesis that was to become an independent religious movement did emerge from the form of Jewish Christian baptismal sect that appears to have played such a prominent role in the development of Sethian Gnosticism during the earlier period.[52] The visions of a young man brought up in the Elkesaite sect gave birth to a religious movement that provided a more stunning challenge to catholic Christianity than any of the earier gnostic groups.[53]

Mani transformed the eclectic intellectual universalism of the school type of *hairesis* evident in gnostic mythologizing by founding a religious movement that sought to embrace all of humanity. Manicheism was not merely addressed to Christians living within the Roman Empire or outside its borders in the east. Manichean teaching spoke to Persian and even Buddhist religious speculation. Mani also perceived the potential of the new codex medium. He used the codex form to preserve and to circulate religious teaching. I have mentioned that in Egypt the codices containing the orthodox canon were much better produced than those containing tracts like the Nag Hammadi texts.

Manichean codices put even canonical Christian texts to shame. The beauty and careful execution of the Manichean writings make their Christian counterparts appear poor and slovenly.[54]

Mani may have been responsible for teaching his followers to regard him as the Christian Paraclete, the messianic offspring of Zarathustra, and the Buddhist Maitreya.[55] He reportedly claimed that God revealed to him a knowledge that embraced all the wisdom contained in the earlier religious traditions. He combined this revelation with new teaching. Consequently, the Manichean church could embrace all the earlier communities (*Kephalaia,* chap. 154). Mani insisted that all earlier religions were insufficient because they were tied to particular places and nations:

> But my hope will go to the West and will also go to the East. And they will hear the voice of its preaching in all languages and they will preach it in all cities. My religion surpasses in this first point all earlier religions, for the earlier traditions were founded in individual places and individual cities. My religion will go out to all cities and its message will reach every land.[56]

Manicheism was eradicated in the West by the sixth century C.E. Its long history in the East, especially in central Asia and China, indicates that the movement was able to sustain these universalist claims.[57] Manicheism recognized the need for a religious perspective that would embrace all of humanity. Mani also attempted a syncretism that was more systematic than the scattered cultural borrowings and reinterpretation of old traditions typical of the Hellenistic reformulations of religion. Sociologically the dual structure of elect and hearers permitted the group to embrace many followers who would not be unduly burdened by its ascetic precepts, among them the young Augustine. The elect were destined to return to the realm of light upon death and had to purify the light substance within. The hearers, who supported the elect, had no such immediate concern. Future incarnations would bring them to the status of "elect" unless the end of the world were to come first. Consequently, the only persons excluded from salvation were those enemies who remained deaf to the call of the redeemer.[58]

Summary

Even though the amorphous pluralism of oral tradition and particular, local interpretations inherited from the first century had been shaped by the necessity of establishing communal boundaries, second-century

Christianity remains pluralistic. Those gnostic writings that engage in reformulating common Christian *theologoumena* should not be accused of deceit. Indeed, those gnostic writers who oppose the apparent accommodation of gnostic mythology and cult to general Christian practices, such as *Testimony of Truth* and possibly *Apocalypse of Adam*, show that Gnostics had no more consensus about the boundaries of the various sects than Christian apologists had.

Irenaeus rightly insisted that theological and exegetical issues formed the basis for dispute between the conventional understanding of Christianity and that propagated by Gnostics, who also claimed to teach Christian truth. He fastened upon historical realism, proximity to the apostolic generation, and the link between Christian teaching and the historical Jesus as evidence of a true reading of the Christian Scripture. Gnostic allegory, symbolic associations between Gospel narratives and gnostic myth, as well as deconstruction of the biblical text are all anathema.

Some gnostic writings such as *Apocryphon of James* and *Gospel of Mary* appear to recognize that the Gospel canon and apostolic authority must be claimed for gnostic exegesis. Individual disciples of Jesus, James and Mary Magdalene, are shown to have possessed insight superior to that of the apostles as a group. On the one hand, *Apocryphon of James* suggests that the Twelve were so hostile to the coming gnostic race that they could not remain in Jerusalem to participate in salvation. On the other hand, *Gospel of Mary* suggests that the Twelve were unable to fulfill the commission to preach throughout the world until they had been awakened to gnosis. Gnostic Christians might even accept a canon of four Gospels and Acts as public teaching. But that canon will not lead to knowledge of the Father unless the revelations of the heavenly Christ are used to interpret its content. Both the meditation on the book in *Gospel of Truth* and the docetic passion account of *Apocalypse of Peter* provide examples of such teaching. *Apocalypse of Peter* even sets the authority of the apostle Peter over against the attempts by ignorant bishops and deacons to stamp out the Gnostics.

ABBREVIATIONS

Targumic Material

Tg. Ps.-J.	*Targum Pseudo-Jonathan*

Jewish Pseudepigrapha

Apoc. Mos.	*Apocalypse of Moses*
2 Bar.	Syriac *Apocalypse of Baruch*
1 Clem.	*1 Clement*
1 Enoch	Ethiopic *Enoch*
2 Enoch	Slavonic *Enoch*
Ep. Arist.	*Epistle of Aristeas*
Jos. Asen.	*Joseph and Asenath*
Jub.	*Jubilees*
T. Naph.	*Testament of Naphtali*
T. Reuben	*Testament of Reuben*

Dead Sea Scrolls and Related Writings

CD	Cairo *Damascus Document*
1QapGen	*Genesis Apocryphon*
1QH	*Hôdāyôt (Thanksgiving Hymns)*
1QpHab	*Pesher on Habakkuk*
1QS	*Community Rule (Manual of Discipline)*

Philo of Alexandria

Fug.	*On Flight and Finding*
Leg. All.	*Allegorical Interpretation*

Opif. Mund.	*On the Creation*
Spec. Leg.	*The Special Laws*
Vit. Mos.	*Life of Moses*

Early Christian Writers

Adv. Haer.	Irenaeus, *Against Heresies (Adversus Haereses)*
1 Apol.	Justin Martyr, *1 Apology*
Bib. Ant.	Ps.-Philo, *Biblical Antiquities*
Com. on Joh.	Origen, *Commentary on John*
Exc. Theod.	Theodotos, *Excerpts from Theodotos*
Hist. Laus.	Palladius, *Lausiac History*
Leg.	Athenagoras, *Embassy for the Christians*
PL	*Patrologiae Series Latina* (Migne)
Ps.-Clem. Hom.	*Pseudo-Clementine Homilies*
Ref.	Hippolytus, *Refutation of all Heresies*
Serm.	Augustine, *Sermones*
Strom.	Clement of Alexandria, *Stromata (Miscellanies)*

Gnostic Writings

Allogenes	*Allogenes*
Ap. Jas.	*Apocryphon of James*
Ap. John	*Apocryphon of John*
Apoc. Adam	*Apocalypse of Adam*
1 Apoc. Jas.	*First Apocalypse of James*
2 Apoc. Jas.	*Second Apocalypse of James*
Apoc. Pet.	*Apocalypse of Peter*
Auth. Teach.	*Authoritative Teaching*
BG	(Codex) Berolinensis Gnosticus
CG	(Codex) Cairensis Gnosticus
C.H.	Corpus Hermetica
Dial Sav.	*Dialogue of the Savior*
Ep. Pet. Phil.	*Letter of Peter to Philip*
Eugnostos	*Eugnostos the Blessed*
Exeg. Soul	*Exegesis on the Soul*
Gos. Eg.	*Gospel of the Egyptians*
Gos. Mary	*Gospel of Mary*
Gos. Phil.	*Gospel of Philip*

Gos. Thom.	*Gospel of Thomas*
Gos. Truth	*Gospel of Truth*
Hyp. Arch.	*Hypostasis of the Archons*
NH	*Nag Hammadi*
NHC	Nag Hammadi Codex
Orig. World	*On the Origin of the World*
Pist. Soph.	*Pistis Sophia*
Soph. Jes. Chr.	*Sophia of Jesus Christ*
Steles Seth	*Three Steles of Seth*
Testim Tr.	*Testimony of Truth*
Treat. Res.	*Treatise on Resurrection*
Treat. Seth	*Second Treatise of the Great Seth*
Tri. Trac.	*Tripartite Tractate*
Trim. Prot.	*Trimorphic Protennoia*
Zost.	*Zostrianos*

Periodicals, Reference Works, and Serials

AB	Anchor Bible
BCNH	Bibliothèque Copte de Nag Hammadi
BETL	Bibliotheca ephemeridum theologicarum lovaniensium
BZNW	Beihefte zur *ZNW*
CBQ	*Catholic Biblical Quarterly*
CBQMS	Catholic Biblical Quarterly—Monograph Series
CRINT	Compendia rerum iudicarum ad novum testamentum
HDR	Harvard Dissertations in Religion
HeyJ	*Heythrop Journal*
HTR	*Harvard Theological Review*
HTS	Harvard Theological Studies
ICC	International Critical Commentary
Int	*Interpretation*
JAC	*Jahrbuch für Antike und Christentum*
JBL	*Journal of Biblical Literature*
JRS	*Journal of Roman Studies*
JSNT	*Journal for the Study of the New Testament*
JTS	*Journal of Theological Studies*
Mus.	*Muséon*

NHLE	*The Nag Hammadi Library in English*, ed. James M. Robinson (San Francisco: Harper & Row, 1988, third edition)
NHS	Nag Hammadi Studies
NICNT	New International Commentary on the New Testament
NovT	*Novum Testamentum*
NTS	*New Testament Studies*
OBT	Overtures to Biblical Theology
PTS	Patristische Texte und Studien
RelSRev	*Religious Studies Review*
RevScRel	*Revue des sciences religieuses*
SBLDS	SBL Dissertation Series
SBT	Studies in Biblical Theology
SJT	*Scottish Journal of Theology*
SNTSMS	Society for New Testament Study Monograph Series
SR	*Studies in Religion/Sciences religieuses*
ST	*Studia theologica*
VC	*Vigiliae christianae*
WBC	Word Biblical Commentary
WUNT	Wissenschaftliche Untersuchungen zum Neuen Testament
ZNW	*Zeitschrift für die neutestamentliche Wissenschaft*
ZPE	*Zeitschrift für Papyrologie und Epigraphik*

NOTES

Introduction

1. For the convenience of the reader, the references to the Coptic text of the Nag Hammadi tractates will be followed by the page number in the standard English translation (*NHLE;* see Abbreviations).

2. C. Kannengiesser points out that by the beginning of the fourth century C.E. Alexandrian Christianity shifted away from the theoretical speculative theology of the intellectuals to the basic catechesis of the populist majority ("Athanasius of Alexandria vs. Arius: The Alexandrian Crisis," *The Roots of Egyptian Christianity* [ed. B. A. Pearson and J. E. Goehring; Philadelphia: Fortress, 1986] 204–15). On the decline of Manicheism in the Roman world see P. Brown, "The Diffusion of Manichaeism in the Roman Empire," *JRS* 59 (1969) 92–103.

3. See the account of the discovery by J. M. Robinson, "Introduction," in *NHLE,* 1–26.

4. Cf. R. McL. Wilson, *Gnosis and the New Testament* (Oxford: Oxford Univ. Press, 1968).

5. Cf. R. Bultmann, *The Gospel of John* (trans. G. R. Beasley-Murray; Philadelphia: Westminster, 1971). Bultmann insists that the gnostic metaphors, not their Jewish antecedents, are necessary to understand John's Gospel. Even the image of Jesus, the revealer, as shepherd derives from that variant (pp. 366–69).

6. Cf. the detailed studies of individual exegetical traditions from their origins in Judaism into the gnostic writings found at Nag Hammadi by B. Pearson, *Gnosticism, Judaism, and Egyptian Christianity* (Minneapolis: Fortress, 1990) 10–123.

7. For evidence of such developments, see G. A. G. Stroumsa, *Another*

Seed: Studies in Gnostic Mythology (NHS 24; Leiden: Brill, 1984).

8. Cf. B. Pearson, "Jewish Sources in Gnostic Literature," in *Jewish Writings of the Second Temple Period* (ed. M. Stone; CRINT II/2; Assen: Van Gorcum; Philadelphia: Fortress, 1984) 443–81.

9. Ibid., 479.

10. Cf. B. Pearson, "Jewish Haggadic Traditions in the *Testimony of Truth* from Nag Hammadi (CG IX,3)," in *Gnosticism*, 39–51. In its present form *Testimony of Truth* is an attack on the heresies of both orthodox Christianity and nonascetic gnostic groups. However, the sections of haggadah are derived from inner-Jewish exegetical debates.

11. H.-M. Schenke, "The Phenomenon of Gnostic Sethianism," in *The Rediscovery of Gnosticism*, vol. 2, *Sethian Gnosticism* (ed. B. Layton; Leiden: Brill, 1981) 607–12.

12. See the more judicious evaluation of the evidence for non-Christian Gnosticism by G. W. MacRae, "Nag Hammadi and the New Testament," in *Gnosis: Festschrift für Hans Jonas* (ed. B. Aland; Göttingen: Vandenhoeck & Ruprecht, 1978) 144–57.

Chapter 1
The Search for Pre-Christian Gnosticism

1. See the introductions and conclusions to the *Apocryphon of James* (I 1,1—2,23; *NHLE*, 30; 16,3-30; *NHLE*, 37) and the *Apocryphon of John* (II 1,1-32; *NHLE*, 105; 3,29—32,5; *NHLE*, 122–23); also P. Perkins, *The Gnostic Dialogue* (New York: Paulist, 1980) 37–58.

2. For example, the *Apocalypse of Adam* (V 85,19-31; *NHLE*, 286); the *Hypostasis of the Archons* (II 96,19-35; *NHLE*, 169); *Zostrianos* (VIII 129,26—130,13; *NHLE*, 430); *Paraphrase of Shem* (VII 1,1-25; *NHLE*, 341–42; 48,8—49,9; *NHLE*, 361).

3. Cf. Irenaeus, *Adv. Haer.* 1.23–31 (W. Foerster, *Gnosis*, vol. 1, *Patristic Evidence* [trans. R. McL. Wilson; Oxford: Clarendon, 1972] 27–43). For an argument that the sectarian divisions were a creation of the church fathers, see F. Wisse, "The Nag Hammadi Library and the Heresiologists," *VC* 25 (1971) 205–23.

4. Irenaeus, *Adv. Haer.* 1.23.2–4 (Foerster, *Gnosis*, 1:30–31); on the recent scholarly attempts to discover the "historical" Simon see W. Meeks, "Simon Magus in Recent Research," *RelSRev* 3 (1977) 137–42.

5. Cf. G. Lüdemann, *Untersuchungen zur simonianischen Gnosis* (Göttingen: Vandenhoeck & Ruprecht, 1975) 41–47.

6. Hippolytus, *Ref.* 6.20.3 (Foerster, *Gnosis*, 1:31).

7. Justin Martyr, *1 Apol.* 26.56; Irenaeus, *Adv. Haer.* 1.23.1. See the reproduction in K. Rudolph, *Gnosis* (trans. P. W. Coxon and K. H. Kuhn; ed. R. McL. Wilson; San Francisco: Harper & Row, 1983) 394–95.

8. Foerster, *Gnosis*, 1:32–33.

9. Rudolph, *Gnosis*, 297–98.

10. K. Beyschlag, *Simon Magus und die christliche Gnosis* (WUNT 16; Tübingen: Mohr-Siebeck, 1975) 77–79.

11. Meeks, "Simon Magus," 141.

12. Cf. Rudolph, *Gnosis*, 30–32; E. Yamauchi has consistently rejected all arguments for a pre-Christian Gnosticism ("Some Alleged Evidences for Pre-Christian Gnosticism," in *New Dimensions in New Testament Study* [ed. R. N. Longenecker and M. C. Tenney; Grand Rapids: Zondervan, 1974] 46–70).

13. A. Veilleux ("Monasticism and Gnosis," in *The Roots of Egyptian Christianity* [ed. B. A. Pearson and J. E. Goehring; Philadelphia: Fortress, 1986] 271–306) downplays the significance scholars have attached to the letters in the binding of Codex VII and the burial in the vicinity of early Pachomian monastic sites. These contingent facts are not sufficient to explain why the manuscripts were collected in the first place or why and by whom they were eventually buried.

14. Rudolph, *Gnosis*, 329–30.

15. Ibid., 363–64.

16. A. Segal, *Two Powers in Heaven* (Leiden: Brill, 1977).

17. Cf. Origen, *Contra Celsum* 5.61–62; 6.24–38.

18. Rudolph, *Gnosis*, 277–82.

19. On Gnosticism and early Christianity as emerging religious phenomena, see Rudolph, *Gnosis*, 286–89.

20. H. Jonas, *The Gnostic Religion* (rev. ed.; Boston: Beacon, 1963).

21. Cf. M. Tardieu, *Trois Mythes Gnostiques: Adam, Éros et les animaux d'Égypte dans un écrit de Nag Hammadi (II, 5)* (Paris: Études Augustiniennes, 1974); G. A. G. Stroumsa, *Another Seed: Studies in Gnostic Mythology* (NHS 24; Leiden: Brill, 1984).

22. Stroumsa, *Another Seed*, 1–4.

23. Cf. H. M. Jackson, "The Origin in Ancient Incantory *Voces Magicae* of Some of the Names in the Sethian Gnostic System," *VC* 43 (1989) 69–79.

24. See the discussion of the text-critical, source-critical, and form-critical work that remains sorely lacking in Nag Hammadi studies by H.-M. Schenke, "The Phenomenon of Gnostic Sethianism," in *The Rediscovery of Gnosticism*, vol. 2, *Sethian Gnosticism* (ed. B. Layton; Leiden: Brill, 1981) 598–602.

25. Cf. Rudolph, *Gnosis*, 53–59, 307–8; Schenke, "Phenomenon," 597–607; J. Turner, "Sethian Gnosticism: A Literary History," in *Nag Hammadi, Gnosticism and Early Christianity* (ed. C. W. Hedrick and R. Hodgson, Jr.; Peabody, Mass.: Hendrickson, 1986) 57–59.

26. A. Cook, *Myth and Language* (Bloomington: Indiana Univ. Press, 1980) 3.

27. The abstract terminology itself requires communal learning. Unlike concrete imagery, it does not belong to the common sense world of individ-

uals. Nor could gnostic readings of Genesis be formulated on the basis of a naive or first-level reading of the text.

28. Cf. Jonas, *Gnostic Religion*, 320–40.

29. Cf. P. Ricoeur, "Preface to Bultmann," in *The Conflict of Interpretations* (ed. D. Ihde; Evanston: Northwestern Univ. Press, 1974) 392.

30. *2 Bar.* 56:10-14 blames the women for seducing the angels.

31. See the detailed discussion of this whole mythological complex in Stroumsa, *Another Seed*, 38–70.

32. *Tg. Ps. J.* on Gen 4:1; Stroumsa, *Another Seed*, 47–48. These traditions are attached to Gen 4:1, "I have begotten a man with the Lord," and Gen 3:13, "the serpent tempted me," in which "tempted" is understood to mean "seduced."

33. John 8:44; 1 John 3:8; Stroumsa, *Another Seed*, 49.

34. Cf. B. Pearson, "The Figure of Norea in Gnostic Literature," in *Gnosticism, Judaism, and Egyptian Christianity* (Minneapolis: Fortress, 1990) 84–94.

35. J. Neyrey, "Body Language in 1 Corinthians: The Use of Anthropological Models for Understanding Paul's Opponents," *Semeia* 35 (1986) 129–70.

36. P. Brown, *The Making of Late Antiquity* (Cambridge: Harvard Univ. Press, 1978) 75.

37. *Kephalaia* VI 33.29-32; cf. Stroumsa, *Another Seed*, 101–2; L. Koenen, "From Baptism to the Gnosis of Manichaeism," in *Rediscovery of Gnosticism*, 2:734–56.

38. Stroumsa, *Another Seed*, 101.

Chapter 2
Gnosticism and the Jewish Connection

1. Cf. I. Gruenwald, "Aspects of the Jewish Gnostic Controversy," in *The Rediscovery of Gnosticism*, vol. 2, *Sethian Gnosticism* (ed. B. Layton; Leiden: Brill, 1981) 713–23.

2. E.g., J. E. Fossum, *The Name of God and the Angel of the Lord* (WUNT 36; Tübingen: Mohr-Siebeck, 1985).

3. Justin's *Baruch* (Hippolytus, *Ref.* 5.26.14–18; W. Foerster, *Gnosis*, vol. 1, *Patristic Evidence* [trans. R. McL. Wilson; Oxford: Clarendon, 1972] 54–55); and the repentance of Sabaoth (*Hyp. Arch.* II 95,13—96,3; *NHLE*, 168; *Orig. World* II 103,32—106,19; *NHLE*, 175–76); cf. F. Fallon, *The Enthronement of Sabaoth: Jewish Elements in Gnostic Creation Myths* (NHS 10; Leiden: Brill, 1978).

4. Fallon, *Enthronement*, 80–87.

5. The throne-chariot motif must derive from Judaism. It does not appear in this form in the NT; so Fallon, ibid., 57–59.

6. Ibid., 101–4.

7. Cf. G. A. G. Stroumsa, *Another Seed: Studies in Gnostic Mythology* (NHS 24; Leiden: Brill, 1984) 11–13.

8. Cf. M. Williams, *The Immovable Race: A Gnostic Designation and the Theme of Stability in Late Antiquity* (NHS 29; Leiden: Brill, 1985).

9. Fossum, *Name of God*, 121–22.

10. Cf. Williams, *Immovable Race*, 54–68.

11. *Hyp. Arch.* 89,31-32; *NHLE*, 164 (cf. *Orig. World* 113,21-34; *NHLE*, 181); M. Tardieu, *Trois Mythes Gnostiques* (Paris: Études Augustiniennes, 1974) 106–7.

12. *Orig. World* 113,34—114,1; *NHLE*, 181.

13. Possibly associated with the tradition that the Grigori were larger than the giants (*2 Enoch* 18); so Stroumsa, *Another Seed*, 55 n. 77.

14. Ps.-Philo, *Bib. Ant.* 1.1; see the extensive discussion of Norea's name in B. Pearson, "The Figure of Norea in Gnostic Literature," in *Gnosticism, Judaism, and Egyptian Christianity* (Minneapolis: Fortress, 1990) 88–92.

15. So Pearson, "Norea," 92.

16. *Norea* IX 27,11—29,5; *NHLE*, 447.

17. Stroumsa, *Another Seed*, 56.

18. Ibid., 57.

19. The interpretation of Adamas as "adamantine earth" has been introduced by the author of *Origin of the World*. The expression "adamantine earth" appears in *Hypostasis of the Archons* (CG II 88,13-14; *NHLE*, 163) without any connection to the name Adamas. There it refers to the heavenly realm from which the spirit comes (cf. Williams, *Immovable Race*, 65).

20. Hippolytus, *Ref.* 5.7.35-36; Williams, *Immovable Race*, 65.

21. B. Pearson, "Jewish Sources in Gnostic Literature," in *Jewish Writings of the Second Temple Period* (ed. M. Stone; CRINT II/2; Assen: Van Gorcum; Philadelphia: Fortress, 1984) 443–81.

22. Ibid., 453–54.

23. The descent of the angels (= archons) to teach magic arts reappears in *Origin of the World* (123,4-15; *NHLE*, 186) and the *Pistis Sophia* (1,15). Echoes of *2 Enoch* have been suggested in *Zostrianos:* the seer becomes like the glories that he beholds in the heavenly world (*Zost.* CG VIII 5,15-17; *NHLE*, 408; *2 Enoch* 9); even the angels do not know the secrets told the seer (*Zost.* 128,15-18; *NHLE*, 429). See M. Scopello, "The Apocalypse of Zostrianos (NH VIII,1) and the Book of the Secrets of Enoch," *VC* 34 (1980) 376–85.

24. Cf. I. Gruenwald, "Manichaeism and Judaism in Light of the Cologne Mani Codex," *ZPE* 50 (1983) 29–45; for a detailed treatment of the preservation of Sethian gnostic mythemes in Manichean traditions see Stroumsa, *Another Seed*, 145–67.

25. See the judicious discussion of this problem by Stroumsa, *Another Seed*, 164–67.

26. B. Pearson, "Jewish Haggadic Traditions in *The Testimony of Truth*," in *Gnosticism*, 39–51. The beginning of the first example has been marked by the scribe with a horizontal line in the margin of the manuscript (ibid., 41).

27. B. Pearson, "The Testimony of Truth," in *Nag Hammadi Codices IX and X* (ed. B. Pearson; NHS 15; Leiden: Brill, 1981) 192–93.

28. Ibid., 167–68.

29. Ibid., 164–65; K. Koschorke, *Die Polemik der Gnostiker gegen das kirchliche Christentum* (NHS 12; Leiden: Brill, 1978) 150–51.

30. T. Tobin, *The Creation of Man: Philo and the History of Interpretation* (CBQMS 14; Washington: Catholic Biblical Association, 1983), 37–38.

31. G. A. G. Stroumsa, "Form(s) of God: Some Notes on Metatron and Christ," *HTR* 76 (1983) 269–88.

32. Pearson, "Jewish Sources," 458.

33. Cf. Pearson, "Philo, Gnosis and the New Testament," in *Gnosticism*, 175–77.

34. But the next sentence says that Epinoia awakened them. Clearly the earlier reading of the text had the female Wisdom figure as the agent of revelation.

35. The short version acknowledges a single descent of the Mother prior to the coming of the Savior (BG 76,1-2; Foerster, *Gnosis*, 1:120).

36. K. King ("Sophia and Christ in the *Apocryphon of John*," in *Images of the Feminine in Gnosticism* [ed. K. King; Philadelphia: Fortress, 1988] 168–71) claims that in general the long version has gone further in substituting male savior figures for the feminine Wisdom than the short version.

37. Cf. P. Perkins, "Apocalypse of Adam: Genre and Function of a Gnostic Apocalypse," *CBQ* 39 (1977) 382–95.

38. Cf. B. Pearson, "Jewish Elements in *Corpus Hermeticum I (Poimandres)*," in *Gnosticism*, 138–39.

39. Ibid., 142–44.

40. So Stroumsa, *Another Seed*, 98.

Chapter 3
Gnostic Influence and the New Testament

1. Cf. the discussion of NT Christology as the formation of a new communal identity by Maurice Casey, *From Jewish Prophet to Gentile God: The Origins and Development of New Testament Christology* (Cambridge: James Clarke; Louisville: Westminster/John Knox, 1991) 11–40.

2. Cf. W. Schmithals, *Neues Testament und Gnosis* (Darmstadt: Wissenschaftliche Buchgesellschaft, 1984).

3. H. Jonas, *The Gnostic Religion* (rev. ed.; Boston: Beacon, 1963) 31–97.

4. H.-M. Schenke, "Die neutestamentliche Christologie und der gnostische Erlöser," in *Gnosis und Neues Testament* (ed. K.-W. Tröger; Berlin: Evangelische Verlagsanstalt, 1973) 208–9; also Schmithals, *Gnosis*, 14–15.

5. Schenke, "Christologie," 210.

6. This tendency is most marked in the Fourth Gospel, where it belongs to the polemic against the claims of the Jewish tradition to "know God." Moses, Jacob, Abraham, and Isaiah are all restricted to having seen Jesus.

7. F. Wisse, "Prolegomena to the Study of the New Testament and Gnosis," in *The New Testament and Gnosis: Essays in honour of Robert McL. Wilson* (ed. A. H. B. Logan and A. J. M. Wedderburn; Edinburgh: T. & T. Clark, 1983) 140–42.

8. J. Blenkinsopp, "Interpretation and the Tendency to Sectarianism: An Aspect of Second Temple History," in *Jewish and Christian Self-Definition*, vol. 2, *Aspects of Judaism in the Greco-Roman Period* (ed. E. P. Sanders; Philadelphia: Fortress, 1981) 14–26.

9. H. Koester, "One Jesus, Four Primitive Gospels," in *Trajectories Through Early Christianity* (with J. M. Robinson; Philadelphia: Fortress, 1971) 158–204.

10. Wisse, "Prolegomena," 143.

11. See A. Segal, *Paul the Convert* (New Haven: Yale Univ. Press, 1990) 34–71. Segal does insist that an apocalyptic mysticism is critical if one is to account for Paul's willingness to depart from major elements in the religious identity of Judaism. This insistence highlights the importance of Schenke's claim ("Christologie," 210) that ecstatic identification with the revealer is a formal feature of gnostic religious experience.

12. Schmithals, *Gnosis*, 30–33.

13. Although this general observation certainly appears to be true from what the church fathers say about gnostic founders, the texts themselves do not give direct evidence for such a sociological conclusion. Schmithals gives a pneumatic reading to the terms *apostle* (1 Cor 14:37-38) and *prophet* (1 Cor 12:28; Eph 2:20; 4:11), but there is no evidence for their derivation from Jewish Christian gnosticizing (ibid., 33–34).

14. Ibid., 48–67.

15. Ibid., 63–64.

16. H. Koester, "The History-of-Religions School, Gnosis, and the Gospel of John," *ST* 40 (1986) 115–36.

17. Ibid., 119–26.

18. Ibid., 123–24.

19. Ibid., 125–26.

20. Ibid., 129–31.

21. The missionary efforts attested in Paul's epistles are all attached to cities that are Roman colonies. Despite Acts 17, it is probable that Paul's efforts in a city that had an ancient and continuing tradition were much less successful. Note the apparent lack of success at Athens suggested by 1 Thess 3:1-5.

22. Koester, "History-of-Religions School," 131.

23. Wisse, "Prolegomena," 139–41.

24. Ibid., 143.

Chapter 4
Reconstructing Gnostic History

1. G. Filoramo (*A History of Gnosticism* [trans. A. Alcock; Oxford: Black-well, 1990]) provides a synthetic overview rather than a detailed hypothesis about the origins and development of Gnosticism.

2. S. Pétrement's attempt to maintain the traditional view that gnostic speculation emerges as a Christian heresy (*An Alien God* [trans. C. Harrison; San Francisco: HarperCollins, 1990) is simply outdated in its analysis of the tradition history of the Nag Hammadi materials.

3. Cf. G. W. MacRae, "The Jewish Background of the Gnostic Sophia Myth," *NovT* 12 (1970) 86–101.

4. E.g., *The Hymn of the Pearl* (*Acts of Thomas* 108-13; cf. W. Foerster, *Gnosis*, vol. 1, *Patristic Evidence* (trans. R. McL. Wilson; Oxford: Clarendon, 1972) 355–58; H. Jonas, *The Gnostic Religion* (rev. ed.; Boston: Beacon, 1963) 112–29; K. Rudolph, *Gnosis* (trans. P. W. Coxon and K. H. Kuhn; ed. R. McL. Wilson; San Francisco: Harper & Row, 1983) 283; P.-H. Poirier, *L'Hymne de la Perle des Actes de Thomas* (Louvain: Louvain-La-Neuve, 1981). Poirier's commentary on the *Hymn of the Pearl* points to numerous linguistic and geographical features that indicate that the hymn originated in an Iranian-Parthian milieu probably no later than the beginning of the third century C.E. (p. 317).

5. *Apoc. Adam* V 77,27—82,19; *NHLE*, 282–85; D. Parrott, "The Thirteen Kingdoms of the Apocalypse of Adam: Origin, Meaning and Significance," *NovT* 31 (1989) 67–87.

6. Cf. Rudolph, *Gnosis*, 214–15, 285–87. Rudolph does not consider the possibility that cultic practice may have preceded new mythological formulations.

7. M. Casey, *From Jewish Prophet to Gentile God: The Origins and Development of New Testament Christology* (Cambridge: James Clarke; Louisville: Westminster/John Knox, 1991) 11–16.

8. Ibid., 16.

9. Cf. B. Pearson, *Gnosticism, Judaism, and Egyptian Christianity* (Minneapolis: Fortress, 1990) 9.

10. E.g., *Hyp. Arch.*, II 95,13—96,3; *NHLE*, 168.

11. Cf. R. Lane Fox, *Pagans and Christians* (New York: Knopf, 1986) 38–261.

12. Ibid., 318–19, 479–82.

13. For a discussion of the impact of such status dissonance on conversions to Christianity in this period see W. Meeks, *The First Urban Christians* (New Haven: Yale Univ. Press, 1983) 52.

14. Cf. Rudolph, *Gnosis*, 288–94; H. A. Green, *The Economic and Social Origins of Gnosticism* (SBLDS 77; Atlanta: Scholars Press, 1985).

15. Rudolph, *Gnosis*, 9–25.

16. Ibid., 294–95.

17. Hippolytus, *Ref.* 6.9-18 (M. Marchovich, *Hippolytus Refutatio Omnium Haeresium* [PTS 25; New York and Berlin: de Gruyter, 1986] 214–25); for an argument that this section of Hippolytus paraphrases a Simonian gnostic work, *Apophasis Megale*, see J. Frickel, *Die Apophasis Megale in Hippolys Refutatio VI, 9–18: Eine Paraphrase zur Apophasis Simons* (Orientalia Christiana Analecta 182; Rome: Pontificium Institutum Orientalium Studiorum, 1968) 88–202.

18. Cf. *Ps.-Clem. Hom.* 3.29-58; *Acts of Peter* 2-8.

19. Rudolph, *Gnosis*, 158–59.

20. R. E. Brown, *The Epistles of John* (AB 30; Garden City: Doubleday, 1982) 73–79.

21. Rudolph, *Gnosis*, 298–308.

22. Cf. G. Lüdemann, "Zur Geschichte des ältesten Christentums in Rom I. Valentin und Marcion II. Ptolemäus und Justin," *ZNW* 70 (1979) 86–114; Ptolemy may have been the Christian martyr referred to in Justin, *Apol.* 2.2.9 (pp. 100–102).

23. Irenaeus, *Adv. Haer.* 1.24.3-7; Foerster, *Gnosis*, 1.58–62; Hippolytus, *Ref.* 7.20-27; Foerster, *Gnosis*, 1.64–74; (cf. Rudolph, *Gnosis*, 310–12; B. Layton, *Gnostic Scriptures* [Garden City: Doubleday, 1987] 417).

24. Cf. C. Osborne, *Rethinking Early Greek Philosophy* (London: Duckworth, 1987) 68–84.

25. Cf. Hippolytus's reference to the "universal serpent" (*ho katholikē ophis*; *Ref.* 5.16.8).

26. E.g., *Orig. World* CG II 97,26—98,7; *NHLE*, 171–72.

27. Marchovich, *Refutatio*, 35–51.

28. Cf. *Tri. Trac.* CG I 118,14—119,32; *NHLE*, 94–96.

29. Rudolph, *Gnosis*, 323–24.

30. Cf. Foerster, *Gnosis*, 1:154–61.

31. J. Turner, "Sethian Gnosticism: A Literary History," in *Nag Hammadi, Gnosticism and Early Christianity* (ed. C. W. Hedrick and R. Hodgson, Jr.; Peabody, Mass.: Hendrickson, 1986).

32. Ibid., 59–62.

33. CG II 30,12—31,25; *NHLE*, 122; Turner, "Sethian Gnosticism," 62.

34. A similar equation appears in the fragment of a cosmological source similar to *Apocryphon of John* preserved in Irenaeus (*Adv. Haer.* 1.29.1-4; Foerster, *Gnosis*, 1:104–5; cf. Turner, "Sethian Gnosticism," 64).

35. This section is replete with images that are also found in the prologue to the Fourth Gospel.

36. It is typical of the second century to treat the expression "Son of man" as a reference to the humanity of Jesus rather than to his identification with a heavenly figure as depicted in Dan 7:14.

37. Turner, "Sethian Gnosticism," 64–65.

38. Turner associates these developments with a similar transformation

in the Fourth Gospel ("Sethian Gnosticism," 67–68). There Wisdom and Word speculation have created a Christology that emphasizes the descent of the divine revealer. Baptism has been reinterpreted as well. The traditional story becomes John the Baptist's recognition of Jesus' divine status. Jesus is the source of living water (John 4:7-15; 7:37-39).

39. B. Layton, *Gnostic Scriptures* (Garden City: Doubleday, 1987) 359–61. Layton thinks that the Thomas tradition may have influenced the emergence of the heavenly twin theme in Mani's autobiography.

40. Ibid., xv–xvi.

Chapter 5
Jesus as Teacher of Wisdom

1. Cf. B. Layton, ed., *Nag Hammadi Codex II, 2-7* (NHS 20; Leiden: Brill, 1989) 1:38–93; J. S. Kloppenborg, M. W. Meyer, S. J. Patterson, and M. G. Steinhauser, *Q/Thomas Reader* (Sonoma: Polebridge, 1990) 77–155.

2. The Greek fragments of *Gospel of Thomas* are variants of the sayings that formed the basis for the Coptic collection. H. Attridge thinks that the Coptic translator might have used one of the Greek texts ("Greek Fragments," in *Nag Hammadi Codex II, 2-7*, 96–112).

3. Cf. W. D. Davies and D. C. Allison, *A Critical and Exegetical Commentary on the Gospel According to Saint Matthew*, vol. 1, *Matthew I–VII* (ICC; Edinburgh: T. & T. Clark, 1988) 116–24.

4. Cf. Kloppenborg et al., *Q/Thomas*, 23–25.

5. Cf. J. M. Robinson, "On Bridging the Gulf from Q to the Gospel of Thomas (or Vice Versa)," in *Nag Hammadi, Gnosticism and Early Christianity* (ed. C. W. Hedrick and R. Hodgson, Jr.; Peabody, Mass.: Hendrickson, 1986) 145–64; H. Koester (*Ancient Gospels* [Philadelphia: Trinity, 1990] 87–99) admits this point in theory but tends to violate it in practice, preferring reconstructions of sayings material from gnostic sources to the Synoptic tradition. See the criticism of the excessive claims of Koester and his students by J. Meier, *A Marginal Jew* (Garden City: Doubleday, 1991) 142–51.

6. Cf. Koester, *Ancient Gospels*, 95.

7. E.g., 1 Cor 2:9; Matt 11:25-30; Luke 7:35; Matt 23:37-39 (Koester, *Ancient Gospels*, 56–59).

8. A phenomenon that is also evident in Matthew's use of Mark. On this point see Meier, *A Marginal Jew*, 162 n. 122.

9. As in the sayings on wealth (Luke 14:11-26); see L. Schottroff and W. Stegemann, *Jesus and the Hope of the Poor* (trans. M. J. O'Connell; Maryknoll, N.Y.: Orbis, 1986) 72–92.

10. The text is extremely fragmentary. Koester has alleged that *Dialogue of the Savior* contains a development of the sayings traditions that is intermediate between the individual sayings in a collection and the extended discourses of the Fourth Gospel (*Ancient Gospels*, 173–87); H. Koester and

E. Pagels, "Introduction," *Nag Hammadi Codex III, 5* [ed. S. Emmel; NHS 26; Leiden: Brill, 1984] 9–17).

11. Cf. the list in Koester, *Ancient Gospels*, 176–85.

12. This example along with the fragmentary nature of the manuscript makes it difficult to accept Koester's use of *Dialogue of the Savior* to reconstruct pre-Johannine discourse material. Koester has been too confident in asserting a lack of NT allusions in *Dialogue of the Savior.* J. V. Hills is forced to reconstruct an elaborate history of the transmission of proverbial sayings to escape the conclusion that *Dialogue of the Savior* alludes to Matthew ("The Three 'Matthean' Aphorisms in *Dialogue of the Savior* 53," *HTR* 84 [1991] 43–58).

13. For a verbal analysis of the NT allusions in the *Gospel of Truth* see J. A. Williams, *Biblical Interpretation in the Gnostic Gospel of Truth from Nag Hammadi* (SBLDS 79; Atlanta: Scholars Press, 1988) 16–173.

14. The fact that modern scholars read this passage as ironic, because the disciples prove to be as uncomprehending as the crowds, does not discredit the principle of secret teaching. It only moves the level of discerning hearers from within the narrative to the author's audience or reader.

15. Cf. H. Attridge, "The Gospel of Truth as an Exoteric Text," in *Nag Hammadi, Gnosticism and Early Christianity*, 239–55.

16. The Lucan parallel (Luke 14:5) has a "son" or an "ox" instead of a sheep. This substitution increases the value of what has fallen into the pit. But the issue of sheep or cattle who give birth to young in a pit and must be abandoned if the Sabbath law is to be kept appears in Essene legislation. Therefore Matthew appears to represent the earliest version of the saying, and *Gospel of Truth* is dependent on Matthew (Williams, *Biblical Interpretation*, 125).

17. Cf. the Sethian-Ophite system described in Irenaeus (*Adv. Haer.* 1.30.14; W. Foerster, *Gnosis*, vol. 1, *Patristic Evidence* [trans. R. McL. Wilson; Oxford: Clarendon, 1972] 93). Christ is enthroned at the right hand of Ialdabaoth in order to receive the souls of the elect.

18. E.g., *Adv. Haer.* 1.pref.2.

19. Also Prov 1:28; Sir 15:7. The prophets are rejected messengers of divine wisdom (Luke 11:49-51).

20. See the discussion of these sayings in R. A. Piper, *Wisdom in the Q-Tradition: The Aphoristic Teaching of Jesus* (SNTSMS 61; Cambridge: Cambridge Univ. Press, 1989) 161–84.

21. Cf. Sir 24:23-29; Bar 4:1; Piper, *Wisdom*, 173–74.

22. E.g., J.-É. Ménard, *L'Évangile selon Thomas* (NHS 5; Leiden: Brill, 1975) 89–90.

23. See H. Koester's protest against such gratuitous interpretations of *Gospel of Thomas* ("Three Thomas Parables," in *The New Testament and Gnosis: Essays in honour of Robert McL. Wilson* [ed. A. H. B. Logan and A. J. M. Wedderburn; Edinburgh: T. & T. Clark, 1983] 196–97, 201).

24. As in the *Hymn of the Pearl*; Ménard (*Évangile selon Thomas*, 176–77) assumes that this allegorical interpretation applies to the *Gospel of Thomas* version.

25. Cf. J. A. Fitzmyer, *The Gospel According to Luke* (AB 28, 28A; 2 vols.; Garden City: Doubleday, 1981–85) 2:982.

26. Cf. J. D. Crossan, *Finding Is the First Act* (Philadelphia: Fortress; Missoula, Mont.: Scholars Press, 1979) 60–70.

27. Cf. ibid., 65–66.

28. Ibid., 104–6.

29. C. Hedrick, "The Treasure Parable in Matthew and Thomas," *Foundations and Facets Forum* 2 (1986) 41–55.

30. Ibid., 44–47.

31. Ibid., 48.

32. Hedrick (ibid., 52–53) goes to the extent of arguing that the parable involves a reversal of values that may have deliberately challenged the Torah's rule on lending.

33. Koester, "Three Thomas Parables," 195–203.

34. *Gos. Thom.* 9; Koester, "Three Thomas Parables," 195–96.

35. Koester, "Three Thomas Parables," 198.

36. Ibid., 199.

37. Cf. the extensive discussion of this tradition by D. MacDonald, *There Is No Male and Female: The Fate of a Dominical Saying in Paul and Gnosticism* (HDR 20; Philadelphia: Fortress, 1987) 20–29.

38. Philo, *Opif. Mund.* 134–35; MacDonald, *No Male and Female*, 26–30.

39. See G. Theissen, *Sociology of Early Palestinian Christianity* (trans. J. Bowden; Philadelphia: Fortress, 1978) 10–14. E. Boring rightly insists that the existence of written collections requires some form of settled community and leadership. Itinerant prophets could not produce and circulate written material (*Sayings of the Risen Jesus: Christian Prophecy in the Synoptic Tradition* [SNTSMS 46; Cambridge: Cambridge Univ. Press, 1982] 149).

40. Robinson, "Bridging," 135–42.

41. Cf. Luke 14:1-14; H. Moxnes, *The Economy of the Kingdom* (OBT; Philadelphia: Fortress, 1988) 127–38.

42. Cf. Philo, *Spec. Leg.* 2.30.

43. Contrast 1 Tim 2:8-15 and Paul's insistence that Christians who are married should not seek to change that state or renounce sexuality within marriage (1 Cor 7:1-9).

44. Cf. M. W. Meyer, "Making Mary Male: The Categories 'male' and 'female' in the Gospel of Thomas," *NTS* 31 (1985) 554–70.

45. Cf. R. Cameron, *Sayings Traditions in the Apocryphon of James* (HTS 34; Philadelphia: Fortress, 1984).

46. Ibid., 12–16.

47. Cf. P. Perkins, *The Gnostic Dialogue* (New York: Paulist, 1980) 145–55.

Chapter 6
Gnosis and the Pauline Tradition

1. Cf. W. Schmithals, "The *Corpus Paulinum* and Gnosis," in *The New Testament and Gnosis: Essays in Honour of Robert McL. Wilson* (ed. A. H. B. Logan and A. J. M. Wedderburn; Edinburgh: T. & T. Clark, 1983) 107–13.

2. Ibid., 107. Colossians and Ephesians present a special case. Schmithals argues for the Pauline authorship of a prior version of Colossians that was edited later to produce the version we have by the author of Ephesians (ibid., 119–21).

3. Cf. P. Perkins, "Pauline Anthropology in Light of Nag Hammadi," *CBQ* 48 (1986) 512–22.

4. W. Schmithals, *Neues Testament und Gnosis* (Darmstadt: Wissenschaftliche Buchgesellschaft, 1984) 26–32.

5. Given the spectrum of options for assimilation to the larger culture, it is possible that Paul did advocate accommodating various marks of Jewish identity (1 Cor 9:19-23). On the circumcision of Timothy, see A. Segal, *Paul the Convert* (New Haven: Yale Univ. Press, 1990) 218–23.

6. Schmithals, "*Corpus Paulinum*," 110–11.

7. H. D. Betz (*Galatians* [Hermeneia; Philadelphia: Fortress, 1979] 5–9) provides a cautious assessment of Schmithals's proposal. Betz recognizes that Paul's rhetorical agenda makes it difficult to accept polemical statements as descriptions of the opponents' views. At the same time, it remains difficult to point to any concrete evidence of gnostic mythemes in Galatians.

8. Cf. *Apocryphon of James* (CG I,2), *First Apocalypse of James* (CG V,3) and *Second Apocalypse of James* (CG V,4); C. Gianotto, "La letteratura apocrifa attribuit a Giacomo a Nag Hammadi (NHC I,2; V,3; V,4)," *Augustinianum* 23 (1983) 111–21.

9. Although this is the conventional reading of Galatians, the paucity of evidence leads to widely differing views of what the impulse for Judaizing was. For example, Betz hypothesizes that the practical ethical problems of living "in the Spirit" led the Galatians to seek to place themselves under the Law (*Galatians*, 8–9).

10. Schmithals, "*Corpus Paulinum*," 115–17.

11. Ibid., 121–23.

12. A. T. Lincoln, *Ephesians* (WBC 42; Dallas: Word, 1990) xlviii–lviii.

13. Ibid., lvi.

14. The division of holy days, new moons, festivals, and Sabbaths was common in the postexilic period (cf. 2 Chron 8:13; 31:3; on the sacrifices appropriate to each type of day cf. Ezek 46:1-12).

15. Although the expression "worship of angels" is sometimes taken to imply that followers of this cult worshiped angelic beings (as in the mistaken homage paid to the revealing angel), some interpreters think that

the expression must refer to participation in the heavenly worship of God (so F. O. Francis, "Humility and Angelic Worship in Col 2:18," *ST* 16 [1962] 109–34). Desire to participate in the angelic cult is evident both in the ecstatic speech attached to gnostic baptismal rituals and in the conviction that the enlightened did participate in the praises that the heavenly powers offer to the highest God (cf. *Gos. Eg.* III 44,1-24; *NHLE*, 210). Most scholars continue to maintain that the references to cultic acts in this section imply that "of angels" is an objective genitive designating the recipients of veneration. Although this posture would be unthinkable in a Jewish environment, the syncretism of the Colossians makes it a plausible interpretation (cf. E. Lohse, *Colossians and Philemon* [trans. W. R. Poehlmann and R. J. Karris; Hermeneia; Philadelphia: Fortress, 1971] 117–19).

16. Cf. K. Rudolph, *Gnosis* (trans. P. W. Coxon and K. H. Kuhn; ed. R. McL. Wilson; San Francisco: Harper & Row, 1983) 336–42.

17. Schmithals, "*Corpus Paulinum*," 118–20.

18. Ibid., 121.

19. Col 3:5-11; cf. E. Schweizer, *The Letter to the Colossians* (trans. A. Chester; Minneapolis: Augsburg, 1982) 183–201.

20. R. Yates, "Colossians and Gnosis," *JSNT* 27 (1986) 53–56.

21. Ibid., 58–59.

22. *Gos. Truth* CG II 19,35–21,1; *NHLE*, 41–42; cf. Yates, "Colossians," 60–62.

23. Cf. H. Attridge, "The Gospel of Truth as an Exoteric Text," in *Nag Hammadi, Gnosticism and Early Christianity* (ed. C. W. Hedrick and R. Hodgson, Jr.; Peabody, Mass.: Hendrickson, 1986) 244–47.

24. Schmithals, "*Corpus Paulinum*," 122.

25. Lincoln, *Ephesians*, 352–63.

26. Schmithals, "*Corpus Paulinum*," 122–23. Also see Lincoln, *Ephesians*, lxxvi–lxxxvii.

27. Cf. Lincoln, *Ephesians*, 225–26.

28. Cf. *Tri. Trac.* I 57,34; 58,30; 59,2; *NHLE*, 63–64.

29. *Tri. Trac.* I 94,20-22; *NHLE*, 82.

30. Cf. H. Attridge and E. Pagels, "The Tripartite Tractate," in *Nag Hammadi Codex I (The Jung Codex): Notes* (ed. H. Attridge; NHS 23; Leiden: Brill, 1985) 457–59.

31. Lincoln (*Ephesians*, 259) argues that the author has no particular group of false teachers in mind. Rather, Ephesians seeks to guard the unity of the received apostolic tradition from other possible contenders. The polemic is similar to that in the Pastoral Epistles (e.g., 2 Tim 3:1-9; Titus 1:10-16).

32. E.g., CG II 24,26-31; 26,20-22; 27,31—28,32; *NHLE*, 119–21.

33. Scholars are sharply divided over whether Paul thought that Christ as son of God was preexistent (see J. D. G. Dunn, *Christology in the Making* [Philadelphia: Westminster, 1980] 176–96).

34. C. B. Cousar, *A Theology of the Cross: The Death of Jesus in the Pauline Letters* (OBT; Minneapolis: Fortress, 1990) 11–18. Cousar notes that Paul's use of the cross is not merely limited to polemical settings. It shapes his understanding of the identity that Christians ought to assume.

35. B. Pearson, "Philo, Gnosis and the New Testament," in *Gnosticism, Judaism, and Egyptian Christianity* (Minneapolis: Fortress, 1990) 168–71.

36. Cf. B. Layton, "Treatise on Resurrection," in *Gnostic Scriptures* (Garden City: Doubleday, 1987) 316–24.

37. Ibid., 321.

38. Ibid., 323.

39. *Vit. Mos.* 1.158-59.; cf. M. Williams, *The Immovable Race* (NHS 29; Leiden: Brill, 1985) 14.

40. Pearson, "Philo, Gnosis," 169.

41. Also see P. Perkins, "Pauline Anthropology in Light of Nag Hammadi," *CBQ* 48 (1986) 512–22.

42. E. Käsemann, *Commentary on Romans* (trans. G. W. Bromiley; Grand Rapids: Eerdmans, 1980) 233–34.

43. Although not a sufficient account for all the nuances in his thought, J. C. Beker's apocalyptic reading of Pauline theology is certainly right on the point of Paul's central convictions (*Paul's Apocalyptic Gospel* [Philadelphia: Fortress, 1982]).

44. Betz, *Galatians*, 181–85.

45. Some manuscripts read τὰ πάντα, "the All," a common expression for the Pleroma in second-century gnostic authors.

46. E. Thomassen, *Le Traité Tripartite (NH I, 5)* (BCNH "Textes" 19; Quebec: Presses de l'Université Laval, 1989) 448–49.

47. See the extensive treatment of this tradition in D. MacDonald, *There Is No Male and Female* (HDR 20; Philadelphia: Fortress, 1987). Although most interpreters insist that this tradition is ascetic, J. J. Buckley has defended a contrary view (*Female Fault and Fulfilment in Gnosticism* [Chapel Hill: University of North Carolina Press, 1986] 84–104).

48. Augustine, *Serm.* 216.10; *PL* 38.1082; MacDonald, *No Male and Female*, 61.

49. Cf. *Exeg. Soul* CG II,6 131,29—132,2; 132,34—133,39; *NHLE*, 194–95. On the spiritual marriage as reconstituting androgyny cf. M. Scopello, *L'Exégèse de l'Âme* (NHS 25; Leiden: Brill, 1985) 140–42.

50. Scholars have extensively debated the precise practices to which Paul alludes and the extent to which he is enforcing on the Corinthians a rule grounded in different social circumstances. Some scholars have even argued that this passage was a non-Pauline interpolation (cf. the detailed treatment of exegetical work on this passage in G. Fee, *The First Epistle to the Corinthians* [NICNT; Grand Rapids: Eerdmans, 1987] 491–530).

51. Ibid., 515.

52. So ibid.

53. Cf. Dunn, *Christology*, 106.

54. Cf. the covenant between God and Noah after the flood in *Apoc. Adam* V 70,16—71,8; *NHLE*, 280.

55. Contrast *Gos. Thom.* 114 (*NHLE*, 138); MacDonald, *No Male and Female*, 98–111.

Chapter 7
Redeemer Myths and New Testament Hymns

1. Harnack sees Gnosticism as the extreme instance of the process of hellenizing that created Christian dogma (A. Harnack, *History of Dogma* [trans. N. Buchanan; Boston: Roberts Brothers, 1897] 41–57; 222–42); R. Bultmann, *The Gospel of John* [trans. G. R. Beasley-Murray; Philadelphia: Westminster, 1971] 7–9, 25–31. Cf. H.-M. Schenke, "Die neutestamentliche Christologie und der gnostiche Erlöser," in *Gnosis und Neues Testament* (ed. K.-W. Tröger; Berlin: Evangelische Verlagsanstalt, 1973) 205–29; J. D. G. Dunn, *Christology in the Making* (Philadelphia: Westminster, 1980) 98–101, 113–25.

2. G. W. MacRae, "Gnosticism and the Church of John's Gospel," in *Nag Hammadi, Gnosticism and Early Christianity* (ed. C. W. Hedrick and R. Hodgson, Jr.; Peabody, Mass.: Hendrickson, 1986) 92–93.

3. So A. L. Helmbold, "Redeemer Hymns—Gnostic and Christian," in *New Dimensions in New Testament Study* (ed. R. N. Longenecker and M. C. Tenney; Grand Rapids: Zondervan, 1974) 74.

4. Cf. the criticism of those who inject a concern with incarnational Christology and the earthly Jesus into the debate in the Johannine epistles by M. C. de Boer, "The Death of Jesus Christ and His Coming in the Flesh (1 John 4:2)," *NovT* 33 (1991) 332–44.

5. M. Tardieu (*Codex de Berlin* [Paris: Cerf, 1984] 339–42) proposes a complex tradition history for this hymn that includes Jewish wisdom texts and the prologue to the Fourth Gospel.

6. Although the hymnic lines are clearly independent of the surrounding discourse, they are suited to the exchange between James and Jesus. Therefore the hymnic passage was not a later insertion into the text (so A. Veilleux, *Les Deux Apocalypses de Jacques* [BCNH "Textes" 17; Quebec: Presses de l'Université Laval, 1986] 75).

7. Helmbold, "Redeemer Hymns," 74.

8. For the identification with the suffering servant in Isaiah texts cf. G. W. MacRae, "The Coptic Gnostic Apocalypse of Adam," *HeyJ* 6 (1965) 32–35. L. Schottroff ("Animae naturaliter salvandae," in *Christentum und Gnosis* [ed. W. Eltester; BZNW 37; Berlin: Töpelmann, 1969] 72) suggests that the references to persecution concern the fate of the enlightened Gnostic, not the revealer.

9. At most such editing has introduced minor expansions into what is essentially a sectarian apocalypse dependent on Jewish traditions. See the discussion of the editing of *Apocalypse of Adam* in C. Hedrick, *The Apocalypse of Adam: A Literary and Source Analysis* (SBLDS 46; Chico, Calif.:

Scholars Press, 1980), and B. Pearson, "Jewish Sources in Gnostic Literature," in *Jewish Writings of the Second Temple Period* (ed. M. Stone; CRINT II/2; Assen: Van Gorcum; Philadelphia: Fortress, 1984) 472–74. F. Morard (*L'Apocalypse d'Adam* [NH V,5] [BCNH "Textes" 15; Quebec: Presses de l'Université Laval, 1985] 100) uses the reference to the suffering illuminator as evidence for the Christian character of *Apocalypse of Adam*. Only Christians, she insists, identified suffering with the redeemer. But the references to suffering affliction that the Qumran texts associate with the Righteous Teacher, who is also depicted as one who gives knowledge (of the Law) to those who had been lost in darkness, weakens this argument. G. W. MacRae ("Apocalypse of Adam," in *Nag Hammadi Codices V,2-5 and VI* [NHS 11; ed. D. Parrott; Leiden: Brill, 1979] 178) points to 1QpHab 9:2.

10. Gnostic texts that refer explicitly to the crucifixion of Jesus provide docetic interpretations of the event so that the reader is not deceived into thinking that the revealer actually suffered (e.g., *Treat. Seth* VII 52,25-30; 55,15—56,18; *NHLE*, 364-65).

11. Cf. MacRae, "Apocalypse of Adam," 178–79. This suggestion is rejected by D. Parrott ("The Thirteen Kingdoms of the Apocalypse of Adam: Origin, Meaning and Significance," *NovT* 31 [1989] 75–80). Parrott reaches back to ancient Egyptian religious phraseology in which "being on" or "walking on" the deity's water is a sign of submission to the commandments of the god or goddess. In order to make this idiom fit the *Apocalypse of Adam* examples, Parrott must conclude that receiving glory and power implies that the figures referred to are commissioned as servants of the lower powers.

12. G. A. G. Stroumsa (*Another Seed: Studies in Gnostic Mythology* [NHS 24; Leiden: Brill, 1984] 89–90) suggests that the first twelve explanations all come under the category of "lustful begetting" proper to the rulers of the lower world (V 74,3-4).

13. But the first explanation is badly preserved. The first and twelfth might have been intended to correspond to each other.

14. The cosmology of *Eugnostos the Blessed* (III 84,2-4; *NHLE*, 234) links the divisions of the calendar to the twelve powers and their associates.

15. See Stroumsa, *Another Seed*, 94–96.

16. Ibid., 97–98.

17. Thus there is some textual support for distinguishing the thirteenth from the previous twelve explanations. But scholars have failed to reach any commonly accepted conclusions about the significance of the thirteen items or the origin of this catalog of explanations (see the survey in Parrott, "Thirteen Kingdoms," 70–75).

18. E.g., G. M. Shellrude, "The Apocalypse of Adam: Evidence for a Christian Gnostic Provenance," in *Gnosis and Gnosticism* (ed. M. Krause; NHS 17; Leiden: Brill, 1981) 82–91; F. Morard, "L'Apocalypse d'Adam du

Codex V de Nag Hammadi et sa polémique anti-baptismale," *RevScRel* 51 (1977) 214–33.

19. Stroumsa, *Another Seed*, 100–103.

20. Ibid., 100.

21. Cf. Parrott, "Thirteen Kingdoms," 70.

22. Most notably Hedrick (*Apocalypse of Adam*, 185–215), whose basic source analysis has been adopted by others (cf. Pearson, "Jewish Sources," 471–72).

23. Cf. *Apoc. Adam* V 83,8—84,3; *NHLE*, 285; so Schottroff, "Animae," 69–70, 81.

24. K. Rudolph, *Gnosis* (trans. P. W. Coxon and K. H. Kuhn; ed. R. McL. Wilson; San Francisco: Harper & Row, 1983) 152.

25. See P. Perkins, "New Testament Christologies in Gnostic Transformation," in *The Future of Early Christianity: Essays in Honor of Helmut Koester* (ed. B. A Pearson; Minneapolis: Fortress, 1991) 433–41.

26. So John 1:1-18 with references to John the Baptist as the one who testifies to the Word (vv. 6-8, 15).

27. Helmbold, "Redeemer Hymns," 74–77.

28. P. Perkins, "Gnostic Christologies and the New Testament," *CBQ* 43 (1981) 590–606.

29. Cf. P. Perkins, *The Gnostic Dialogue* (New York: Paulist, 1980) 122–23.

30. Ibid., 77–82.

31. M. Scopello, "The Apocalypse of Zostrianos (NH VIII, 1) and the Book of the Secrets of Enoch," *VC* 34 (1980) 376–85.

32. Ibid., 382.

33. Porphyry, *Vita Plotini* 16; J. Sieber, "Introduction to Zostrianos," in *Nag Hammadi Codex VIII* (ed. J. Sieber; NHS 31; Leiden: Brill, 1991) 19–25.

34. So Sieber, "Introduction," 25–27.

35. Sieber, *Codex VIII*, 107.

36. Sieber, "Introduction," 27.

37. Sieber *(Codex VIII*, 118 note to 48, 27–29) considers this a reference to a "heavenly power." But a discussion of forms of things in the material world seems to be indicated just before this section (48,10-21; *NHLE*, 416).

38. Sieber, "Introduction," 11–12.

39. J. Turner, "Sethian Gnosticism: A Literary History," in *Nag Hammadi, Gnosticism and Early Christianity*, 79–83.

40. The revelation in *Zostrianos* may have included ascetic practices of standing meditation and fasting that were copied by members of the sect (cf. Williams, *Immovable Race*, 89–99).

41. Ibid., 198–99.

42. C. W. Hedrick, "Christian Motifs in the *Gospel of the Egyptians*: Method and Motive," *NovT* 23 (1981) 242–60.

43. E.g., IV 56,26-27 has added "the great Christ" and so broken up a

genitive and personified the conquering power; IV 59,16-17, which may have originally had the son as the one from silence; IV 60,7-8, the antecedent of "the great Christ" is lost. It is unclear whether the author is claiming that the Word is the Son of the great Christ; in III 68,25-26 (*NHLE*, 218), *monogenēs*, "only begotten," has probably been taken from the NT, because it does not occur elsewhere in *Gospel of the Egyptians*; in III 54,18-20 (*NHLE*, 213), introducing "the great Christ" has confused the antecedents of the verbs.

44. Cf. the docetic accounts of the crucifixion in *Treat. Seth* VII 55,14—56,19; *NHLE*, 365; *Apoc. Pet.* VII 81,6-24; *NHLE*, 377.

45. E. Schweizer, *The Letter to the Colossians* (trans. A. Chester; Minneapolis: Augsburg, 1982) 143–49.

46. Ibid., 151.

47. Cf. H.-F. Weiss, "Gnostiche Motive und antignostische Polemik im Kolosser- und im Epheserbrief," in *Gnosis und Neues Testament*, 311–24.

48. So Schweizer, *Colossians*, 151.

49. E.g., *Ap. John* II 28,11-32; *NHLE*, 121.

50. Schweizer, *Colossians*, 80.

51. Ibid., 85.

52. Williams, *Immovable Race*, 144–46.

53. Ibid., 147–48.

54. Ibid., 149–50.

55. Cf. B. Layton, *Gnostic Scriptures* (Garden City: Doubleday, 1987) 277.

56. J. T. Sanders, "Nag Hammadi, Odes of Solomon, and NT Christological Hymns," in *Gnosticism and the Early Christian World: In Honor of James M. Robinson* (ed. J. E. Goehring, C. W. Hedrick, J. T. Sanders, with H. D. Betz; Sonoma: Polebridge, 1990) 65.

Chapter 8
Jesus as Word

1. E.g., R. E. Brown, *The Gospel According to John* (AB 29, 29A; 2 vols.; Garden City: Doubleday, 1966–70) 1:3–36; R. Schnackenburg, *The Gospel According to St. John* (trans. K. Smyth et al.; 3 vols.; New York: Herder and Herder, Crossroad, 1968–82) 1:224–31; J. D. G. Dunn, *Christology in the Making* (Philadelphia: Westminster, 1980) 239–40.

2. A. Culpepper, *Anatomy of the Fourth Gospel* (Philadelphia: Fortress, 1983) 185.

3. So Brown (*Gospel*, 1:28), who takes v. 9 as an editorial transition to the second strophe of the hymn (vv. 10-12b).

4. Cf. R. Bultmann, *The Gospel of John* (trans. G. R. Beasley-Murray; Philadelphia: Westminster, 1971) 8–18.

5. Cf. Dunn, *Christology*, 217–43.

6. Bultmann, *John*, 21–25.

7. Ibid., 23-27.

8. E.g., B. Pearson, "Jewish Sources in Gnostic Literature," in *Jewish Writings of the Second Temple Period* (ed. M. Stone; CRINT II/2; Assen: Van Gorcum; Philadelphia: Fortress, 1984) 443–81.

9. See the discussion of this transition as a stage in the history of the Johannine community by R. E. Brown, *Community of the Beloved Disciple* (New York: Paulist, 1979) 25–58.

10. Bultmann, *John*, 9.

11. J. Ashton, "The Transformation of Wisdom: A Study of the Prologue of John's Gospel," *NTS* 32 (1986) 161–86.

12. G. A. G. Stroumsa, *Another Seed: Studies in Gnostic Mythology* (NHS 24; Leiden: Brill, 1984) 81–88.

13. 1QH 11:11; also 1QH 10:2; Schnackenburg, *John*, 1:238.

14. Schnackenburg, *John*, 1:239.

15. Cf. W. Schoedel, "Topological Theology and Some Monistic Tendencies in Gnosticism," in *Essays on the Nag Hammadi Texts* (ed. M. Krause; NHS 6; Leiden: Brill, 1975) 88–108.

16. Cf. H. Jonas, *The Gnostic Religion* (rev. ed.; Boston: Beacon, 1963) 57–58.

17. Bultmann, *John*, 29. Bultmann does assert that the dualism in the prologue represents an early stage that had not undergone speculative elaboration.

18. This passage shifts from speaking about the Word of God to the more common second-century term, "Son" (cf. P. Perkins, "Logos Christologies in the Nag Hammadi Codices," *VC* 35 [1981] 383).

19. Cf. R. E. Brown, *The Epistles of John* (AB 30; Garden City: Doubleday, 1982) 155–87.

20. Schnackenburg, *John*, 1:277–80.

21. Ibid., 279.

22. Admittedly the evangelist later attributes to Moses the ability to testify to Christ as the "one from God" (e.g., John 5:46-47), but he never suggests that the Scriptures provide independent knowledge of God. Indeed, they cannot be properly understood without the appearance of the revealer.

23. Cf. F. T. Fallon, *The Enthronement of Sabaoth: Jewish Elements in Gnostic Creation Myths* (NHS 10; Leiden: Brill, 1978) 45–53.

24. Cf. II 13,19-20; 22,22-23; 23,3; 29,6; *NHLE*, 112, 117–21; B. Pearson, *Gnosticism, Judaism, and Egyptian Christianity* (Minneapolis: Fortress, 1990), 129.

25. II 95,19-25; *NHLE*, 168.

26. See the discussion of this section and the relationship of its theology to that of the Gnostics reported in Irenaeus, *Adv. Haer.* 1.30, in Fallon, *Enthronement*, 73–78.

27. Cf. the seminal essay by W. Meeks, "The Man from Heaven in Johannine Sectarianism," *JBL* 91 (1972) 44–72. Meeks argues that the gnosticizing of the Johannine tradition occurred after the Gospel was composed, fueled by the symbolic possibilities in the Gospel itself and the further experiences of the community.

28. Cf. J. Turner, "The Trimorphic Protennoia," *NHLE*, 511.

29. Cf. C. Colpe, "Heidnische, jüdische und christliche Überlieferung in den Schriften aus Nag Hammadi III," *JAC* 17 (1974) 120–22; Y. Janssens, *La prôtennoia (NH XIII,1)* (BCNH "Textes" 4; Quebec: Presses de l'Université Laval, 1978); idem, "The Trimorphic Protennoia and the Fourth Gospel," in *New Testament and Gnosis: Essays in Honour of R. McL. Wilson* (ed. A. H. B. Logan and A. J. M. Wedderburn; Edinburgh: T. & T. Clark, 1983), 229–44; J. Turner, "Trimorphic Protennoia," in *Nag Hammadi Codices XI, XII, XIII* (ed. C. Hedrick; NHS 28; Leiden: Brill, 1990) 374–75.

30. For a more detailed list of parallels to the prologue of John see Y. Janssens, "Une source gnostique du Prologue?" *L'Évangile de Jean: Sources, rédaction, théologie* (BETL 44; Gembloux: Duculot, 1977) 355–58.

31. For a general survey of the initial stages of the debate see J. M. Robinson, "Sethians and Johannine Thought: The *Trimorphic Protennoia* and the Prologue of the Gospel of John," in *The Rediscovery of Gnosticism*, vol. 2, *Sethian Gnosticism* (ed. B. Layton; Leiden: Brill, 1981) 643–62.

32. So Turner, "Trimorphic Protennoia," in *NHLE*, 512–13.

33. Cf. B. Layton, *Gnostic Scriptures* (Garden City: Doubleday, 1987) 86–87.

34. J. Turner, "Sethian Gnosticism: A Literary History," in *Nag Hammadi, Gnosticism and Early Christianity* (ed. C. W. Hedrick and R. Hodgson, Jr.; Peabody, Mass.: Hendrickson, 1986) 65.

35. C. A. Evans, "On the Prologue and the Trimorphic Protennoia," *NTS* 27 (1981) 395–401.

36. Ibid., 397.

37. Ibid., 398.

38. Cf. the discussion in P. Hofrichter, *Im Anfang war der "Johannesprolog": Das urchristliche Logosbekenntnis—die Basis neutestamentlicher und gnostischer Theologie* (Regensburg: Friedrich Pustet, 1986) 39–82.

39. E.g., John 3:3-8; 4:10-15; 7:37-39. Janssens ("Trimorphic Protennoia," 238) links the passage on the Word as life-giving water to John 4:10-14.

40. Cf. Perkins, "Logos Christologies," 381–82.

41. A. H. B. Logan, "John and the Gnostics: The Significance of the Apocryphon of John for the Debate about the Origins of Johannine Literature," *JSNT* 43 (1991) 50–57. Logan holds that both *Apocryphon of John* and *Trimorphic Protennoia* have reshaped their mythological material under the influence of the Johannine prologue.

42. Ibid., 52–53.

43. Janssens, "Trimorphic Protennoia," 239–41.

44. Cf. J. Daniélou, *Gospel Message and Hellenistic Culture* (trans. and ed. J. A. Baker; Philadelphia: Westminster, 1973) 370.

45. Cf. ibid., 345–57.

46. Origen, *Com. in Joh.* 1.21.125; cf. Perkins, "Logos Christologies," 382.

47. Bultmann, *John*, 13 n. 1.

48. J. Dillon, *The Middle Platonists* (London: Duckworth, 1977) 166.

49. Cf. Schnackenburg, *John*, 1:245–47.

50. Dillon, *Middle Platonists*, 166.

51. See H. Conzelmann, "The Mother of Wisdom," in *The Future of Our Religious Past: Essays in Honour of Rudolf Bultmann* (ed. J. M. Robinson; London: SCM, 1971) 230–43. Conzelmann detects this syncretism in Hellenistic Judaism. Sir 24:3-7 employs the liturgical form of the Isis aretalogy. This form recurs in gnostic writings that use a paradoxical "I Am" style to depict the cosmological and soteriological role of Wisdom/Eve. See *Thunder: Perfect Mind* (VI,2) and the discussion of its paradoxical language of divine self-predication by B. Layton, "The Riddle of the Thunder (NHC VI, 2): The Function of Paradox in a Gnostic Text from Nag Hammadi," in *Nag Hammadi, Gnosticism and Early Christianity*, 37–54.

52. Dillon, *Middle Platonists*, 163–66.

53. See B. Pearson, "Jewish Elements in *Corpus Hermeticum I (Poimandres),*" in *Gnosticism*, 136–47. Pearson thinks that the syncretistic combination of Jewish traditions, a sectarian piety of self-knowledge through meditative identification with the divine, and gnosticizing cosmology probably originated among Egyptian Jewish proselytes early in the second century C.E. Jewish revolts in Egypt (115–17 C.E.) deprived Judaism of its popularity. A cult devoted to the Egyptian Hermes-Thoth provided a new focus of religious identity. Jewish elements would be less evident in later Hermetic tracts (pp. 146–47).

54. On the philosophical call to awaken from irrational passion and be saved by reason cf. A. Malherbe, *Paul and the Thessalonians* (Philadelphia: Fortress, 1987) 21–28.

Chapter 9
Discourses of the Revealer

1. Jesus' rejection of Mary Magdalene's gesture in John 20:17 also suggests a sharp distinction between the glorified Lord and the earthly appearance of Jesus.

2. Cf. P. Perkins, *The Gnostic Dialogue* (New York: Paulist, 1980) 49–52.

3. The Matthean version of that appearance tradition (Matt 28:16-17) lacks all the traditional elements of a vision except the reference to worship. No unusual appearance, no fear of the recipients, and no words of

reassurance, typical elements in a theophany, occur in the Matthean passage. But the transfiguration can also be understood as an appropriation of the visionary traditions associated with Moses and Elijah. See P. Perkins, *Resurrection: New Testament Witness and Contemporary Reflection* (Garden City: Doubleday, 1984) 95–99.

4. The formula is extended to Paul's own case in v. 8. On the ecstatic character of the experience referred to in Gal 1:16 see H. D. Betz, *Galatians* (Hermeneia; Philadelphia: Fortress, 1979) 70–71.

5. P. Hofrichter, *Im Anfang war der "Johannesprolog"* (Regensburg: Friedrich Pustet, 1986) 89–97.

6. The manuscript evidence is divided on the reading of this verse. Although I consider "god" the more difficult and more likely reading, the two terms would be equivalent in a gnostic reading of the text.

7. P. Perkins, "Johannine Traditions in *Ap. Jas.* (CG I,2)," *JBL* 101 (1982) 403–14.

8. V 33,10—35,18; *NHLE*, 265–66; Irenaeus, *Adv. Haer.* 1.13.16 (Marcosian version); A. Veilleux, *Les Deux Apocalypses de Jacques* (BCNH "Textes" 17; Quebec: Presses de l'Université Laval, 1986) 85–86.

9. Veilleux (*Deux Apocalypses,* 80) notes the unusual shift to the plural "us" in a revelation that is made to James alone. When the risen Jesus appears, James is walking with the other disciples (42,20-23). This plural may also be an indication that the gnostic authors are just as dependent as the canonical Gospels on narratives of resurrection appearances that refer only to Jesus' return to a group of disciples. No primitive narrative tradition of an appearance to an individual male disciple is extant, although there may be such a tradition concerning the appearance to Mary Magdalene (see P. Perkins, "I Have Seen the Lord (John 20:18): Women Witnesses to the Resurrection," *Int* 46 [1992] 31–41).

10. Veilleux, *Deux Apocalypses,* 80. The break in the text at the bottom of the codex page 29 makes it difficult to tell who is being referred to as the object of the archons' hostility. Although James would appear to be the logical subject, the third-person reference to him is awkward.

11. Cf. the discussion of the Paraclete sayings as a group in R. E. Brown, *The Gospel According to John* (AB 29, 29A; 2 vols.; Garden City: Doubleday, 1966–70) 2:1135–44.

12. The prophetic character of the Spirit's revelation is indicated by the expression "things to come" in v. 13. The Paraclete cannot replace Jesus as revealer, because what the Spirit reveals belongs to Jesus (cf. R. Schnackenburg, *The Gospel According to St. John* [trans. K. Smyth, et al.; 3 vols.; New York: Seabury, 1980–82] 3:133).

13. Apparently an echo of the earlier debate in John 8:21-28. The Jews who are "of this world" cannot believe that Jesus is the divine Son. When he departs, they will die in their sin (of disbelief).

14. Cf. Veilleux, *Deux Apocalypses,* 73.

15. Ibid., 73–74.

16. Cf. J. Collins, *The Apocalyptic Imagination* (New York: Crossroad, 1984) 5–7.

17. Cf. Schnackenburg, John, 2:200.

18. See G. W. MacRae, "The Ego-Proclamation in Gnostic Sources," in *The Trial of Jesus: Cambridge Studies in Honour of C. F. D. Moule* (ed. E. Bammel; SBT 2/13; London: SCM, 1970) 123–29.

19. See the aretalogies of Isis and Karpocrates in F. C. Grant, *Hellenistic Religions* (Indianapolis: Bobbs-Merrill, 1953) 131–36.

20. Cf. Veilleux, *Deux Apocalypses*, 68.

21. Cf. MacRae, "Ego-Proclamation," 129–34.

22. Such mythological associations are also evident in the lengthy aretalogy, *Thunder: Perfect Mind*, whose apparent paradoxes point to the incompatibility of gnosis with the structures of the lower world. Cf. G. W. MacRae, "Discourses of the Gnostic Revealer," in *Proceedings of the International Colloquium on Gnosticism, Stockholm, August 20–25, 1973* (ed. G. Widengren; Stockholm: Almqvist & Wiksell; Leiden: Brill, 1977) 121–22; and B. Layton, *Gnostic Scriptures* (Garden City: Doubleday, 1987) 78.

23. Cf. the discussion of Johannine misunderstandings in R. Culpepper, *Anatomy of the Fourth Gospel* (Philadelphia: Fortress, 1983) 152–65.

24. The evangelist then interprets the saying as a reference to the coming of the Spirit (v. 39).

25. R. Bultmann, *The Gospel of John* (trans. G. R. Beasley-Murray; Philadelphia: Westminster, 1971) 7–8.

26. Cf. H. Koester, "Gnostic Sayings and Controversy Traditions in John 8:12-59," in *Nag Hammadi, Gnosticism and Early Christianity* (ed. C. W. Hedrick and R. Hodgson, Jr.; Peabody, Mass.: Hendrickson, 1986) 99–110.

27. *Dial. Sav.* III 127,1-6; *NHLE*, 248.

28. Cf. W. Kelber, *The Oral and Written Gospel* (Philadelphia: Fortress, 1983) 2–36.

29. Koester, "Sayings," 99.

30. Ibid., 106.

31. Ibid., 109–10.

32. Cf. I. P. Couliano, *The Tree of Gnosis: Gnostic Mythology from Early Christianity to Modern Nihilism* (San Francisco: HarperCollins, 1992) 106–7, 137, 173–76.

33. Couliano (ibid., xv, 108–11) identifies the *anthropic principle*, the commensurability between humans and the cosmos in which they live as a fundamental given of religious and philosophical experience in the first century C.E., which is rejected in gnostic systems. The persistent use of "the world" for what is hostile to revelation and to the believer in the Fourth Gospel (e.g., John 1:5, 9-11; 7:4-7; 15:18-19) delivers a similar message.

34. Couliano (ibid., 120–21) notes that from a structuralist point of view "*the sequences of gnostic myth are transformations of another myth,* that is, the myth of creation according to the Book of Genesis."

35. As Couliano apparently does by referring to the Platonizing structures in their exegesis, although he then appears to return to the assumption that the gnostic mythologizers must have been Jewish Christians (ibid., 126–27).

36. Couliano (ibid., 127) refers to later Neoplatonists who find the gnostic Genesis myth compelling enough to reinterpret while de-Judaizing and de-Christianizing it.

37. Kelber, *Oral and Written Gospel*, 101.

38. Ibid., 98–101.

39. B. Layton, "The Riddle of the Thunder," in *Nag Hammadi, Gnosticism and Early Christianity*, 41–51.

40. MacRae, "Ego-Proclamation," 124.

41. Cf. Layton, "Riddle," 44–47; *Orig. World* II 114,5-15; *NHLE*, 181; *Hyp. Arch.* II 89,11-17; *NHLE*, 164.

42. Layton, "Riddle," 48–51; Couliano (*Tree of Gnosis*, 79) claims that *Thunder* is not gnostic, but that a gnostic reader would recognize the paradoxes of the "holy" and "whore" as references to Sophia. He fails to allow for the riddle as a decoding device for the linguistic transformations of the gnostic pattern—despite the fact that that view would be more appropriate to his overall methodological interests in religious systems as ideal objects that generate their own variations and transformations than this lapse into genetic language.

43. Layton, "Riddle," 39–41; also cf. *Trim. Prot.* XIII 36,23; 40,31; 41,20; 42,12, 25; 45,21; 46,17, 22-24; 48,20.

44. Cf. Layton, *Gnostic Scriptures*, 77, 205.

45. Cf. Schnackenburg, *John*, 2:260–65.

46. E. Pagels, "Conflicting Versions of Valentinian Eschatology: Irenaeus' Treatises vs. the Excerpts from Theodotus," *HTR* 67 (1974) 35–53; the extent to which gnostic writers retained the conviction that the "spiritual persons" were distinct from other humans by nature remains unclear; see E. Mühlenberg, "Wieviel Erlösungen kennt der Gnostiker Herakleon," *ZNW* 66 (1975) 170–93.

47. Cf. H. Koester, "The History-of-Religions School, Gnosis, and the Gospel of John," *ST* 40 (1986) 122.

48. Ibid., 128–31; Couliano (*Tree of Gnosis*, 8–28) cautions against the assumption that communal experience can be read off the transformations in religious symbols, which have a logic of their own as ideal objects.

49. Koester, "History-of-Religions School," 130.

50. Ibid., 129.

51. An embarrassment not suffered by gnostic revelations that are spoken by a primordial heavenly figure or the risen Jesus.

52. Cf. Brown, *John*, 1:273.

53. Bultmann, *John*, 234–37.

54. R. E. Brown, *Community of the Beloved Disciple* (New York: Paulist, 1979) 157–58.

55. Schnackenburg, *John*, 2:56–69.

56. G. Luck, "The Doctrine of Salvation in the Hermetic Writings," *Second Century* 8 (1991) 34–35.

Chapter 10
Gnostic Identity

1. Cf. P. Brown, *The Body and Society: Men, Women and Sexual Renunciation in Early Christianity* (New York: Columbia Univ. Press, 1988) 65–258.

2. I. P. Couliano, *The Tree of Gnosis* (San Francisco: HarperCollins, 1992) 127.

3. Cf. the comments on *Gospel of Truth* by J. Fineman, "Gnosis and the Piety of Metaphor: The *Gospel of Truth*," in *The Rediscovery of Gnosticism*, vol. 1, *Valentinianism* (ed. B. Layton; Leiden: Brill, 1981) 289–312.

4. Cf. the discussion of H. Jonas's parallels between ancient Gnosticism and modern nihilism by Couliano, *Tree of Gnosis*, 255–64.

5. This dynamic made it possible for earlier scholars to conclude that a gnosticizing movement was already evident in the Pauline communities. Cf. W. Schmithals, "The *Corpus Paulinum* and Gnosis," in *The New Testament and Gnosis: Essays in Honour of Robert McL. Wilson* (ed. A. H. B. Logan and A. J. M. Wedderburn, Edinburgh: T. & T. Clark, 1983) 107–10.

6. As in *Ep. Arist.* 140-71; L. Gaston, "Angels and Gentiles in Early Judaism and in Paul," *SR* 11 (1982) 65–75.

7. Cf. H. D. Betz, *Galatians* (Hermeneia; Philadelphia: Fortress, 1979) 213–18; E. Schweizer, *The Letter to the Colossians* (trans. A. Chester; Minneapolis: Augsburg, 1982) 125–30, 140–45; in Philippians the connection is less evident if one separates 3:2-21 as a fragment of a different letter from the hymn that asserts Christ's victory over the powers in 2:6-11. But 3:21 does affirm Christ's rule over all things.

8. Betz, *Galatians*, 28–33.

9. Cf. E. R. Dodds (*Pagan and Christian in an Age of Anxiety* [New York: Norton, 1965] 1–36) on the vague, persistent anxiety about the divine in the early Christian period.

10. J. L. Martyn has insisted that Judaizing need not have been the result of Jewish Christian attacks on the Pauline mission but could reflect an indigenous local movement fostered by Gentiles ("A Law-Observant Mission to Gentiles: The Background of Galatians," *SJT* 38 [1985] 307–24).

11. See the discussion of the language of the passage and the various proposals about its origin in V. P. Furnish, *II Corinthians* (AB 32A; Garden City: Doubleday, 1984) 271–83. Because it is difficult to explain how such a passage would have been placed in its present position by someone other than Paul, Furnish concludes that it is most likely a non-Pauline fragment used by the apostle himself.

12. Cf. J. Neyrey, "Body Language in 1 Corinthians: The Use of Anthropological Models for Understanding Paul's Opponents," *Semeia* 35 (1986) 129–70.

13. E.g., G. Fee, *The First Epistle to the Corinthians* (NICNT; Grand Rapids: Eerdmans, 1987) 491–530.

14. Fee (ibid., 491, 530) finds Paul detached and unemotional. He concludes that the issue was of little importance to the apostle. The tormented argument in this section contrasts sharply with the certainty of that in vv. 17-34 and suggests considerable anxiety on the apostle's part, as J. Murphy-O'Connor rightly points out ("Sex and Logic in 1 Corinthians 11:2-16," *CBQ* 42 [1980] 482–500).

15. Cf. G. Theissen, *The Social Setting of Pauline Christianity: Essays on Corinth* (trans. J. H. Schütz; Philadelphia: Fortress, 1982) 145–74.

16. Fee, *1 Corinthians*, 544.

17. Ibid., 560–61.

18. According to *T. Reuben* 5:6-7, human women provoked lust in the archons. Cf. H. Conzelmann, *1 Corinthians* (trans. J. W. Leitch; Hermeneia; Philadelphia: Fortress, 1975) 189.

19. Cf. M. Williams, *The Immovable Race* (NHS 29; Leiden: Brill, 1985) 129–31.

20. P. Brown, *The Making of Late Antiquity* (Cambridge: Harvard Univ. Press, 1978) 75.

21. V. Turner, *The Ritual Process* (Chicago: Aldine, 1969) 166–89.

22. Cf. J. Neyrey, *An Ideology of Revolt* (Philadelphia: Fortress, 1988) 115–50.

23. Ibid., 142–49.

24. Ibid., 185–207.

25. Williams, *Immovable Race*, 163–79.

26. Ibid., 161–63.

27. Cf. ibid., 86–92.

28. Cited in ibid., 88.

29. Ibid., 90 n. 37.

30. Ibid., 99–100.

31. Cf. A. Veilleux's caution against excessive enthusiasm for a monastic context in evaluating the origins of the Nag Hammadi material ("Monasticism and Gnosis," in *The Roots of Egyptian Christianity* [ed. B. A. Pearson and J. E. Goehring; Philadelphia: Fortress, 1986] 278–89).

32. Cf. H. Attridge, "The Gospel of Truth as an Exoteric Text," in *Nag Hammadi, Gnosticism and Early Christianity* (ed. C. W. Hedrick and R. Hodgson, Jr.; Peabody, Mass.: Hendrickson, 1986) 239–40.

33. Cf. W. R. Schoedel, "Topological Theology and Some Monistic Tendencies in Gnosticism," in *Essays on the Nag Hammadi Texts* (ed. M. Krause; NHS 6; Leiden: Brill, 1975) 88–108.

34. Cf. A. McGuire, "Conversion and Gnosis in the *Gospel of Truth*," *NovT* 28 (1986) 346–47.

35. Williams, *Immovable Race*, 172–73.

36. Ibid., 146–48.

37. Cf. McGuire, "Conversion," 344–48.

38. Ibid., 351.

39. Cf. J. Heldermann, *Die Anapausis im Evangelium Veritatis* (NHS 17; Leiden: Brill, 1984) 227–28.

40. C. M. Tuckett, "Synoptic Tradition in the *Gospel of Truth* and the *Testimony of Truth*," *JTS*, n.s., 35 (1984) 131–45.

41. B. Standaert, "L'évangile de Vérité: critique et lecture," *NTS* 22 (1975) 243–75. A similar perspective is evident in John 17, where Jesus speaks to the Father as though he were already glorified in heaven. But the distance that separates Jesus from the disciples is preserved by the constant references to their situation "in the world" (e.g., John 17:11, 14-15).

42. Fineman, "Piety," 289–318; H. Attridge, *Nag Hammadi Codex I (The Jung Codex): Notes* (NHS 23; Leiden: Brill, 1985) 117–19.

43. This emphasis also highlights the importance of the Nag Hammadi material for understanding the development of Christology in the second and third centuries (cf. Couliano, *Tree of Gnosis*, 9–19).

44. Fineman, "Piety," 288–312.

45. Ibid., 294–97.

46. Ibid., 311.

47. Ibid., 302–5.

48. Ibid., 305–6.

49. S. Gero, "With Walter Bauer on the Tigris: Encratite Orthodoxy and Libertine Heresy in Syro-Mesopotamian Christianity," in *Nag Hammadi, Gnosticism and Early Christianity*, 287–307.

50. Ibid., 293–94.

51. Ibid., 305–6.

52. Cf. K. Koschorke, *Die Polemik der Gnostiker gegen das kirchliche Christentum* (NHS 12; Leiden: Brill, 1978) 91–174.

53. Cf. B. Pearson, *Gnosticism, Judaism, and Egyptian Christianity* (Minneapolis: Fortress, 1990) 39–51.

54. Ibid., 51.

55. Cf. B. Pearson, "Gnostic Interpretation of the Old Testament in the *Testimony of Truth* (NHC IX,3)," *HTR* 73 (1980) 311–19.

56. Pearson, *Gnosticism*, 191.

57. Koschorke, *Polemik*, 158–60.

58. Fineman, "Piety," 306–8.

59. Ibid., 309.

60. Ibid., 310–11.

61. His example will be invoked by *1 Clement* in addressing a later conflict over communal leadership (cf. *1 Clem.* 47.1-6).

62. This tradition has been continued in R. E. Brown's extensive commentary (*The Epistles of John* [AB 30; Garden City: Doubleday, 1982]

47–115). Although the epistles show no clear evidence of gnosticizing speculation by the opponents, Brown concludes that the dissident Johannine Christians may have been the bridge by which the Fourth Gospel came to play an extensive role in second- and third-century Gnosticism (pp. 104–6).

63. Cf. ibid., 71–72.

64. Cf. ibid., 174–87.

65. Cf. P. Perkins, "The Johannine Epistles," in *New Jerome Biblical Commentary* (ed. R. Brown, J. Fitzmyer, and R. Murphy; Englewood Cliffs: Prentice-Hall, 1990) 62:4–5.

66. J. Lieu, *The Theology of the Johannine Epistles* (Cambridge: Cambridge Univ. Press, 1991) 22–23.

67. Attridge, "Gospel of Truth," 242–43.

68. J. Ménard (*L'Évangile de Vérité* [NHS 2; Leiden: Brill, 1972] 72) notes that John 1:1 appears frequently in Valentinian texts. He emphasizes the parallels between this section of *Gospel of Truth* and the poetry of the *Odes of Solomon*.

69. Attridge, "Gospel of Truth," 245.

70. Ibid., 249.

71. McGuire, "Conversion," 353.

72. So Attridge, "Gospel of Truth," 241–42.

73. McGuire, "Conversion," 355.

Chapter 11
Women Disciples and Worshipers

1. Cf. R. F. Stoops, "Patronage in the *Acts of Peter*," *Semeia* 38 (1986) 91–100.

2. Irenaeus also notes a Valentinian exegesis of the rule that women must veil themselves when prophesying as an instance in which gnostic exegetes found the story of the lower Sophia, Achamoth, hidden in Scripture (*Adv. Haer.* 1.8.2). He does not provide an alternate interpretation of the text.

3. Cf. the collection of reports of women prophets in A. C. Wire, *The Corinthian Women Prophets* (Philadelphia: Fortress, 1990) 237–69.

4. Cf. R. S. Kraemer, *Her Share of the Blessings* (New York: Oxford Univ. Press, 1992) 80–92, 174–90.

5. Cf. Stoops, "Patronage," 95–98.

6. The charge that one's opposition could sway only weak-minded women was commonplace in ancient polemic. It is already firmly established in the Pastoral Epistles (e.g., 2 Tim 3:6).

7. Even if this section is taken to be a later addition to 1 Corinthians, it represents an understanding of the Pauline tradition that was established by the time the Pastorals were written (cf. 1 Tim 2:12).

8. Cf. E. Schüssler-Fiorenza, "Rhetorical Situation and Historical Reconstruction in 1 Corinthians," *NTS* 33 (1987) 386–403; Wire, *Corinthian Women Prophets*, 8–9, 181–93.

9. Wire, *Corinthian Women Prophets*, 62–71.

10. Ibid., 102.

11. On the surviving icons of the saint and the celebration of her feast day, see D. R. MacDonald and A. D. Scrimgeour, "Pseudo-Chrysostom's Panegyric to Thecla: The Heroine of the *Acts of Paul* in Homily and Art," *Semeia* 38 (1986) 151–59.

12. Cf. P. Perkins, "I Have Seen the Lord (John 20:18): Women Witnesses to the Resurrection," *Int* 46 (1992) 31–41.

13. Cf. P. Perkins, *The Gnostic Dialogue* (New York: Paulist, 1980) 133–37, 144.

14. Cf. A. Veilleux, *Les Deux Apocalypses de Jacques* (BCNH "Textes" 17; Quebec: Presses de l'Université Laval, 1986) 94–95. The names in the list of four women are reconstructed on the basis of Manichean sources.

15. The whole range of issues associated with the feminine in Gnosticism are dealt with in the symposium on this topic, K. L. King, ed., *Images of the Feminine in Gnosticism* (Philadelphia: Fortress, 1988).

16. Cf. J. M. Robinson, "Very Goddess and Very Man: Jesus' Better Self," in *Images of the Feminine*, 113–27.

17. Cf. E. A. Fischer-Mueller, "Yaldabaoth: The Gnostic Female Principle in Its Fallenness," *NovT* 32 (1990) 79–95. Fisher-Mueller's conclusion exalts the gnostic quest for redemption and integration of the fallen female beyond what the ancient evidence demonstrates.

18. Scholars continue to be divided over the extent to which *Gospel of Philip* reinterprets common Christian sacraments in the light of gnostic mythologizing or represents an independent cultic system (cf. D. H. Tripp, "The Sacramental System of the Gospel of Philip," *Studia Patristica*, vol. 17/1 [ed. E. A. Livingstone; Oxford: Pergamon, 1982] 251–60).

19. On the philosophical background to this speculation see H.-J. Krämer, *Der Ursprung der Geistmetaphysik* (Amsterdam: P. Schippers, 1964) 93–96.

20. D. Good, "Sophia in Valentinianism," *Second Century* 4 (1984) 193–201.

21. I cannot agree with Good (ibid., 200) that *Exc. Theod.* 45,2 is evidence for the earlier Valentinian view that retains the ambiguity of Wisdom's position. Good herself recognizes that this section is dominated by Christian gnostic apologetic. It makes the savior responsible for the emergence of the world outside the Pleroma (Good, "Sophia," 199). *Excerpts from Theodotos* represents a Christianization of the Wisdom myth, which had already been Platonized. *Adversus Haereses* preserves the earlier, philosophical variant better than *Excerpts from Theodotos*.

22. I disagree with Good's decision to reject the view that this text refers to the savior making Wisdom passionless and to read it to say that

the savior brought Wisdom into being outside the Pleroma ("Sophia," 199 n. 25). Conversion of the soul to a passionless state is the basic require-ment of salvation in the Platonized form of the myth.

23. See M. Williams, *The Immovable Race* (NHS 29; Leiden: Brill, 1985) 120.

24. Ibid., 139. Williams distinguishes this tradition from those which speak of a mystical *anchōrēsis* that allows the enlightened to stand in the Self-Begotten aeon.

25. Ibid., 144–45.

26. Repentance is purely an agent of salvific power. She is not a variant of the wandering, repentant Wisdom who needs to be healed. Although the seed of Seth is the primary object of salvation, she prays for the other seed as well. *Gospel of the Egyptians* suggests that some of the seed of the archon will also repent (cf. A. Böhlig and F. Wisse, *Nag Hammadi Codices III,2 and IV,2* [NHS 4; Leiden: Brill, 1975] 185–86).

27. Williams (*Immovable Race*, 146–47) notes that while the erring planets are "nailed to the cross," stability is conferred on the gnostic race, not the stars.

28. So ibid., 161–64.

29. Cf. M. Scopello, "Jewish and Greek Heroines in the Nag Hammadi Library," in *Images of the Feminine*, 71–90; idem, *L'Exégèse de l'Âme* (NHS 25; Leiden: Brill, 1985) 45–55.

30. Scopello, *L'Exégèse de l'Âme*, 86.

31. Ibid., 88–92.

32. Ibid., 91–93.

33. Ibid., 18–27.

34. Thus G. W. MacRae's tentative suggestion that the polemic in *Authoritative Teaching* might refer to Jewish unwillingness to accept the gospel ("Authoritative Teaching," in *NHLE*, 304–5) does not seem to be a likely description of the provenance of this work.

35. Scopello, "Heroines," 89–90.

36. Cf. D. M. Parrott, "Response to 'Jewish and Greek Heroines in the Nag Hammadi Library,'" in *Images of the Feminine*, 91–95.

37. Cf. the discussion of initiation rites in W. Burkert, *Structure and History in Greek Myth and Ritual* (Berkeley and Los Angeles: Univ. of California Press, 1979) 6–7.

38. This fact is particularly evident in the Valentinian *Tripartite Tractate* (CG I,5). In that work, the Word is entirely responsible for the origins of the lower world. The Word takes over functions that other Valentinian myths attribute to the higher and lower Wisdom figures.

Chapter 12
Christians: Gnostic and Orthodox

1. E. Pagels's best-selling popular account of Gnosticism (*The Gnostic Gospels* [New York: Random House, 1979]) took this approach. The

Gnostics are depicted as champions of individual freedom in an oppressive church. Her later work (e.g., *Adam, Eve, and the Serpent* [New York: Random House, 1988]) is more nuanced.

2. J.-M. Sevrin, *L'Exégèse de l'Âme* (BCNH "Textes" 9; Quebec: Presses de l'Université Laval, 1983) 26–29.

3. H. Attridge and E. Pagels, "The Tripartite Tractate: Introduction," in *Nag Hammadi Codex I (The Jung Codex): Introductions, Texts, Translations, Indices* (ed. H. Attridge: NHS 23; Leiden: Brill, 1985) 190.

4. See E. Thomassen, *Le Traité Tripartite(NH I,5)* (BCNH "Textes" 19; Quebec: Presses de l'Université Laval, 1989) 19.

5. Cf. Attridge and Pagels, *Nag Hammadi Codex I*, 417.

6. Ibid., 421.

7. See P. Perkins, "Irenaeus and the Gnostics," *VC* 30 (1976) 193–200.

8. Cf. D. Parrott, "Gnostic and Orthodox Disciples in the Second and Third Centuries," in *Nag Hammadi, Gnosticism and Early Christianity* (ed. C. W. Hedrick and R. Hodgson, Jr.; Peabody, Mass.: Hendrickson, 1986) 193–219.

9. Ibid., 203–210.

10. Cf. P. Perkins, *The Gnostic Dialogue* (New York: Paulist, 1980) 115.

11. T. Orlandi, "Coptic Literature," in *Roots of Egyptian Christianity* (ed. B. A. Pearson and J. E. Goehring; Philadelphia: Fortress, 1986) 55–56. Orlandi notes that the writings of Shenoute against the Origenists are preserved in a physical form that is more like that of the Nag Hammadi material.

12. Cf. A. Pasquier, *L'Évangile selon Marie (BG 1)* (BCNH "Textes" 10; Quebec: Presses de l'Université Laval, 1983) 26, 74.

13. Cf. ibid., 56–62.

14. Ibid., 69.

15. Cf. ibid., 72, 101–4.

16. Cf. *Gos. Thom.* 114; *NHLE*, 138.

17. Pasquier, *L'Évangile*, 99–101.

18. Several pages are missing from the beginning as well as from the middle of Mary's revelation. Their absence makes all interpretations of the structure of the work as a whole tentative. I am not concerned with analyzing the probable sources and redaction of *Gospel of Mary.* Pasquier suggests a double redaction of source material gave rise to the extant text (*L'Évangile*, 7–13).

19. *Gospel of Mary* may imply that the apostles' ability to interpret the sayings of Jesus was also initiated through Mary's exhortation (cf. Perkins, *Gnostic Dialogue*, 136).

20. Pasquier (*L'Évangile*, 64) points out that Irenaeus's polemic against the Gnostics includes a defense of the positive role of the Law (e.g., in making human sinfulness known, *Adv. Haer.* 3.18.7).

21. So G. L. Borchert, "Insights into the Gnostic Threat to Christianity as Gained through the Gospel of Philip," in *New Dimensions in New Testa-*

ment Study (ed. R. N. Longenecker and M. C. Tenney; Grand Rapids: Zondervan, 1974) 79–93.

22. So most recently, B. Layton, *Gnostic Scriptures* (Garden City: Doubleday, 1987) 325–53. Layton suggests that *Gospel of Philip* is a Valentinian anthology whose individual selections may represent different Valentinian schools (p. 325).

23. M. Desjardins gives a Pauline reconstruction of the doctrine of sin in *Gospel of Philip* (*Sin in Valentinianism* [SBLDS 108; Atlanta: Scholars Press, 1990] 91–100). *Gospel of Philip* does not pick up Pauline language about the atoning death of Christ (p. 99 n. 76).

24. The bride chamber restores the integrity of the human image of God, which was lost with the division of Eve from Adam (70,5-20). Whether the text envisages an actual marriage rite between earthly partners remains a matter of dispute. For a detailed analysis that concludes that *Gospel of Philip* does not refer to such a rite, see J.-M. Sevrin, "Les Noces Spirituelles dans l'Évangile selon Philippe," *Mus.* 87 (1974) 143–93. J. Buckley insists that *Gospel of Philip* refers to earthly marriage ("A Cult Mystery in the *Gospel of Philip*," *JBL* 99 [1980] 569–81).

25. So J. S. Siker, "Gnostic Views on Jews and Christians in the Gospel of Philip," *NovT* 31 (1989) 279 n. 6.

26. Ibid., 284.

27. Desjardins, *Sin*, 92–95.

28. So Borchert, "Insights," 84–85. Borchert sees this overt similarity as evidence of the insidious evil of Gnosticism. It corrupts the Christian message from within.

29. Parrott ("Gnostic and Orthodox Disciples," 217–19) rejects the claim that Peter is treated positively in gnostic circles. He interprets all use of the Peter figure as antiorthodox polemic.

30. Desjardins, *Sin*, 91.

31. Cf. ibid., 85–86.

32. See the sensitive discussion of Arius's place in the Alexandrian church and the subsequent anti-Arian orthodoxy of Athenagoras, who was not party to the original dispute, by C. Kannengiesser, "Athanasius of Alexandria vs. Arius: The Alexandrian Crisis," in *Roots*, 204–15.

33. H. A. Green, "The Socio-Economic Background of Christianity in Egypt," in *Roots*, 110.

34. Ibid., 111.

35. Kannengiesser, "Athanasius," 213. Arius adapted Plotinus's thought in the framework of an inherited Jewish Christian cosmology: "Arius, as a man trained in the spirit of the third century, conceived theology as a faith-filled scholarly exercise but one that became esoteric under the pressure of the transcendency that was the ultimate pole of his fascination" (p. 214).

36. See H. von Staden, "Hairesis and Heresy: The Case of *haireseis iatrikai*," in *Jewish and Christian Self-Definition*, vol. 3, *Self-Definition in*

the Greco-Roman World (ed. B. F. Meyer and E. P. Sanders; Philadelphia: Fortress, 1982) 76–100.

37. Ibid., 96.

38. Cf. J. Blenkinsopp, "Interpretation and the Tendency to Sectarianism: An Aspect of Second Temple History," in *Jewish and Christian Self-Definition*, vol. 2, *Aspects of Judaism in the Greco-Roman Period* (ed. E. P. Sanders; Philadelphia: Fortress, 1981) 3–5.

39. K. Rudolph, *Gnosis* (trans. P. W. Coxon and K. H. Kuhn: ed. R. McL. Wilson; San Francisco: Harper & Row, 1983) 294–96.

40. G. Lüdemann, "Zur Geschichte des ältesten Christentums in Rom I. Valentin und Marcion II. Ptolemäus und Justin," *ZNW* 70 (1979) 86–114.

41. On the intellectual background of this eclectic work, see P. Perkins, "On the Origin of the World (C.G. II,5): A Gnostic Physics," *VC* 34 (1980) 36–46; L. Painchaud ("The Redactions of the Writing Without Title [CG II,5]," *Second Century* 8 [1991] 221–34) proposes a complex redactional history in which the rhetorical introduction belongs to the first stage of the document, which came from a Hellenistic Jewish milieu.

42. Cf. Perkins, *Dialogue*, 94–98; Painchaud ("Redactions," 223 n. 22) detects the same rhetorical framework behind *Eugnostos* and *Origin of the World*.

43. See R. van den Broek, "Jewish and Platonic Speculation in Early Alexandrian Theology: Eugnostos, Philo, Valentinus, and Origen," in *Roots*, 191–94. Van den Broeck argues that Anthropos speculation is more primitive than Philo's hellenizing substitution of the Logos for the primary manifestation of God's powers (p. 195).

44. G. A. G. Stroumsa, *Another Seed: Studies in Gnostic Mythology* (NHS 24; Leiden: Brill, 1984) 102–3.

45. For these primordial senses of Scripture as sacred book see W. Graham, *Beyond the Written Word: Oral Aspects of Scripture in the History of Religion* (Cambridge: Cambridge Univ. Press, 1987) 50–51.

46. See H. Attridge and G. W. MacRae in *Nag Hammadi Codex I*, 55–71.

47. Cf. D. Rouleau, *L'Épître Apocryphe de Jacques* (BCNH "Textes" 18; Quebec: Presses de l'Université Laval, 1987) 93–100.

48. So Parrott, "Gnostic and Orthodox Disciples," 211–12.

49. Rouleau, *L'Épître*, 10–18.

50. Ibid., 95–96.

51. On the distance between the internal audience and the audience to which the work speaks see ibid., 131, 136.

52. On the development of Sethian mythical themes in Manichean literature see Stroumsa, *Another Seed*, 145–67.

53. Cf. Stroumsa, "The Manichaean Challenge to Egyptian Christianity," in *Roots*, 307–19. Stroumsa concludes that the vigorous persecution of Manicheans under Diocletian merely led them to merge into the Christian populace. It was particularly easy for the Manichean elect to join groups of desert monks (p. 309). Also see R. Lane Fox, *Pagans and Chris-*

tians (New York: Knopf, 1986) 561–69; Rudolph, *Gnosis*, 326–42; I. Couliano, *The Tree of Gnosis* (San Francisco: HarperCollins, 1992) 161–88. Couliano's attempt to distinguish Manicheism from its Sethian gnostic origins by claiming that it accepts an "eco-systemic intelligence" because the Demiurge of the world is a living Spirit (p. 181) simply attaches more value to such statements in Manicheism than to the revisions of the Sethian scheme that are already evident in Christian gnostic authors of the Valentinian school.

54. Lane Fox, *Pagans*, 569; Rudolph, *Gnosis*, 332–34.

55. So Rudolph, *Gnosis*, 335.

56. Unpublished text quoted in ibid., 332.

57. On the history of Manicheism in China, which continued to the seventeenth century, see S. N. Lieu, *Manichaeism in the Later Roman Empire and Medieval China* (Manchester: Manchester Univ. Press, 1985) 178–264.

58. Lane Fox, *Pagans*, 568–69.

GLOSSARY

Achamoth. The "lower Wisdom" (from Hebrew *hokhmōth*, "wisdom") whose fall outside the divine world generates the material world and its ruler. The doubled Wisdom figure appears in Valentinian systems.

aeon. Greek for "period of time," is used in gnostic writings to refer to the various heavenly beings or levels of reality that have come forth from the Divine and make up the divine world.

androgynous. From Greek "male/female," refers to stage of human existence or psychological reality in which the gender division between male and female does not exist.

anthropomorphism. From Greek "in human form," refers to representations of God with human characteristics.

antinomian. From Greek "against law or custom," refers to those sects that claim to demonstrate their superior spiritual status by violating religious or cultural norms.

apocalyptic. From Greek for "revelation," refers both to writings that claim to provide secret information about the divine plan or about the heavenly world and to concepts commonly found in such writings, such as predictions of the timetable until the end of the world or descriptions of the soul's ascent through the heavens to a vision of God's throne.

apocrypha. From Greek for "hidden," refers to both Jewish and early Christian writings that are outside the accepted canon. Some of the Jewish apocrypha were part of the Greek OT.

apologist. From Greek for "defense" (in a legal sense), refers to early Christian writers who sought to defend the truth of Christianity.

archon. From Greek for "ruler," in gnostic writings refers to the demonic powers that are thought to govern the material world.

aretalogy. From Greek for "virtue" or "excellence," a term used by scholars to refer to the catalogs of miracles or great deeds of a god, a healer, or a ruler that were often circulated as propaganda for particular temples or cults.

ascetic. From Greek for "training" or "way of life," in early Christianity refers to those who adopt a life that renounces such things as sex, certain foods, a fixed home, or the pursuit of wealth in order to attain holiness.

Autogenes. From Greek for "self-begotten," refers to third level of divine being to come forth from the Father. Often identified with the heavenly Christ.

Barbelo. The second divine being in many systems, possesses an obscure non-Greek name, frequently a female Wisdom figure. After she comes forth the rest of the divine world emerges.

cosmogony. From Greek for "generation of the cosmos," refers to the mythic account of the origins of the material world and its rulers.

demythologizing. A form of biblical interpretation that seeks to state the meaning of the Bible in terms that do not use the mythological images and categories of ancient times.

Docetism. From Greek "to seem," refers to the view that the Savior (Christ) only appeared in human form but was not a mortal, human being. Docetic accounts of the crucifixion depict the Savior departing from the human body before it was hung on the cross.

Ennoia. Greek for "thought" or "conception," in gnostic systems a term used for the first divine being that comes forth from the Father or as an attribute of the Father.

Epinoia. Greek for "thinking" or "power of thought," in gnostic systems a term for the heavenly power who comes to enlighten Adam.

Essene. A Jewish sect with its own interpretation of the Torah, community rules, and messianic reading of the prophets referred to by Josephus and Philo of Alexandria. The sectarian writings found in caves near the Dead Sea at Qumran appear to have been the work of Essenes.

form criticism. Analysis of gospel materials into distinctive genres ("forms") that could be collected and transmitted orally such as miracle stories, parables, and various types of sayings.

haggadah. In Jewish writings the retelling of biblical stories with additional details and interpretation that goes beyond the biblical narrative; that part of the Talmud that does not deal with legal interpretation.

hellenize. To adopt the civic arrangements, religious, educational, and cultural patterns typical of Greek city states.

heresiologist. From Greek *hairesis*, originally a "school" of philosophy or medicine; in Christian sources referred to sects considered unacceptable by the majority. The heresiologist is an orthodox writer who devotes some of his writing to the refutation of the doctrines of heretical sects.

hermeneutics. From Greek "to explain" or "to interpret," a modern term used to designate the theory about the methods and conditions for interpreting texts.

hierophant. Person in a mystery cult who "shows the holy," that is, initiates others into the secret wisdom of the sect.

Ialdabaoth. The origins of the name are uncertain; one of the most common names in gnostic mythology for the god who rules the material world.

libertinism. Permits the violation of moral conventions (often associated with sexuality) in the name of religion.

Mandaean. A dualist sect that understands the world as a place of conflict between light and darkness; practices baptismal rites and seeks to free its members from the control of the powers of darkness. Originated sometime in the first or second century C.E. and continues to exist as a tiny minority in Iran/Iraq.

Manicheism. A dualist sect founded in Persia by the prophet Mani in the middle of the third century C.E. Manicheism combines elements of gnosticizing Jewish Christian baptismal sects with elements of Buddhism and traditional Persian religion.

Marcosian. A gnostic sect founded by a prophet called Marcus which included Valentinian mythology, numerical speculation, and permitted women to celebrate the sacraments.

midrash. From Hebrew "to search" or "to interpret," detailed interpretations of the biblical text, word by word or phrase by phrase. The Midrashim are rabbinic commentaries on Scripture, but the term has been extended to refer to earlier texts of Jewish origin that employ a similar method.

mytheme. A term taken from structuralist studies of myth to refer to the individual narrative units that are combined to make up each variant of a myth.

Naasene. From the Greek form of the Hebrew for "serpent," refers to a gnostic sect in which the world is derived from the interaction of three cosmic powers; concerned with allegorical interpretations of Greek myths and said to praise the serpent that is the source of all religious wisdom.

Nag Hammadi. Region in Egypt where a collection of Coptic codices was found buried in a jar. These codices contained mostly gnostic treatises. The writings found there are referred to as the Nag Hammadi codices.

Neoplatonism. A school of interpretation of the philosophical work of Plato that originated with the philosopher Plotinus in the middle of the third century C.E. Its emphasis on the emanation of all things from a transcendent divine principle, the One, and its religious interest in ascent to contemplate the divine are reflected in several Nag Hammadi writings.

ontological. From Greek for "being," refers to speculation about the nature of Being and the essential characteristics of beings that make up the universe.

Pleroma. Greek for "fullness," a technical term in gnostic writings for the divine realm.

pneumatic. From Greek for "spirit," refers to that class of people, "spiritual persons," who are capable of the insight into the divine conveyed by gnostic teaching.

powers, the. See *archon*.

Pronoia. Greek for "providence" or "forethought," another term used in gnostic writings for the first being who comes forth from the Father. Often refers to her function as wisdom in establishing the cosmic plan of salvation that will bring enlightenment to the gnostic race.

Protennoia. From Greek, "first thought," a term constructed by gnostics for the first series of aeons to come forth from the Father. Identified with Barbelo.

pseudepigrapha. From Greek, "false writings," refers to texts that claimed to be composed by ancient prophets and holy men like Adam, Moses, and Enoch.

psychic. From Greek "soul," in gnostic systems like the Valentinian that divide humankind into three categories, the "spiritual" or "gnostic," the "psychic," and the "material persons." The so-called "psychics" are frequently orthodox Christians who lack gnostic insight but are not completely ignorant of the redeemer.

Q. Abbreviation from German *Quelle*, "source," used by modern scholars to designate the source of sayings and parables of Jesus employed by Luke and Matthew.

redaction criticism. Studies how an author has employed and edited traditional materials in composing a text.

revelation discourse. Refers to the speeches attributed to the heavenly revealer in gnostic writings. The revelation discourse often identifies its speaker as one who is fully enlightened.

Sethian. A term used by modern scholars to describe those writings that have similar mythemes connected with the figure of Seth as the source of the gnostic race.

Simon Magus. In Acts 8, a Samaritan magician who attempts to buy the power of the Holy Spirit from the apostles. Later assumed to be the founder of a gnostic sect with Samaritan origins. Simon was said to have enacted the fall and redemption of Wisdom by taking up with a prostitute.

syncretism. From Greek for "mix together," a term used by modern scholars for the process by which religious traditions in the Greco-Roman period adopted new features of both ritual and mythology from other cultural and religious traditions.

tradition history. Analyzes the surviving examples of sayings, stories, or texts to construct a possible history of their development from earlier to later forms.

Valentinian. Refers to the views of several gnostic teachers, all of whom belong to schools of gnostic practice and interpretation founded by the Christian gnostic leader, Valentinus, who flourished in Rome in the middle of the second century C.E.

BIBLIOGRAPHY

Texts

Attridge, Harold, ed. *Nag Hammadi Codex I (The Jung Codex): Notes*. NHS 23; Leiden: Brill, 1985.

Böhlig, Alexander, and Frederik Wisse. *Nag Hammadi Codices III,2 and IV,2*. NHS 4; Leiden: Brill, 1975.

Emmel, Stephen, ed. *Nag Hammadi Codex III,5*. NHS 26; Leiden: Brill, 1984.

Foerster, Werner. *Gnosis*. Vol. 1, *Patristic Evidence*. Trans. R. McL. Wilson; Oxford: Clarendon, 1972.

Hedrick, Charles, ed. *Nag Hammadi Codices XI, XII, XIII*. NHS 28; Leiden: Brill, 1990.

Janssens, Yvonne. *La prôtennoia (NH XIII,1)*. BCNH "Textes" 4; Quebec: Presses de l'Université Laval, 1978.

Kloppenborg, John S., Marvin W. Meyer, Stephen J. Patterson, and Michael G. Steinhauser. *Q/Thomas Reader*. Sonoma: Polebridge, 1990.

Layton, Bentley. *Gnostic Scriptures*. Garden City: Doubleday, 1987.

Layton, Bentley, ed. *Nag Hammadi Codex II, 2-7: Volume One*. NHS 20; Leiden: Brill, 1989.

Marchovich, Miroslav. *Hippolytus Refutatio Omnium Haeresium*. PTS 25; New York and Berlin: de Gruyter, 1986.

Morard, Françoise. *L'Apocalypse d'Adam* [NH V,5]. BCNH "Textes" 15; Quebec: Presses de l'Université Laval, 1985.

Parrott, Douglas, ed. *Nag Hammadi Codices V,2-5 and VI*. NHS 11; Leiden: Brill, 1979.

Pasquier, Anne. *L'Évangile selon Marie (BG 1)*. BCNH "Textes" 10; Quebec: Presses de l'Université Laval, 1983.

Pearson, Birger, ed. *Nag Hammadi Codices IX and X*. NHS 15; Leiden: Brill, 1981.

239

Poirier, Paul-Hubert. *L'Hymne de la Perle des Actes de Thomas*. Louvain: Louvain-La-Neuve, 1981.

Robinson, James M., ed. *The Nag Hammadi Library in English*. 3d ed. San Francisco: Harper & Row, 1988.

Rouleau, Donald. *L'Épître Apocryphe de Jacques*. BCNH "Textes" 18; Quebec: Presses de l'Université Laval, 1987.

Sevrin, J.-M. *L'Exégèse de l'Âme*. BCNH "Textes" 9; Quebec: Presses de l'Université Laval, 1983.

Sieber, John, ed. *Nag Hammadi Codex VIII*. NHS 31; Leiden: Brill, 1991.

Thomassen, Einar. *Le Traité Tripartite (NH I, 5)*. BCNH "Textes" 19; Quebec: Presses de l'Université Laval, 1989.

Veilleux, Armand. *Les Deux Apocalypses de Jacques*. BCNH "Textes" 17; Quebec: Presses de l'Université Laval, 1986.

Secondary Literature

Ashton, John. "The Transformation of Wisdom: A Study of the Prologue of John's Gospel." *NTS* 32 (1986) 161–86.

Attridge, Harold. "The Gospel of Truth as an Exoteric Text." In *Nag Hammadi, Gnosticism and Early Christianity*, 239–55. *See* Hedrick and Hodgson.

Beker, J. Christiaan. *Paul's Apocalyptic Gospel*. Philadelphia: Fortress, 1982.

Betz, Hans Dieter. *Galatians*. Hermeneia. Philadelphia: Fortress, 1979.

Beyschlag, Karlmann. *Simon Magus und die christliche Gnosis*. WUNT 16; Tübingen: Mohr-Siebeck, 1975.

Blenkinsopp, Joseph. "Interpretation and the Tendency to Sectarianism: An Aspect of Second Temple History." In *Jewish and Christian Self-Definition*. Vol. 2, *Aspects of Judaism in the Greco-Roman Period*. Ed. E. P. Sanders, 1–26. Philadelphia: Fortress, 1981.

Boer, Martinus C. de. "The Death of Jesus Christ and His Coming in the Flesh (1 John 4:2)." *NovT* 33 (1991) 332–44.

Borchert, Gerald L. "Insights into the Gnostic Threat to Christianity as Gained through the Gospel of Philip." In *New Dimensions in New Testament Study*, 79–93. *See* Longenecker and Tenney.

Boring, Eugene. *Sayings of the Risen Jesus: Christian Prophecy in the Synoptic Tradition*. SNTSMS 46; Cambridge: Cambridge Univ. Press, 1982.

Broek, Roelof van den. "Jewish and Platonic Speculation in Early Alexandrian Theology: Eugnostos, Philo, Valentinus, and Origen." In *The Roots of Egyptian Christianity*, 190–203. *See* Pearson and Goehring.

Brown, Peter. *The Body and Society: Men, Women and Sexual Renunciation in Early Christianity*. New York: Columbia Univ. Press, 1988.

———. "The Diffusion of Manichaeism in the Roman Empire." *JRS* 59 (1969) 92–103.

———. *The Making of Late Antiquity*. Cambridge: Harvard Univ. Press, 1978.

Brown, Raymond E. *Community of the Beloved Disciple*. New York: Paulist, 1979.

———. *The Epistles of John*. AB 30. Garden City: Doubleday, 1982.

———. *The Gospel According to John*. AB 29, 29A. 2 vols. Garden City: Doubleday, 1966–70.

Buckley, Jorunn J. "A Cult Mystery in the *Gospel of Philip*." *JBL* 99 (1980) 569–81.

———. *Female Fault and Fulfilment in Gnosticism*. Chapel Hill: Univ. of North Carolina Press, 1986.

Bultmann, Rudolph. *The Gospel of John*. Trans. G. R. Beasley-Murray; Philadelphia: Westminster, 1971.

Burkert, Walter. *Structure and History in Greek Myth and Ritual*. Berkeley and Los Angeles: Univ. of California Press, 1979.

Cameron, Ron. *Sayings Traditions in the Apocryphon of James*. HTS 34; Philadelphia: Fortress, 1984.

Casey, Maurice. *From Jewish Prophet to Gentile God: The Origins and Development of New Testament Christology*. Cambridge: James Clarke; Louisville: Westminster/John Knox, 1991.

Collins, John. *The Apocalyptic Imagination*. New York: Crossroad, 1984.

Colpe, Carsten. "Heidnische, jüdische und christliche Überlieferung in den Schriften aus Nag Hammadi III." *JAC* 17 (1974) 109–25.

Conzelmann, Hans. *1 Corinthians*. Trans. J. W. Leitch. Hermeneia. Philadelphia: Fortress, 1975.

———. "The Mother of Wisdom." In *The Future of Our Religious Past*: *Essays in Honour of Rudolf Bultmann*. Ed. J. M. Robinson, 230–43. London: SCM, 1971.

Cook, A. *Myth and Language*. Bloomington: Indiana Univ. Press, 1980.

Couliano, Ioan P. *The Tree of Gnosis: Gnostic Mythology from Early Christianity to Modern Nihilism*. San Francisco: HarperCollins, 1992.

Cousar, Charles B. *A Theology of the Cross: The Death of Jesus in the Pauline Letters*. OBT. Minneapolis: Fortress, 1990.

Crossan, John Dominic. *Finding Is the First Act*. Philadelphia: Fortress; Missoula, Mont.: Scholars Press, 1979.

Culpepper, R. Alan. *Anatomy of the Fourth Gospel*. Philadelphia: Fortress, 1983.

Daniélou, Jean. *Gospel Message and Hellenistic Culture*. Trans. and ed. J. A. Baker. Philadelphia: Westminster, 1973.

Desjardins, Michel. *Sin in Valentinianism*. SBLDS 108; Atlanta: Scholars Press, 1990.

Dillon, John. *The Middle Platonists*. London: Duckworth, 1977.

Dunn, James D. G. *Christology in the Making*. Philadelphia: Westminster, 1980.

Evans, Craig A. "On the Prologue and the Trimorphic Protennoia." *NTS* 27 (1981) 395–401.

Fallon, Francis T. *The Enthronement of Sabaoth: Jewish Elements in Gnostic Creation Myths*. NHS 10; Leiden: Brill, 1978.

Fee, Gordon. *The First Epistle to the Corinthians*. NICNT. Grand Rapids: Eerdmans, 1987.

Filoramo, Giovanni. *A History of Gnosticism*. Trans. A. Alcock. Oxford: Blackwell, 1990.

Fineman, Joel. "Gnosis and the Piety of Metaphor: The *Gospel of Truth*." In *The Rediscovery of Gnosticism*. Vol. 1, *Valentinianism*. Ed. B. Layton, 289–312. Leiden: Brill, 1981.

Fischer-Mueller, E. Aydeet. "Yaldabaoth: The Gnostic Female Principle in Its Fallenness." *NovT* 32 (1990) 79–95.

Fossum, Jarl E. *The Name of God and the Angel of the Lord*. WUNT 36; Tübingen: Mohr-Siebeck, 1985.

Francis, Fred O. "Humility and Angelic Worship in Col 2:18." *ST* 16 (1962) 109–34.

Frickel, Josef. *Die Apophasis Megale in Hippolys Refutatio VI, 9-18: Eine Paraphrase zur Apophasis Simons*. Orientalia Christiana Analecta 182; Rome: Pontificium Institutum Orientalium Studiorum, 1968.

Furnish, Victor P. *II Corinthians*. AB 32A. Garden City: Doubleday, 1984.

Gaston, Lloyd. "Angels and Gentiles in Early Judaism and in Paul." *SR* 11 (1982) 65–75.

Gero, Stephen. "With Walter Bauer on the Tigris: Encratite Orthodoxy and Libertine Heresy in Syro-Mesopotamian Christianity." In *Nag Hammadi, Gnosticism and Early Christianity*, 287–307. *See* Hedrick and Hodgson.

Gianotto, C. "La letteratura apocrifa attribuit a Giacomo a Nag Hammadi (NHC I,2; V,3; V,4)." *Augustinianum* 23 (1983) 111–21.

Good, Deirdre. "Sophia in Valentinianism." *Second Century* 4 (1984) 193–201.

Green, Henry A. *The Economic and Social Origins of Gnosticism*. SBLDS 77; Atlanta: Scholars Press, 1985.

———. "The Socio-Economic Background of Christianity in Egypt." In *The Roots of Egyptian Christianity*, 100–113. *See* Pearson and Goehring.

Gruenwald, Ithamar. "Aspects of the Jewish Gnostic Controversy." In *The Rediscovery of Gnosticism*. Vol. 2, 713–23. *See* Layton, ed.

———. "Manichaeism and Judaism in Light of the Cologne Mani Codex." *ZPE* 50 (1983) 29–45.

Hedrick, Charles. *The Apocalypse of Adam: A Literary and Source Analysis*. SBLDS 46; Chico, Calif.: Scholars, 1980.

———. "Christian Motifs in the *Gospel of the Egyptians*: Method and Motive." *NovT* 23 (1981) 242–60.

———. "The Treasure Parable in Matthew and Thomas." *Foundations and Facets Forum* 2 (1986) 41–55.

Hedrick, Charles W., and Robert Hodgson, Jr., eds. *Nag Hammadi, Gnosticism and Early Christianity*. Peabody, Mass.: Hendrickson, 1986.

Heldermann, Jan. *Die Anapausis im Evangelium Veritatis*. NHS 17; Leiden: Brill, 1984.

Helmbold, Andrew L. "Redeemer Hymns—Gnostic and Christian." In *New Dimensions in New Testament Study*, 71–78. *See* Longenecker and Tenney.

Hills, Julian V. "The Three 'Matthean' Aphorisms in *Dialogue of the Savior* 53." *HTR* 84 (1991) 43–58.

Hofrichter, Peter. *Im Anfang war der "Johannesprolog": Das urchristliche Logosbekenntnis—die Basis neutestamentlicher und gnostischer Theologie.* Regensburg: Friedrich Pustet, 1986.

Jackson, H. M. "The Origin in Ancient Incantory *Voces Magicae* of Some of the Names in the Sethian Gnostic System." *VC* 43 (1989) 69–79.

Janssens, Yvonne. "Une source gnostique du Prologue?" In *L'Évangile de Jean: Sources, rédaction, théologie.* Ed. M. de Jonge, 355–58. BETL 44; Gembloux: Duculot, 1977.

———. "The Trimorphic Protennoia and the Fourth Gospel." In *The New Testament and Gnosis*, 229–44. *See* Logan and Wedderburn.

Jonas, Hans. *The Gnostic Religion.* Rev. ed. Boston: Beacon, 1963.

Kannengiesser, Charles. "Athanasius of Alexandria vs. Arius: The Alexandrian Crisis." In *The Roots of Egyptian Christianity*, 204–15. *See* Pearson and Goehring.

Käsemann, Ernst. *Commentary on Romans.* Trans. G. W. Bromiley. Grand Rapids: Eerdmans, 1980.

Kelber, Werner H. *The Oral and Written Gospel.* Philadelphia: Fortress, 1983.

King, Karen L. "Sophia and Christ in the *Apocryphon of John*." In *Images of the Feminine in Gnosticism.* Ed. K. King, 158–76. Philadelphia: Fortress, 1988.

———, ed. *Images of the Feminine in Gnosticism.* Philadelphia: Fortress, 1988.

Koenen, L. "From Baptism to the Gnosis of Manichaeism." In *The Rediscovery of Gnosticism.* Vol. 2, 734–56. *See* Layton, ed.

Koester, Helmut. *Ancient Gospels.* Philadelphia: Trinity, 1990.

———. "Gnostic Sayings and Controversy Traditions in John 8:12-59." In *Nag Hammadi, Gnosticism and Early Christianity*, 97–110. *See* Hedrick and Hodgson.

———. "The History-of-Religions School, Gnosis, and the Gospel of John." *ST* 40 (1986) 115–36.

———. "One Jesus, Four Primitive Gospels." In *Trajectories Through Early Christianity.* With J. M. Robinson, 158–204. Philadelphia: Fortress, 1971.

———. "Three Thomas Parables." In *The New Testament and Gnosis*, 195–203. *See* Logan and Wedderburn.

Koschorke, Klaus. *Die Polemik der Gnostiker gegen das kirchliche Christentum.* NHS 12; Leiden: Brill, 1978.

Krämer, J. *Der Ursprung der Geistmetaphysik.* Amsterdam: P. Schippers, 1964.

Kraemer, Ross S. *Her Share of the Blessings.* New York: Oxford Univ. Press, 1992.

Lane Fox, Robin. *Pagans and Christians*. New York: Knopf, 1986.

Layton, Bentley. "The Riddle of the Thunder (NHC VI, 2): The Function of Paradox in a Gnostic Text from Nag Hammadi." In *Nag Hammadi, Gnosticism and Early Christianity*, 37–54. *See* Hedrick and Hodgson.

———, ed. *The Rediscovery of Gnosticism*. Vol. 2, *Sethian Gnosticism*. Leiden: Brill, 1981.

Lieu, Judith. *The Theology of the Johannine Epistles*. Cambridge: Cambridge Univ. Press, 1991.

Lieu, Samuel N. C. *Manichaeism in the Later Roman Empire and Medieval China*. Manchester: Manchester Univ. Press, 1985.

Lincoln, Andrew T. *Ephesians*. WBC 42. Dallas: Word, 1990.

Logan, Alastair H. B. "John and the Gnostics: The Significance of the Apocryphon of John for the Debate about the Origins of Johannine Literature." *JSNT* 43 (1991) 50–57.

Logan, A. H. B., and A. J. M. Wedderburn, eds. *The New Testament and Gnosis: Essays in Honour of Robert McL. Wilson*. Edinburgh: T & T. Clark, 1983.

Lohse, Eduard. *Colossians and Philemon*. Trans. W. R. Poehlmann and R. J. Karris. Hermeneia. Philadelphia: Fortress, 1971.

Longenecker, Richard N., and Merrill C. Tenney, eds. *New Dimensions in New Testament Study*. Grand Rapids: Zondervan, 1974.

Luck, Georg. "The Doctrine of Salvation in the Hermetic Writings." *Second Century* 8 (1991) 31–41.

Lüdemann, Gerd. "Zur Geschichte des ältesten Christentums in Rom I. Valentin und Marcion II. Ptolemäus und Justin." *ZNW* 70 (1979) 86–114.

———. *Untersuchungen zur simonianischen Gnosis*. Göttingen: Vandenhoeck & Ruprecht, 1975.

MacDonald, Dennis. *There Is No Male and Female: The Fate of a Dominical Saying in Paul and Gnosticism*. HDR 20; Philadelphia: Fortress, 1987.

MacDonald, Dennis, and Andrew D. Scrimgeour. "Pseudo-Chrysostom's Panegyric to Thecla: The Heroine of the *Acts of Paul* in Homily and Art." *Semeia* 38 (1986) 151–59.

MacRae, George W. "The Coptic Gnostic Apocalypse of Adam." *HeyJ* 6 (1965) 27–35.

———. "Discourses of the Gnostic Revealer." In *Proceedings of the International Colloquium on Gnosticism, Stockholm, August 20–25, 1973*. Ed. G. Widengren, 111–24. Stockholm: Almqvist & Wiksell; Leiden: Brill, 1977.

———. "The Ego-Proclamation in Gnostic Sources." In *The Trial of Jesus: Cambridge Studies in Honour of C. F. D. Moule*. Ed. E. Bammel, 123–34. SBT 2/13. London: SCM, 1970.

———. "Gnosticism and the Church of John's Gospel." In *Nag Hammadi, Gnosticism and Early Christianity*, 89–96. *See* Hedrick and Hodgson.

———. "The Jewish Background of the Gnostic Sophia Myth." *NovT* 12 (1970) 86–101.

————. "Nag Hammadi and the New Testament." In *Gnosis: Festschrift für Hans Jonas*. Ed. B. Aland, 144–57. Göttingen: Vandenhoeck & Ruprecht, 1978.

Martyn, J. Louis. "A Law-Observant Mission to the Gentiles: The Background of Galatians." *SJT* 38 (1985) 307–24.

McGuire, Anne. "Conversion and Gnosis in the *Gospel of Truth*." *NovT* 28 (1986) 338–55.

Meeks, Wayne. *The First Urban Christians*. New Haven: Yale Univ. Press, 1973.

————. "The Man from Heaven in Johannine Sectarianism." *JBL* 91 (1972) 44–72.

————. "Simon Magus in Recent Research." *RelSRev* 3 (1977) 137–42.

Ménard, Jacques-É. *L'Évangile selon Thomas*. NHS 5; Leiden: Brill, 1975.

————. *L'Évangile de Vérité*. NHS 2; Leiden: Brill, 1972.

Meyer, Marvin W. "Making Mary Male: The Categories `male' and `female' in the Gospel of Thomas." *NTS* 31 (1985) 554–70.

Morard, Françoise. "L'Apocalypse d'Adam du Codex V de Nag Hammadi et sa polémique anti-baptismale." *RevScRel* 51 (1977) 214–33.

Moxnes, Halvor. *The Economy of the Kingdom*. OBT. Philadelphia: Fortress, 1988.

Mühlenberg, Ekkehard. "Wieviel Erlösungen kennt der Gnostiker Herakleon." *ZNW* 66 (1975) 170–93.

Murphy-O'Connor, Jerome. "Sex and Logic in 1 Corinthians 11:2-16." *CBQ* 42 (1980) 482–500.

Neyrey, Jerome. "Body Language in 1 Corinthians: The Use of Anthropological Models for Understanding Paul's Opponents." *Semeia* 35 (1986) 129–70.

————. *An Ideology of Revolt*. Philadelphia: Fortress, 1988.

Orlandi, Tito. "Coptic Literature." In *The Roots of Egyptian Christianity*. 51–81. *See* Pearson and Goehring.

Osborne, Catherine. *Rethinking Early Greek Philosophy*. London: Duckworth, 1987.

Pagels, Elaine. *Adam, Eve, and the Serpent*. New York: Random House, 1988.

————. "Conflicting Versions of Valentinian Eschatology: Irenaeus' Treatises vs. the Excerpts from Theodotus." *HTR* 67 (1974) 35–53.

————. *The Gnostic Gospels*. New York: Random House, 1979.

Painchaud, Louis. "The Redactions of the Writing Without Title (CG II,5)." *Second Century* 8 (1991) 221–34.

Parrott, Douglas. "Gnostic and Orthodox Disciples in the Second and Third Centuries." In *Nag Hammadi, Gnosticism and Early Christianity*, 193–219. *See* Hedrick and Hodgson.

————. "Response to 'Jewish and Greek Heroines in the Nag Hammadi Library.'" In *Images of the Feminine in Gnosticism*, 91–95. See King, ed.

————. "The Thirteen Kingdoms of the Apocalypse of Adam: Origin, Meaning and Significance." *NovT* 31 (1989) 67–87.

Pearson, Birger. "Gnostic Interpretation of the Old Testament in the *Testimony of Truth* (NHC IX,3)." *HTR* 73 (1980) 311–19.

——. *Gnosticism, Judaism, and Egyptian Christianity*. Minneapolis: Fortress, 1990.

——. "Jewish Sources in Gnostic Literature." In *Jewish Writings of the Second Temple Period*. Ed. M. Stone, 443–81. CRINT II/2. Assen: Van Gorcum; Philadelphia: Fortress, 1984.

——, ed. *The Future of Early Christianity: Essays in Honor of Helmut Koester*. Minneapolis: Fortress, 1991.

Pearson, Birger A., and James E. Goehring, eds. *The Roots of Egyptian Christianity*. Philadelphia: Fortress, 1986.

Perkins, Pheme. "Apocalypse of Adam: Genre and Function of a Gnostic Apocalypse." *CBQ* 39 (1977) 382–95.

——. "Gnostic Christologies and the New Testament." *CBQ* 43 (1981) 590–606.

——. *The Gnostic Dialogue*. New York: Paulist, 1980.

——. "I Have Seen the Lord (John 20:18): Women Witnesses to the Resurrection." *Int* 46 (1992) 31–41.

——. "Irenaeus and the Gnostics." *VC* 30 (1976) 193–200.

——. "Johannine Traditions in *Ap. Jas*. (CG I,2)." *JBL* 101 (1982) 403–14.

——. "Logos Christologies in the Nag Hammadi Codices." *VC* 35 (1981) 379–96.

——. "New Testament Christologies in Gnostic Transformation." In *The Future of Early Christianity*, 433–41. See Pearson, ed.

——. "On the Origin of the World (CG II,5): A Gnostic Physics." *VC* 34 (1980) 36–46.

——. "Pauline Anthropology in Light of Nag Hammadi." *CBQ* 48 (1986) 512–22.

——. *Resurrection: New Testament Witness and Contemporary Reflection*. Garden City: Doubleday, 1984.

Pétrement, Simone. *An Alien God*. Trans. C. Harrison. San Francisco: HarperCollins, 1990.

Piper, Ronald A. *Wisdom in the Q-Tradition: The Aphoristic Teaching of Jesus*. SNTSMS 61; Cambridge: Cambridge Univ. Press, 1989.

Ricoeur, Paul. "Preface to Bultmann." In *The Conflict of Interpretations*. Ed. D. Ihde, 381–401. Evanston: Northwestern Univ. Press, 1974.

Robinson, James M. "On Bridging the Gulf from Q to the Gospel of Thomas (or Vice Versa)." In *Nag Hammadi, Gnosticism and Early Christianity*, 127–75. See Hedrick and Hodgson.

——. "Sethians and Johannine Thought: The *Trimorphic Protennoia* and the Prologue of the Gospel of John." In *The Rediscovery of Gnosticism*. Vol. 2, 643–62. See Layton, ed.

——. "Very Goddess and Very Man: Jesus' Better Self." In *Images of the Feminine in Gnosticism*, 113–27. See King, ed.

Rudolph, Kurt. *Gnosis*. Trans. P. W. Coxon and K. H. Kuhn. Ed. R. McL. Wilson; San Francisco: Harper & Row, 1983.

Sanders, Jack T. "Nag Hammadi, Odes of Solomon, and NT Christological Hymns." In *Gnosticism and the Early Christian World: In Honor of James M. Robinson*. Ed. J. E. Goehring, C. W. Hedrick, J. T. Sanders, with H. D. Betz, 51–66. Sonoma: Polebridge, 1990.

Schenke, Hans-Martin. "Die neutestamentliche Christologie und der gnostische Erlöser." In *Gnosis und Neues Testament*. Ed. K.-W. Tröger, 205–29. Berlin: Evangelische Verlagsanstalt, 1973.

———. "The Phenomenon of Gnostic Sethianism." In *The Rediscovery of Gnosticism*. Vol. 2, 588–616. *See* Layton, ed.

Schmithals, Walter. "The *Corpus Paulinum* and Gnosis." In *The New Testament and Gnosis*, 107–24. *See* Logan and Wedderburn.

———. *Neues Testament und Gnosis*. Darmstadt: Wissenschaftliche Buchgesellschaft, 1984.

Schnackenburg, Rudolf. *The Gospel According to St. John*. Trans. K. Smyth et al. 3 vols. New York: Herder and Herder, Crossroad, 1980–82.

Schoedel, William R. "Topological Theology and Some Monistic Tendencies in Gnosticism." In *Essays on the Nag Hammadi Texts*. Ed. Martin Krause, 88–108. NHS 6; Leiden: Brill, 1975.

Schottroff, Luise. "Animae naturaliter salvandae." In *Christentum und Gnosis*. Ed. Walther Eltester, 65–97. BZNW 37; Berlin: Töpelmann, 1969.

Schüssler-Fiorenza, Elisabeth. "Rhetorical Situation and Historical Reconstruction in 1 Corinthians." *NTS* 33 (1987) 386–403.

Schweizer, Eduard. *The Letter to the Colossians*. Trans. A. Chester. Minneapolis: Augsburg, 1982.

Scopello, Maddalena. "The Apocalypse of Zostrianos (NH VIII,1) and the Book of the Secrets of Enoch." *VC* 34 (1980) 376–85.

———. *L'Exégèse de l'Âme*. NHS 25; Leiden: Brill, 1985.

———. "Jewish and Greek Heroines in the Nag Hammadi Library." In *Images of the Feminine in Gnosticism*, 71–90. *See* King, ed.

Segal, Alan. *Paul the Convert*. New Haven: Yale Univ. Press, 1990.

———. *Two Powers in Heaven*. Leiden: Brill, 1977.

Sevrin, J.-M. "Les Noces Spirituelles dans l'Évangile selon Philippe." *Mus.* 87 (1974) 143–93.

Shellrude, G. M. "The Apocalypse of Adam: Evidence for a Christian Gnostic Provenance." In *Gnosis and Gnosticism*. Ed. Martin Krause, 82–91. NHS 17; Leiden: Brill, 1981.

Siker, Jeffrey S. "Gnostic Views on Jews and Christians in the Gospel of Philip." *NovT* 31 (1989) 275–88.

Staden, Heinrich von. "Hairesis and Heresy: The Case of *haireseis iatrikai*." In *Jewish and Christian Self-Definition*. Vol. 3, *Self-Definition in the Greco-Roman World*. Ed. B. F. Meyer and E. P. Sanders, 76–100. Philadelphia: Fortress, 1982.

Standaert, B. "L'évangile de Vérité: critique et lecture." *NTS* 22 (1975) 243–75.

Stoops, Robert F. "Patronage in the *Acts of Peter*." *Semeia* 38 (1986) 91–100.

Stroumsa, Gedaliahu A. G. *Another Seed: Studies in Gnostic Mythology.*
NHS 24; Leiden: Brill, 1984.
———. "Form(s) of God: Some Notes on Metatron and Christ." *HTR* 76
(1983) 269–88.
———. "The Manichaean Challenge to Egyptian Christianity." In *The Roots
of Egyptian Christianity*, 307–19. See Pearson and Goehring.
Tardieu, Michel. *Codex de Berlin.* Paris: Cerf, 1984.
———. *Trois Mythes Gnostiques: Adam, Éros et les animaux d'Égypte dans
un écrit de Nag Hammadi (II, 5).* Paris: Études Augustiniennes, 1974.
Theissen, Gerd. *The Social Setting of Pauline Christianity: Essays on
Corinth.* Trans. J. H. Schütz; Philadelphia: Fortress, 1982.
———. *Sociology of Early Palestinian Christianity.* Trans. John Bowden.
Philadelphia: Fortress, 1978.
Tobin, Thomas. *The Creation of Man: Philo and the History of Interpreta-
tion.* CBQMS 14. Washington: Catholic Biblical Association, 1983.
Tripp, D. H. "The Sacramental System of the Gospel of Philip." In *Studia
Patristica.* Vol. 17/1. Ed. E. A. Livingstone, 251–60. Oxford: Pergamon,
1982.
Tuckett, Christopher. "Synoptic Tradition in the *Gospel of Truth* and the
Testimony of Truth." *JTS*, n.s., 35 (1984) 131–45.
Turner, John. "Sethian Gnosticism: A Literary History." In *Nag Hammadi,
Gnosticism and Early Christianity*, 55–86. See Hedrick and Hodgson.
Turner, Victor. *The Ritual Process.* Chicago: Aldine, 1969.
Veilleux, Armand. "Monasticism and Gnosis." In *The Roots of Egyptian
Christianity*, 271–306. See Pearson and Goehring.
Weiss, Hans-Friedrich. "Gnostiche Motive und antignostische Polemik im
Kolosser- und im Epheserbrief." In *Gnosis und Neues Testament.* Ed.
K.-W. Tröger, 311–24. Berlin: Evangelische Verlagsanstalt, 1973.
Williams, Jacqueline A. *Biblical Interpretation in the Gnostic Gospel of Truth
from Nag Hammadi.* SBLDS 79; Atlanta: Scholars Press, 1988.
Williams, Michael. *The Immovable Race: A Gnostic Designation and the
Theme of Stability in Late Antiquity.* NHS 29; Leiden: Brill, 1985.
Wilson, Robert McL. *Gnosis and the New Testament.* Oxford: Oxford Univ.
Press, 1968.
Wire, Antoinette Clark. *The Corinthian Women Prophets.* Philadelphia: For-
tress, 1990.
Wisse, Frederik. "The Nag Hammadi Library and the Heresiologists." *VC*
25 (1971) 205–23.
———. "Prolegomena to the Study of the New Testament and Gnosis." In
The New Testament and Gnosis, 138–45. See Logan and Wedderburn.
Yamauchi, Edwin. "Some Alleged Evidences for Pre-Christian Gnosticism."
In *New Dimensions in New Testament Study*, 46–70. See Longenecker
and Tenney.
Yates, Roy. "Colossians and Gnosis." *JSNT* 27 (1986) 49–68.

INDEX OF ANCIENT SOURCES

BIBLICAL BOOKS (WITH APOCRYPHA)

249

EARLY PATRISTIC BOOKS

TARGUMIC LITERATURE
JEWISH PSEUDEPIGRAPHA AND DEAD SEA SCROLLS

NAG HAMMADI TRACTATES
(AND OTHER GNOSTIC WRITINGS)

CLASSICAL AND LATER CHRISTIAN LITERATURE

INDEX OF MODERN AUTHORS

Alliance Theological Seminary
Nyack, N.Y. 10960